SECOND EDITION

CASES IN MACRO
SOCIAL WORK PRACTICE

David P. Fauri
Virginia Commonwealth University

Stephen P. Wernet
St. Louis University

F. Ellen Netting
Virginia Commonwealth University

PEARSON

Boston ■ New York ■ San Francisco
Mexico City ■ Montreal ■ Toronto ■ London ■ Madrid ■ Munich ■ Paris
Hong Kong ■ Singapore ■ Tokyo ■ Cape Town ■ Sydney

Series Editor: Patricia Quinlin
Series Editorial Assistant: Annemarie Kennedy
Marketing Manager: Taryn Wahlquist
Editorial-Production Service: Omegatype Typography, Inc.
Manufacturing Buyer: JoAnne Sweeney
Composition and Prepress Buyer: Linda Cox
Cover Administrator: Joel Gendron
Electronic Composition: Omegatype Typography, Inc.

For related titles and support materials, visit our online catalog at
www.ablongman.com.

Between the time Website information is gathered and then published, it is not
unusual for some sites to have closed. Also, the transcription of URLs can result in
typographical errors. The publishers would appreciate notification where these
errors occur so that they may be corrected in subsequent editions.

Library of Congress Cataloging-in-Publication Data

Cases in macro social work practice / [edited by] David P. Fauri, Stephen P. Wernet,
   F. Ellen Netting.—2nd ed.
      p.   cm.
   Includes bibliographical references and index.
   ISBN 0-205-38114-6
   1. Social service.   2. Social work education.   I. Fauri, David P.   II. Wernet,
Stephen P.   III. Netting, F. Ellen.

HV40.C365 2004
361.3'2—dc21

                                                                        2003041902

CONTENTS

ABOUT THE EDITORS

David P. Fauri is professor of social work at Virginia Commonwealth University (VCU) where he teaches MSW courses in macro practice, policy, administration and planning, and in the Advanced Standing MSW program, Doctoral Program, and BSW program. He has been at VCU for twenty years and was previously at the University of Tennessee, the University of Kentucky, and Southern Illinois University. He has served on the Board of the Council on Social Work Education and has been a site visitor for its accreditation process; has been active in leadership for the National Association of Social Workers in Virginia and Tennessee; and has served and led mental health, public social services, Parents Anonymous, and United Way boards. Practice has included planning community programs for elders and staff work in training and management analysis. Recent writing includes services for the dying and caregiving by professionals, family, and volunteers; bereavement services programming; and political participation of social workers. Currently he is a member of the editorial board of Areté. He earned his doctoral degree at Syracuse University.

Stephen P. Wernet is professor of social work in the School of Social Service and the Department of Public Policy Studies at St. Louis University in Missouri. He previously served on the faculties of Loyola University–Chicago, the University of Illinois at Urbana–Champaign, St. Edward's University, and the University of Texas at Austin. Professor Wernet is known both nationally and internationally for research on nonprofit organizations. His scholarship focuses on the political economy of nonprofit, social service organizations. Current research includes consummated and unconsummated mergers, evaluation of venture grant funding, joint ventures and Web-based education in social work He is editor of Lyceum Books' *Managed Care in Human Services* (1999). Professor

Wernet serves in numerous professional capacities including vice-chair of a United Way of Greater St. Louis Community Investment Panel; chair, Evaluation Subcommittee of the Management Assistance Center of the United Way of Greater St. Louis; site visitor for the Council on Accreditation–Council on Social Work Education. He has served as president of the Association for Community Organization and Social Administration (ACOSA). He earned his doctoral degree at the University of Texas in Austin.

F. Ellen Netting is professor of social work at Virginia Commonwealth University (VCU) where she teaches courses in the area of macro practice, policy, administration, and planning. She has been at VCU for ten years, after ten years at Arizona State University. She is co-author of *Social Work Macro Practice* (with Kettner and McMurtry), just released in its third edition; *Organization Practice* (with O'Connor); *Managing the New Human Service Workforce* (with Perlmutter and Bailey); and *Understanding Religious and Spiritual Aspects of Human Service Practice* (with Ellor and Thibault). She is co-editor of *The Role of Gender in Practice Knowledge: Reclaiming Half the Human Experience* (with Figueira-McDonough and Nichols-Casebolt) and *Enhancing Primary Care of Elderly People* (with Williams). She is author of more than 100 book chapters and refereed journal articles. She received the VCU Distinguished Scholar Award in 1997, was elected to the National Academy of Social Work Practice as a Distinguished Scholar in 1998, and is a fellow in The Gerontological Society of America. She earned her doctoral degree at the University of Chicago.

ACKNOWLEDGMENTS

We would like to thank the following reviewers for their helpful comments and suggestions: Tangerine-Ann Holt, University of Louisville, and Kathleen Nuccio, University of Minnesota, Duluth.

ABOUT THE CONTRIBUTORS

Melissa L. Abell is assistant professor in the School of Social Work at Virginia Commonwealth University where she teaches clinical research and human behavior in the social environment. She received her PhD and MSW degrees from the University of North Carolina–Chapel Hill and her BA from the University of Kentucky in Lexington. Her research interests include families and children and interventions with at-risk families.

D. Veronica Creech is a PhD student in public policy studies and a fellow in the Graduate College at St. Louis University. She received her MSW from the University of North Carolina–Chapel Hill with a concentration in community planning and management. Veronica's dissertation research focuses on senior citizens and fear.

Stephen French Gilson is associate professor at the University of Maine School of Social Work in Orono, where he teaches biology for social workers, human behavior in the social environment, and health policy as well as teaching in the disability studies concentration in the Center for Community Inclusion. He received his PhD from the University of Nebraska Medical Center, his MSW from the University of Denver, and his BA in art from California State University at Long Beach. His research interests are in disability, domestic violence, aging, and health policy.

Cheryl A. Hyde is associate professor at the University of Maryland School of Social Work, where she is co-chair of the management and community organization concentration and coordinator for diversity coursework. She previously held positions at San Francisco State University and Boston University, earned her MSW and PhD degrees from the University of Michigan and is currently chair for the Association for Community Organization and Social Administration (ACOSA). Her research interests are feminist approaches to macro practice, multicultural development in human service agencies, community collaboratives, and multicultural learning in social work education.

Sharon Keigher is professor of social work at the Helen Bader School of Social Welfare, University of Wisconsin–Milwaukee, where she teaches health policy, organizational and community theories, and social services for the aging. She taught previously at the University of Michigan after receiving her PhD and MA from the University of Chicago. Her research interests include the financing of human services, home care, homelessness, and housing risks facing older adults.

Roger A. Lohmann is professor in the Division of Social Work, Eberly College of Arts and Sciences, West Virginia University, where he teaches social administration, nonprofit management, and social policy. He received his PhD from Brandeis University, masters degree from the University of Minnesota, and BA from St. Cloud State University in Minnesota. His research interests include nonprofit theory, management theory, nonprofit financial management, and electronic communications.

Nancy Macduff is an internationally recognized trainer and author on volunteer management and administration and a consultant to organizations such as the Points of Light Foundation. She is an adjunct faculty member at Washington State University, teaching online courses for the Volunteer Management Certificate Program. She has authored six books on volunteer management, contributed to texts on nonprofit and volunteer management, and contributed journal and magazine articles on these topics.

Marsha A. Marley is associate director and instructor at the University of South Florida School of Social Work, where she teaches macro practice and policy. She received her PhD from Tulane University, her MSW from Louisiana State University, and her BS degree from Southwest Missouri State University. Her research interests include leadership, macro practice, health policy, and kinship care.

Jon K. Matsuoka is professor and interim dean at the University of Hawaii in Manoa. He has taught courses in communities and organizations and in human behavior in the social environment. He has experience working with indigenous communities in Hawaii and the Pacific Region in areas related to community assessment, social planning, and community-based economic development. His MSW is from the University of Washington and his PhD is from the University of Michigan.

Steven L. McMurtry is professor in the Helen Bader School of Social Welfare at the University of Wisconsin–Milwaukee, where he teaches courses in research and policy. He received his PhD from the University of Wisconsin–Madison, his MSSW from the University of Texas–Arlington, and his BA from Texas Tech University. His research interests are in out-of-home care for children and brief assessment measures for use in practice and evaluation.

Benjamina Menashe graduated from the University of California, Los Angeles with a BA in history, and obtained her MPA from the University of Washington. She currently resides in Seattle with her husband and two children.

David Menefee is associate professor of social administration at the Columbia University School of Social Work in New York City. He helps health and human service organizations design and install performance improvement systems. His work with medical centers, state government agencies, and private nonprofit organizations focuses on strategic planning and management, business process analysis and improvement, financial management, management information systems, and outcome-based evaluation systems. Articles about his work are published in a variety of nonprofit management journals.

Patricia Miller is director of Early Childhood Services at Southwest Counseling and Development Services in Detroit. She received her MSW from Wayne State University and her BA from Oakland University.

Elizabeth A. Mulroy is professor in the Graduate School of Social Work at the University of Maryland, Baltimore, where she teaches courses in communities and organizations, program management, and community and strategic planning. She received her PhD and her MSW from the University of Southern California. Her research interests include nonprofit, community-based organizations; interorganizational collaboration; and community development, affordable housing, and low-income families.

Risa Sandler, at the time of the original writing of the Ecological Outcomes case for the first edition of this book, was a graduate student at the University of Washington Graduate School of Public Affairs. She is now a budget analyst in San Francisco. Her interests include the evolution of nonprofit organizations, public–private contracting, and child welfare.

Mary E. Rogge is associate professor at the University of Tennessee College of Social Work, and an associate at the university's Energy, Environment, and Resource Center, where she teaches management, community practice, and international sustainability. She is a PhD and MSW graduate of Washington University and holds a BA from Kansas State University. Her research interests center around environmental, social, and economic justice and children's well-being.

Jonathan Scherch is a core faculty member in the Graduate Programs in Environment and Community at Antioch University in Seattle, where he teaches social and environmental change, ecological design principles and methods, and sustainable community development. He received his PhD from the University of Tennessee, his MSW from the University of Pittsburgh, and his BA from West Chester University. His research includes sustainable living innovations and appropriate technology implementation.

Steven Rathgeb Smith is associate professor at the Daniel J. Evans School of Public Affairs at the University of Washington, co-editor of *Public Policy for Democracy,* and editor of the *Nonprofit and Voluntary Sector Quarterly.* He received an MSW from Washington University in St. Louis and a PhD in political science from Massachusetts Institute of Technology. His current scholarly activity includes co-authoring *Nonprofits for Hire: The Welfare State in the Age of Contracting* and *Adjusting the Balance: Federal Policy and Victim Services.*

Diane Vinokur-Kaplan, associate professor at the University of Michigan School of Social Work in Ann Arbor, teaches courses on organizational studies, nonprofit research, and macro practice. She received her graduate degrees—MSW, MA (sociology), and interdisciplinary PhD (social work and sociology)—from the University of Michigan and her BA (cum laude) in sociology from Oberlin College in Ohio. Her recent research includes "The Under One Roof" project on the benefits and challenges of co-locating nonprofit organizations together, and reviews of new trends in the human service workplace.

Bob Wineburg is Jefferson Pilot Excellence Professor in the Department of Social Work at the University of North Carolina at Greensboro, where he teaches social policy, social administration, and macro practice. He received his PhD from the University of Pittsburgh, his MSW from Syracuse University, and his BA from Utica College of Syracuse University. His research interests center on how social polices affect the design and delivery of social services locally, with an emphasis on social service provision from the religious community.

Jeff Wunrow has been active in the GLBT community for ten years and executive director of PROMO, Missouri's statewide GLBT advocacy organization, since 1995. His work has been recognized by the Human Rights Campaign, Missouri Progressive Vote Coalition, the Women's Political Caucus, the *Riverfront Times,* and *The Advocate.*

PART I

INTRODUCTION

USING THE CASE METHOD IN THE CLASSROOM

We want to provide some guidance in using these cases in classroom teaching. This first section is for that purpose. It provides an overview for the student reader. Additionally, in the second section there is general information on the historical development of the case method and two charts to guide in the selection of cases.

Although there is no single best method for effectively teaching with cases, the instructor may want to consider some of the factors that seem to have worked for others, including the editors of this book. When introducing a case to a class, a summary or "mini lecture" may help to alert students to the key concepts, theories, or skills provided earlier in class or in readings that are relevant to the case. On the other hand, some instructors prefer to let students search for this during the case process and then summarize it following case discussion and debriefing.

Potentially, the most valuable learning when using the case method results from group discussion and debate, either in small groups or in the larger classroom setting. The group process of discussing cases tends to encourage participants' investment in the product of the group as individual analyses and views are modified through discussion. When the case method is new to participants, intense group effort may be necessary as the case may be approached broadly and with uncertainty. As more experience is gained, the process becomes more focused and participants become more assured of their abilities and the value of group outcomes. Preparation of each case by class members prior to discussion is essential for good learning outcomes, as is a willingness to constantly fuse the best of individual contributions and group discussion. Such willingness is a critical component of team participation and leadership in today's organizational world.

Small-group processes can be very helpful in case analysis and intervention planning. Addressing a case in small-group settings of five to six students allows each person an opportunity to discuss the case in more depth than might occur in a full-classroom setting. Each small group can be responsible for bringing back a report or recommendation to the larger class for comparison and contrast between group outcomes and possible summary of useful approaches found in the group reports. The instructor's responsibility is to bring together the individual group reports or recommendations into a total group product that is more complete and whole than the individual reports.

If the time available for a class session allows, it can be effective to combine a mini lecture, group meetings, group class reporting, and debriefing into one session. This breaks up the time and provides variety, which students often find aids learning. Normally, such a process would require more time than is available in a one-hour class session, but if sufficient time is not available during a single class, the groups might be asked to meet for discussion outside of class if this is built into the course plan and assignments.

It is important when holding large-group (class) discussions to develop a common, agreed-on base for understanding key elements of a case. One successful approach is to ask the class as a whole to identify the elements of a case in a manner similar to the extraction of key information from a play or work of fiction. This information is listed on a chalkboard, overhead, or flip chart. This can include identification of the setting (time and place), the situation (major events and plot line), exposition (anything one should be aware of that took place prior to the beginning of the case that coincides with it, such as major political events, economic conditions, or cultural factors), and a listing of the key roles (characters) in the story line. Individual instructors can experiment with the process to determine where this is most effectively placed (prior to small-group meetings or prior to full-class discussion). Placing it first in the process has the advantage of helping students, either in a classroom discussion or small groups, to avoid oversight or misinterpretations that set them off in a direction that may prove difficult. On the other hand, when discussing key elements first, there is a temptation, which must be guarded against, to get too far into the events and personalities of the case, essentially tilting the direction of discussion to come. Instructors may also wish to develop their own approach to introducing a case. For example, an instructor with thespian-like abilities developed an approach of entering the classroom in the role of the main character in a case, carrying on about the awful dilemma faced, and asking the class to provide counsel. This became an anticipated event on case days.

Debriefing—the process of having a final discussion of the case and the related theories, concepts, and skills—is important to maximizing learning. It gives the instructor an opportunity to summarize and to shape the learning to fit course objectives and sequencing of course topics, and debriefing provides for the natural movement to the topic and activity of the following class. It also is important for students because it brings a form of closure to the class, allowing students to disengage from the case and its characters as well as from their own positions on the case in which they may have become vested.

To maximize instructor latitude, discussion questions following each case in this book can be used in a range of ways or ignored if the instructor wishes to employ questions that are more relevant to the specific content of the course. Case discussions based on the questions provided or on instructor questions and direction are similar to experiential exercises in that they provide for active participation in learning and allow students to address each case from their perspectives. Many cases provide questions useful for building additional experiential exercises to supplement classroom case discussions, and some of the cases contain attachments that are specifically designed for use in structured, experiential learning (e.g., "The Coffee Break" case).

A final thought on instructional use of cases: Take advantage of potential that exists for constructing new cases by providing for students an opportunity to write their own cases. This could be done as a class or as group projects that are part of class exercises and assignments. Experiences in field instruction, in employment situations, or even in social work education programs might offer relevant and intriguing material for conversion to teaching cases, and practice principles, dilemmas, and challenges would likely flow from them.

Having a second edition of this casebook available for classroom use is in good measure due to those instructors who have explored and used the first edition cases to enliven the teaching of macro social work practice. It is also due to students who have responded positively to this learning. We recognize the wisdom of past and current acquisition editors in being willing to entertain the potential for issuing a text featuring the case method and then following through by encouraging it.

THE CASE METHOD: AN INTRODUCTION

The cases in this book reflect the realities encountered by social work administrators, planners, and community organizers. They describe various problems faced by macro social workers in organization, community, and policy practice, challenging the users' abilities in evaluating situations and problems as well as in coming up with possible solutions or interventions. The editors asked contributors to prepare a case based on their real-life experiences as well as on a knowledge base in keeping with their scholarly or practice experience and education.

Although identifying information about social service agencies and individuals is modified with respect to details and events, cases are based on real situations that the contributors have either observed or been involved with in a professional capacity. In some cases, several real-life situations are combined to provide a comprehensive story that provides integration of applicable theoretical background. In all of the cases, theoretical and conceptual materials (at the beginning of each case) were added by the contributors by using hindsight and their professional expertise to help in understanding what had gone on in the actual situation.

We sought to ensure that each case addressed both the realities of social work practice and the needs of those teaching and studying macro social work practice, that is, to have a theoretical base to which to refer when making practice decisions. In addition, a focused reference list supporting both the theory and the case is inserted between the theory/concept section and the case. Cases provide the user with opportunities to both examine and evaluate the behavior of the main characters in each case as well as to ask, "How would I handle this sort of situation?" In short, each case provides powerful teaching/ learning opportunities while also offering a good and interesting story intended to absorb the reader with the excitement and challenge of professional practice in macro social work.

Conceptual Background: The Case Method in Education for the Professions

The use of cases for teaching and learning is an old and honored tradition within the professions. It goes by many different names—for example, the case method and case teaching. Some date case method teaching to the Greeks and Socrates, hence, the Socratic Method. It has been used with a range of enthusiasm in professional education. Business, law, and medicine use case method as a mainstream teaching technique. In law, there is the tradition of the law casebook and case law. The most famous, contemporary approach to case method teaching is associated with the Harvard Business School and its series of business cases. Nursing, social work, public administration, and education have cycled through periods in which the case method was integral and other times when it was abandoned. Again, Harvard University maintains a series of teaching cases focused on public administration. The Institute for Nonprofit Management at the University of San Francisco maintains a collection of cases for teaching about issues related to "The Nonprofit Sector." The University of Washington Graduate School of Public Affairs houses the consortium-maintained "Electronic Hallway" for public administration and public policy cases. In social work, *Families in Society,* formerly known as *Social Casework,* has a long tradition of publishing cases for teaching social work practice.

There are several advantages to using the case method for teaching in the professions. Professional education seeks to prepare individuals to practice, hence, the need for experience in applying conceptual or theoretical material to real-life situations. Cases can be thought of as the counterpart to the science laboratory. They provide students with problem-solving practice within a protected environment.

Cases encourage analysis of practice situations and flexible thinking, thereby avoiding prescriptive solutions. Potentially the most valuable case method learning results from group discussion and debate, whether in small groups or in a large classroom setting. The process of case discussion challenges participants' analyses and perspectives while providing the opportunity for viewpoints to be modified through discussion of the case. Even though they all start with the same case, the student or groups of students often identify different problem constellations. These differing views can lead to a range of solutions for handling the case situation. Frequently, each view offers substantial insights and learning opportunities. Given variation in viewpoints, as well as time invested in analysis, it can be expected that individuals or work teams will weigh events and facts differently and may uncover aspects of a case others may overlook.

There is a second advantage to using the case teaching method. The professions use clinical experience as an integral component of the educational program. Practice under supervision and grand rounds are a gradual approximation of practice meant to prepare the student for the work world. When practice under supervision is impossible or impractical, case teaching provides this gradual approximation for learning.

Cases parallel real-life situations and the practice world. Cases are powerful learning tools for helping acquire problem-solving skills. One must identify relevant facts, define the problem situation by reviewing a case for one or more issues, analyze and interpret the facts in light of the problem etiology, reach conclusions about the problem and its causes, and plan a solution to the problem(s) inherent in the case.

Cases aid with the integration of theory and practice. This task is perhaps the greatest challenge in professional education. Professionals experience fatigue, stress, burnout, and disillusionment because of the demands in the field and the incongruity between theory and practice. Cases allow bridging the ideal or perfect situation with the variance of the real world. Cases enable the complexity and murkiness of practice to enter into the antiseptic environment of the classroom. They allow us to view theoretical principles through the range and variety of occurrences in the world of practice.

A third advantage concerns client or consumer safety and protection. The recipient of service needs to be protected from exploitation and incompetence in research. Case teaching provides for learning through simulation of a real-world experience. It protects both the recipient of services and the service provider. It protects the recipient by ensuring that the practitioner has had some previous exposure to issues and problems likely to be faced in practice and therefore is less likely to make serious errors in judgment. It protects providers or students by preparing them in advance for fast-paced, split-second, decision-making work. Cases insulate us from potential negative consequences of critical incidents while providing opportunity to insert ourselves into similar situations.

Using Cases as Learning Tools

Cases offer a powerful means of helping social workers acquire problem-identification and problem-solving skills. The user must review the case for one or more problems, identify relevant facts, analyze and interpret those facts in light of the author's presentation of problem etiology, redefine the problem situation if necessary, and finally reach conclusions about the problem and its causes. Many times individual students or groups of students will come up with differing positions even though they all start with the same case. The ability to live with ambiguity should increase as more cases are experienced and it becomes apparent that there is no one right answer to the diverse problems posed. Continued encounters with ambiguity and learning to tolerate it, while avoiding a rush to judgment, can build confidence in meeting similar problems in professional practice. Analytic processes can be learned relatively easily, but it may be more difficult to learn to select and recommend an interventive course of action, including advocating for and defending it in discussion.

The cases in this book vary in complexity, but the reader can approach each case at a variety of levels. Although every case contains a number of issues and themes, students will find familiar elements in each case even if they are relatively new to the field of social work. Similarly, some cases may seem fairly straightforward, when in fact there are multiple management issues, community problems, and policy needs embedded in several levels of understanding.

The reader does not need any special educational prerequisites to begin exploring these cases. What is needed is a determined interest in understanding how multifaceted these human situations can be and a willingness to systematically assess what is known, what assumptions are made, and the importance of critically thinking things through. It is important to carefully assess the contextual framework of each case and to actively seek the practice challenges and dilemmas found therein. As you work with the cases, you will read about both the joys and the trials of social work macro practice. It is hoped that this experience will engage you in an opportunity to go beyond passive learning and to become involved in the search for appropriate interventions. None of the cases provide easy, ready-made answers. By intention, the contributors have left the remainder of the script unwritten, just as in real life. That's the fun in it!

The cases are meant to be appealing and are written in an engaging style, but the amount of learning value in each is tied to the theoretical material at the beginning and the discussion questions listed at the end of each case. We encourage the reader to maximize the use of each case by studying the theoretical and practice perspectives that appear in the beginning and tie each case to the important literature in the field.

THEORIES, CONCEPTS, AND PRACTICE APPLICATIONS: SELECTING CASES IN THIS BOOK ACCORDING TO THEMES

The cases included in this book are real—they reflect practice realities, issues, and difficulties, and each case is unique in its setting. As unique as each case is, the main themes are common to many practice situations in organizations, in communities, and in policy work. These themes can be and should be related to theories that inform social work macro practice, and this book does this through two user-oriented tables presented on pages 8–11. Depending on how an instructor and students wish to use a particular case or emphasize a particular theory area, cases can be used on a stand-alone, one-by-one basis, or they can be combined to emphasize a specific theory area or practice setting.

Cases are grouped into the four parts that provide the organizing framework for the book: problems and populations, communities, organizations, and changing macro systems. As one reads each case, it will become immediately apparent that none of these cases fits only one of the sections. Although they have been categorized according to their major themes, every case contains subthemes and elements that are cross-cutting. Yet these broad categories provide some guidance in managing the large number of cases while fitting them into major arenas or macro social work practice. Obviously, because cases reflect reality, any categorization that moves beyond the major practice areas presents a substantial challenge. Nevertheless, it is assumed that many users of this book will want to pick and choose cases from throughout the book rather than moving through the book in the sequence in which the cases are presented. To facilitate this, two tables follow.

Table 1, Theoretical and Practice Perspectives, provides a means for quickly identifying themes contained in each case, even if these themes are not the major ones identified in the brief theoretical and practice perspectives at the beginning of each case. Themes are advocacy, boards of directors, coalition building, community organization, community relations, diversity, funding, leadership, interorganizational relationships, management information systems (MIS), motivation of staff, needs assessment, organizational culture, organizational life cycle, organizational structure, policy analysis, policy im-

	Advocacy	Boards of Directors	Coalition Building	Community Organization	Community Relations	Diversity	Funding
1 • Lee and the Amazing . . .			•		•		
2 • Hate Crimes			•			•	
3 • Underground Advocates	•		•		•	•	
4 • Guatemalan Stove Project			•	•	•		•
5 • The Reverend and Me			•	•	•	•	
6 • Riverton	•		•	•	•		
7 • Native Hawaiian					•	•	
8 • Lindblom County			•	•	•	•	•
9 • The Consultants							
10 • Women's Coop		•			•	•	•
11 • Managed Care		•					•
12 • Computerizing Welfare							
13 • Ecological Outcomes	•	•	•		•		•
14 • The Coffee Break				•	•		
15 • KingsHaven and YOU			•	•	•		
16 • Carol's Value Dilemmas	•				•		•

TABLE 1   **Theoretical and Practice Perspectives**

plementation, power/authority/conflict, and strategic planning. Thus, it becomes possible to group cases to emphasize a single theme and to look at it in the various and unique contexts each case offers. For example, if one is looking at leadership, cases noted as having a leadership theme could be employed to identify common elements of leadership regardless of the specific practice arena. Similarly, advocacy occurs within all of the practice arenas that provide the organizing framework of this book, and there are several cases that are useful in illustrating various aspects of this important concept.

Leadership	Interorganization Relations	MIS	Motivation of Staff	Needs Assessment	Organization Culture	Organization Life Cycle	Organization Structure	Policy Analysis	Policy Implementation	Power, Authority, and Conflict	Strategic Planning
	•			•							•
	•								•		
•			•							•	
•	•										
	•			•						•	
•					•				•	•	•
	•									•	
•					•	•		•	•	•	•
•						•	•			•	•
•						•					•
		•	•			•		•			
•									•		•
•			•		•					•	
	•	•							•	•	
•		•		•				•	•	•	

	Environmental Setting	Arena
1 • Lee and the Amazing . . .	Urban	Community
2 • Hate Crimes	Statewide	Community
3 • Underground Advocates	Statewide	Community
4 • Guatemalan Stove Project	Rural, Central American	Community
5 • The Reverend and Me	Urban	Community
6 • Riverton	Urban	Community
7 • Native Hawaiian	Urban	Organization
8 • Lindblom County	Rural	Community
9 • The Consultants	Urban	Organization
10 • Women's Coop	Urban	Organization
11 • Managed Care	Urban	Organization
12 • Computerized Welfare	Urban	Organization
13 • Ecological Outcomes	Urban	Organization
14 • The Coffee Break	Rural	Organization
15 • KingsHaven and YOU	Rural	Community
16 • Carol's Value Dilemmas	Urban	Community

TABLE 2   Settings, Arenas, Auspice, and Target Populations

In Table 2, Settings, Arenas, Auspices, and Target Populations, we provide a brief template of environmental setting, arena, auspice, and target population served. Readers interested in combining cases with particular foci can do so by using this table. For example, someone interested in macro practice in a rural setting is able to locate cases that are clearly about rural areas. Similarly, readers wanting nonprofit management content could locate voluntary auspices; or others, focusing on a substantive area targeted to a particular population group, can identify the group by a specific case.

Finally, both tables are designed to enable instructors to go back and use a case already read for a purpose other than that emphasized at the time of original use. Themes, settings, arenas, auspices, and target populations not addressed or developed in the original reading and discussion can be addressed

Auspice	Target Population
Mixed Public–Private	Older Adults
Legislative/State Government	GLBT
Legislative/State Government	Disabled Persons
Voluntary/Faith Community	Latinos
Voluntary/Faith-Based	Women in Poverty
Voluntary/Environmental	At-Risk Youth and Communities
Voluntary/Ethnic	Children, Families, Communities
Voluntary Coalition	
Public Social Services	Families, Adults, Children
Voluntary Feminist	Women
Voluntary with Public $	Mental Health (including prevention)
Public Child Welfare	Families, Children
Voluntary—Housing and Planning	Urban Poor
Public Social Services	Families, Adults, Children
Mixed Public–Private	At-Risk Youth
Public Services	Older and Disabled Persons

in this way without introducing another case for reading, analysis, and discussion. In a similar fashion, a case already read and discussed might be revisited for purposes of comparison and contrast with a case currently under discussion.

PART **II**

UNDERSTANDING PROBLEMS
AND POPULATIONS

In this part, we focus on how practitioners identify situations that need to change and how they begin to understand why these situations are problematic to various population groups. In recognizing the macro practice issues that occur in organizational and community settings, it is important to examine the underlying assumptions that practitioners and others hold. Therefore, we are pleased to have four cases in this part that illustrate a diversity of situations, as well as reveal the underlying tensions that occur when people have different understandings about what approach to take and how to begin to make change happen.

Three themes link the cases in this section. First, practitioners will be struggling to decide how to *get started* in their work, amid differing opinions and perceptions. These cases are not about the work of implementation; they are about the work of knowing where to begin. Second, initial efforts are being made in defining a change opportunity and the reader will witness the constant reassessment that has to occur as the problem emerges in process. It is likely that the reader might identify the problem differently from what the main characters in each case think the problem is. Third, there is a recognition of the diversity among population groups with which social workers engage, including cases that focus primarily on elders; gay, lesbian, bisexual, and transgendered persons; disabled persons; and Latinas.

The practitioners in "Lee and the Amazing Multifaceted Community Needs Assessment" are trying to decide how to go about finding out what older citizens in their community think the priorities need to be. Their way of getting started is a bit ragged as they debate about how to begin the process of learning about needs and what methods could be used to do so. Similarly, in "Hate Crimes Legislation," a social worker recognizes that something has to be done about crimes that are targeted to vulnerable population groups, his particular concern being gay men and lesbians. He, too, seeks support and knowledge from various constituents to begin the process of facilitating the drafting of legislation intended to raise public awareness of the severity of the problem. "The Underground Advocates" are a little farther along in their problem definition process, having already obtained a sponsor for their proposed policy change that would provide assistive technology for disabled persons in the community. Yet, they too are just getting started, knowing that even if legislation is approved, a tedious process of implementation will be necessary to ensure that anyone will actually benefit. "The Guatemalan Stove Project" provides a very different case that is far removed from the legislative corridors in the United States. This case also involves the same dilemma—where does one begin to gather information in the problem-solving process.

Constant reassessment occurs within each case, making the reader aware of how important it is not to jump to premature action. Whereas "The Guatemalan Stove Project" illustrates how persons who do not know a community well can make naive assumptions, "Lee and the Amazing Multifaceted Needs Assessment" reveals how workers in a community with which they have some experience still face barriers to truly understanding how to prioritize a community's concerns. Both "Hate Crimes Legislation" and "The Underground Advocates" raise the stakes to a broader arena, taking on statewide problems and encountering multiple obstacles in the process.

The diversity among client population groups represented in these cases reminds social workers of the number of differences faced by practitioners. Whereas the needs assessment case targets older persons within the local community, "The Underground Advocates" seeks to address the needs of disabled persons. However, advocates for both aged and disabled persons readily recognize that there are overlapping concerns within these communities that at times form ready coalitions and at other times create barriers and misunderstandings. "The Guatemalan Stove Project" provides a more global perspective, taking the reader outside the United States and demonstrating how careful one has to be to respect cultural differences in how one looks at gender in context. Similarly, "Hate Crimes Legislation" provides a perspective on how diverse population groups often have to use windows of opportunity, such as tragic events, to make their voices heard and how practitioners must seize these opportunities in order to effect change.

1

LEE AND THE AMAZING MULTIFACETED COMMUNITY NEEDS ASSESSMENT

MARY ROGGE and MARSHA MARLEY

THEORETICAL AND PRACTICE PERSPECTIVES

This case illustrates the work of a community practitioner assessing the needs of and services for older Americans. The case focuses on three questions. First, what theoretical perspectives are involved in defining community? Second, what is the role of the social worker in helping a community define its needs? Third, what tools can be used in translating theory into assessments and interventions that improve community well-being?

Defining Community

The concept of community has been defined using a variety of theoretical perspectives and parameters (Chaskin, 1997; Fellin, 2001; Figueira-McDonough, 2001; Netting, Kettner, & McMurtry, 2004; Warren, 1978; Weil, 1996; Wellman & Leighton, 1979). Defining community involves the social construction of community boundaries and characteristics, conditions and problems, strengths and weaknesses, distribution of power, and resources for constructive social change (Rogge, 1995). Its outcome determines who will be helped and what social issues, conditions, or problems will be addressed.

Virtually every definition of community highlights those spaces, interactions, and identifications that people share with others in both place-specific and nonplace-specific locations (Netting et al., 2004). Typically, we think of community boundaries in terms of *geographic, spatial,* or *locational* characteristics—geopolitical jurisdictions ranging from smaller units such as city blocks and neighborhoods nested within larger units such as cities, states, and nations. Community boundaries can also be defined by *common intentional or circumstantial attributes* (e.g., beliefs, ethnicity, physical characteristics, or conditions such as age, height, or illness). Communities can be bounded by *interest* (e.g., professional associations, social issue advocacy groups, or sports-oriented groups). In this age of information technology, a new form of community—a computer-accessed *virtual* community—has emerged, and we are learning how individuals around the world can participate in community from a local to a *global* scale. Each individual's *personal* community is comprised of a set of relationships developed through his or her connections within a variety of community types (Fellin, 2001).

Chaskin (1997) offers three definitions of community that center around geographic or spatial locations, and one that centers on an individual's personal community. Chaskin notes that, for each of these four conceptualizations, individual experiences and the social and physical attributes of the community interact to uniquely shape community dynamics. First, in an ecological/systems-based, *natural area/urban village,* geographic areas with commonly acknowledged boundaries, such as ethnic neighborhoods, represent a natural, functional, and organic community that forms to maintain informal, interpersonal relationships. Second, a *community of limited liability,* such as a city or rural county that has governmentally designated geographic boundaries, is defined in large part by those boundaries and a shared reliance on formal institutions for goods and services. Third, communities based on *social system/political economy models* most fully account for the actual complexity of community. In these communities, actors' economic and political interests, both within and outside of the community's commonly acknowledged geographic boundaries, compete against each other to create and maintain a range of social relationships and exchanges. Finally, Chaskin offers a network analysis-based reframing of the individual's personal community as a *community without propinquity,* which emphasizes the influence of individuals' different experiences in shaping the larger community (see also Putnam, 1995; Wellman & Leighton, 1979).

In this case, there are different lenses through which Lee Bartolo and her colleagues in Brookfield can define community. Each lens has consequences for the path the social workers select to create change. The issue of how to define community is intimately connected to the second question: What is the role of the social worker in helping a community define its needs?

The Role of the Community Social Worker, Participatory Processes, and Actors

The second issue, highlighted by this case, is the roles of the various actors in a community assessment process. The key actors include the social worker as well as the variety of community members (Atpeter, Schopler, Galinsky, & Pennell, 1999).

The role of the social worker in community practice is varied (Kondrat & Julia, 1998; Weil & Gamble, 1997). On the one hand, it can be a grassroots organizer who is concerned with procuring broad-based and wide-ranging participation and ensuring the rights of marginalized or oppressed communities. On the other hand, the social worker may operate as a technician whose focus is on implementing a rational choice or decision-making process. There is little unanimity about which role a community social worker should use. There is, however, agreement that the social worker should mix and phase her or his tactics and strategies when working within the political processes of community work (Rothman, 1997).

There can be consensus concerning the pool of community actors from which to select stakeholders in order to identify community needs. Unfortunately, there may be less unanimity about the most appropriate ways and means for involving various stakeholders in the planning and assessment process due to their diversity. Stakeholders are individuals who, and organizations that, can be affected by a given community issue, condition, or problem. Drawing from a range of conceptualizations of community stakeholders, one can assess the relevance of social problems to:

1. target and client populations
2. their extended families and social networks
3. individuals and organizations that provide raw materials (capital, labor, supplies), goods, and services to a community
4. entities that function in regulatory and social control functions
5. media and other entities that disseminate information and ideas within and across communities
6. members of the general public—the most generalized set of stakeholders—not otherwise invested in a given community problem

Given the diversity, from both ecological and political economic perspectives, it is important to identify stakeholders' positions within the subsystems of planned change efforts. For example, what interest does each stakeholder have in terms of change agent, primary or secondary client, controlling, host, implementing and target systems (Hardcastle, Wenocur, & Powers, 1997; Netting et al., 2004)?

Balancing stakeholder influence is a continual, important part of the struggle to produce reliable and valid needs assessments that can lead toward constructive community change. Since the 1980s, a growing interest in participatory action and research methods (Park, Brydon-Miller, Hall, & Jackson, 1993; Sarri & Sarri, 1992; Whyte, 1991) and communitarianism has buoyed efforts to create mechanisms for genuinely meaningful citizen participation in organizational and community settings. Fisher and Karger (1997) note that participatory research, communitarianism, and feminist models of social work practice share an emphasis on capacity building and empowering individuals and communities.

The able practitioner will keep a firm hold on two facts about community and participatory processes. First, community is a dynamic entity in which boundaries, stakeholders, and sources of power can and will change. Second, the ethical, skillful use of this knowledge can be applied to manage power, include or exclude decision makers, and shape community change efforts. Similar choices—and dilemmas—that can affect change efforts are addressed in the third question to be mindful of in your visit to Brookfield: What tools can be (and have been by Lee Bartolo and company) used in translating theory into assessments and interventions that improve community well-being?

Community Needs Assessment Tools and Techniques

A community needs assessment is a systematic examination of the synergistic relationship among a social issue, condition or problem, a target population thought to be affected by the problem, and other community contextual factors such as the nature of the community's service delivery system (Netting et al., 2004). The skeletal structure of community needs assessments resembles the generalist problem-solving and research models. That is, social problems and target populations are identified; actors and methods for analyzing the problem are reviewed, prioritized, and selected; data are collected and analyzed; the process is evaluated and critiqued; and recommendations for change are made. This statement should not lure the reader into an unrealistic sense of security regarding the need to learn specific community needs assessment techniques. Rather, with a well-grounded understanding of basic problem-solving and research processes, the social worker is equipped to move to a deeper level of sophistication in applying theory and technique to understand a community and its members' needs.

There are a number of useful guides for implementing community needs assessments (see, e.g., Balaswamy & Dabelko, 2002; Kretzmann & McKnight, 1997; Netting et al., 2004). In addition to choices about how stakeholders are involved through the assessment process, other key choices involve methods for collecting, aggregating, and triangulating data; and for analyzing, interpreting, and disseminating results (Kettner, Moroney, & Martin, 1999; Krueger

& Casey, 2000; Moore, 1994; Royse, Thyer, Padgett, & Logan, 2000). Rarely do individuals involved in community needs assessments have the luxury of time or other resources to carry out a perfect assessment. More frequently, funding opportunities or constraints, external accountability requirements, service demands, and changing dynamics within the community restrict the time and resources available to accomplish an assessment. Developing creative assessment designs, measures, and collaborative interorganizational processes can be critical factors in implementing assessments that can lead to efficient and effective social change.

In summary, our efforts to understand human relationships are inseparable from our understanding of community. The ways we think about community are inevitably sculpted by complex social, political, and economic influences. Skillful change agents know that choices about how community is defined, who defines community, and how community is explored involve inherently biased choices by multiple actors, including social workers. Social workers, including Lee Bartolo, choose, by action or default, which community members with whom to align to shape the questions asked about community. The choices made can, in turn, shape which community members are nurtured, which symptoms and causes of social problems are targeted for analysis, the location and development of community capacity, and the interventions and measures used to determine the success of community change efforts.

REFERENCES

Altpeter, M., Schopler, J. H., Galinsky, M. J., & Pennell, J. (1999). Participatory research as social work practice: When is it viable? *Journal of Progressive Human Services, 10*(2), 31–53.

Balaswamy, S., & Dabelko, H. I. (2002). Using a stakeholder participatory model in a community-wide service needs assessment of elderly residents: A case study. *Journal of Community Practice, 19*(1), 55–70.

Chaskin, R. J. (1997). Perspectives on neighborhood and community: A review of the literature. *Social Service Review, 71*(4), 522–547.

Fellin, P. (2001). *The community and the social worker* (3rd ed.). Itasca, IL: F. E. Peacock.

Figueira-McDonough, J. (2001). *Community analysis and praxis: Toward a grounded civil society*. Philadelphia: Brunner-Routledge.

Fisher, R., & Karger, H. J. (1997). *Social work and community in a private world: Getting out in public*. New York: Longman.

Hardcastle, D. A., Wenocur, S., & Powers, P. R. (1997). *Community practice: Theories and skills for social workers.* New York: Oxford University Press.

Kettner, P. M., Moroney, R. M., & Martin, L. L. (1999). *Designing and managing programs: An effectiveness-based approach* (2nd ed.). Newbury Park, CA: Sage.

Kondrat, M. E., & Julia, M. (1998). Democratizing knowledge for human social development: Case studies in the use of participatory action research to enhance people's choice and well-being. *Social Development Issues, 20*(2), 1–20.

Kretzmann, J. P., & McKnight, J. L. (1997). *Building communities from the inside out: A path toward finding and mobilizing a community's assets.* Chicago: ACTA.

Krueger, R. A., & Casey, M. A. (2000). *Focus groups: A practical guide for applied research* (3rd ed.). Newbury Park, CA: Sage.

Moore, C. (1994). *Group techniques for idea building* (2nd ed.). Newbury Park, CA: Sage.

Netting, F. E., Kettner, P. M., & McMurtry, S. L. (2004). *Social work macro practice* (3rd ed.). New York: Longman.

Park, P., Brydon-Miller, M., Hall, B., & Jackson, T. (Eds.). (1993). *Voices of change: Participatory research in the United States and Canada.* Westport, CT: Bergin & Garvey.

Putnam, R. (1995). The strange disappearance of civic America. *American Prospect, 24,* 34–48.

Rogge, M. E. (1995). Coordinating theory, evidence, and practice: Toxic waste exposure in communities. *Journal of Community Practice, 2*(2), 55–75.

Rothman, J. (1997). The interweaving of community intervention approaches with personal preface by the author. *Journal of Community Practice. Special Issue, 3*(3/4), 69–99.

Royse, D., Thyer, B., Padgett, D. L., & Logan, T. K. (2000). *Program evaluation: An introduction* (3rd ed.). Chicago: Nelson-Hall.

Sarri, R. C., & Sarri, C. M. (1992). Organizational and community change through participatory action research. *Administration in Social Work, 16*(3/4), 99–122.

Warren, R. L. (1978). *The community in America* (3rd ed.). Chicago: Rand McNally.

Weil, M. (1996). Community building: Building community practice. *Social Work, 41*(5), 481–499.

Weil, M., & Gamble, D. (1997). Model development in community practice: An historical perspective. *Journal of Community Practice. Special Issue, 3*(3/4), 5–67.

Wellman, B., & Leighton, B. (1979). Networks, neighborhoods, and communities: Approaches to the study of the community question. *Urban Affairs Quarterly, 14*(3), 363–390.

Whyte, W. F. (Ed.). (1991). *Participatory action research.* Newbury Park, CA: Sage.

THE CASE

LEE AND THE AMAZING MULTIFACETED COMMUNITY NEEDS ASSESSMENT

HARD TIMES AHEAD?

Lee Bartolo sensed the uncertainty in the air when she walked into the management team meeting at the Brookfield Center for Senior Services. The center had recently been given advance notice by the Federation for Community Giving, an important funding source for the agency, that it would be making major changes in the way member agency funding would be determined. The changes would be implemented during the next cycle of the Federation's budget hearings. The center managers knew all too well that this could have a significant effect on the center's future operations.

Lee had been the center's senior program director for two years. From her point of view, this announcement was just the latest in a recent wave of federal, state, and local policy decisions affecting human services agencies in the metropolitan Brookfield area. Agencies providing social services for elderly persons were particularly hard hit by federal and state cutbacks in Medicare- and Medicaid-funded programs. Prospects for new state-funded pilot projects in case management and long-term care were questionable.

As Jane Fine, the center's administrator, Lee, and the other members of the center management team strategized about the funding issues, the discussion quickly expanded to the current state of services for elders. They realized that any discussion of program planning and funding necessarily involved projecting the needs of elders and anticipating what the service-delivery environment would look like in the next few years. As the discussion continued, comments focused on the need to know more about what was being done by other agencies providing services on behalf of elderly persons. As Jane concluded, "We don't have an accurate picture of what the needs of elders will be or what the service-delivery environment should be. We need a common base of understanding."

By the end of the center management meeting, the team members agreed that the center needed to act on a twofold strategy. First, the implications of the Federation for Community Giving's funding changes on center viability had to be determined. Second, an effort to involve other community agencies in developing a broader perspective of the needs of elderly persons had to be initiated. The idea of starting a discussion with the Case Managers' Alliance (CMA) as an approach to involving other agencies came from Lee. This appealed to Jane who, as administrator of the center, had helped develop the CMA four years earlier. Lee, who was given primary responsibility for beginning discussions with other agencies about developing the broader needs' perspective, decided to bring up the issues at the next monthly meeting of the CMA.

THE WORKER BEES AGREE

Lee was well aware of the center's strong organizational commitment to the Case Managers' Alliance. The CMA had been founded by Jane and agency administrators of four other local agencies: Brookfield Nursing Services, University Medical Center Home Health Agency, Council for Family Services, and Volunteer Resource and Referral Agency. As heads of these agencies, they often supported each other in their dedication to serving the elderly population. Through creating the CMA, they had taken a step toward formalizing their good working relationships to further improve interagency coordination. Although the center was the only agency whose services were exclusively for elders, the agencies served many of the same clients. The CMA seemed to be a natural fit for the five agencies because they provided a range of services, including education, home maintenance and support, counseling, home health services, and information and referral. The primary goal of the CMA was to coordinate case management and referral services among its five member agencies.

Lee had worked with the CMA for two years. In her capacity as the center's senior program director, Lee had also assumed responsibility for the administrative coordination and supervision of the CMA. Each of the five CMA member agencies was represented at CMA meetings by a direct practitioner associated with his or her agency's case management or discharge planning programs. The direct practitioners held monthly meetings to coordinate services for their clients. The agency administrators met quarterly to discuss common issues and address problems identified in case managers' meetings. Lee respected the effort of both case managers and the administrators, who, by and large, had developed a strong network.

From Lee's perspective, the next two CMA meetings couldn't have come at a more opportune time. The CMA case managers' monthly meeting took place the week following the center's team management meeting, and the CMA administrators' quarterly meeting followed only three weeks after the case managers' meeting.

At the CMA meeting, Lee encouraged the case managers to think about the broader picture beyond their agency boundaries and about the problems of the clients they shared and knew so well. She asked them to talk about which elderly persons were and were not served, why they were or were not served, and what the big picture of services for elders would look like in the next 5 to 15 years. She listened very carefully as the discussion of client problems turned to expressions of frustration and concern as gaps in community resources and the lack of services became more and more evident. One of the case managers captured the sentiment of the group when he commented, "It's ironic, the people we help are always outnumbered by the people we can't—and these are our clients. I think we're losing ground."

As the case managers debated the issues Lee had raised, she saw themes emerging that were very similar to those that had been discussed by the center's management team. Outside of the CMA agencies and a few other community agencies, there seemed to be a surprisingly high level of uncertainty about the full range of services offered to, and needed by, elders in the Brookfield area. The CMA case managers were unanimous in their genuine commitment to developing services that were needed and in their fears about the ability to maintain—let alone expand—services in a context of shrinking resources. They concluded that these issues were communitywide problems that required communitywide solutions beyond the capability of the CMA. Lee left the CMA meeting feeling overwhelmed, knowing that the case managers had provided a very important, realistic, troubling perspective on the problems. She hoped that the CMA administrators' quarterly meeting would result in more support and a collective sense of direction.

In the interim between the CMA direct practitioners' and administrators' meetings, a lead story in *The Brookfield Standard* newspaper provided an unexpected focus and impetus to move more quickly than Lee had anticipated.

Federation for Community Giving Announces Funding Priorities

(Brookfield). The Federation for Community Giving, which recently completed its annual fund drive, has unveiled its funding priorities for the upcoming fiscal year. Primary consideration will be given to those programs that emphasize issues of prevention and early intervention in childhood, child care issues, violence in schools, adolescent substance abuse, and domestic violence. Last month, the Federation for Community Giving announced major revisions in its criteria for establishing eligibility for funding. Agencies applying to the Federation for Community Giving for funding will be required to demonstrate not only need but service effectiveness.

Noticeably absent from the article was any mention of funding for elders as a Federation for Community Giving priority. Following this news, Lee and Jane's discussions intensified as they considered how to get the other CMA administrators on board with the center's desire to build a more comprehensive picture of the needs of elders in the Brookfield area. The growing risk of agency competition, the draining away of funds from services to elders to other popular issues, and further splintering of services were of particular concern to them. In Lee's mind, the CMA administrators' meeting couldn't come soon enough.

THE ADMINISTRATORS COMMISERATE

At the next meeting of the CMA administrators, Lee summarized the recent meeting, with a focus on the concerns that had been raised by the direct practitioners about inadequate or nonexistent resources. Lee was not disappointed by the administrators' initial reactions. As one administrator summed it up: "This is not the issue of one agency. This is a community issue that affects all of us. We don't even have a handle on what the needs are or will be, how can we plan?" Jane commented, "The issue is even more complicated. Not only are we experiencing funding decreases, aging issues are losing ground as a priority. We are at serious risk for losing support for the services that we have in place now. We have to face the fact that some of our programs and services for elders may not survive unless we approach these problems very differently from the ways we have in the past."

Lee took careful note as the discussion unfolded. While the administrators expressed genuine concern and commitment for the elders they served, there were many different interpretations about what was happening and the potential impact. Lee could see that the dissimilarity among agency members in terms of size, diversified client populations, programs, and funding sources was definitely a factor. For the first time since she had worked at the center, Lee felt an immediate and real threat to the health of the center itself because of its exclusive focus on elderly persons as a target population.

Although the center had long been seen as a leader in advocating for elders, there was a consensus that the overall aging network in the Brookfield area was fragmented and not harmonious. Based on previous, sometimes less-than-successful experiences in pulling off broad community initiatives, the administrators knew they needed a firm base of agency, community, and political support to successfully plan for the needs of elders and to restore aging issues as a priority. As one CMA administrator woefully reminded the group, "Remember when the Older Americans Act passed and all the problems of older people were going to be solved?" "Sure," said another, "and Mid-State Aging Agency was mandated as the community planning agency?" "Go on, remind us of the painful past," groaned another. Jane spoke up, "The reality is that our local Mid-State Aging Agency covers not only Brookfield but eight adjacent counties, and with a small staff, they're swamped with requests for grant funding. They've never been able to meet the demand." Finally, someone reminded the group, "Let's face it. Mid-State Aging Agency's resources are limited, everybody wants a piece of the pie, and the State Commission on Aging doesn't carry the power it once did." With that, they concurred that their working relationship through the CMA was an important asset on which they could build to lead Brookfield toward achieving its goals. Using CMA leadership as a vehicle was appealing, they reasoned, because it represented a unified, collaborative response rather than one of individual agency self-interest. And, as Lee optimistically added, "It's a planning year for the Mid-State Aging Agency. I saw the schedule for the public hearings they plan to hold in the counties. Maybe there's potential there for some kind of involvement."

WHERE DO WE GO FROM HERE?

But what exactly should the rest of the strategy be? Although each agency kept data on its own clients and services, the CMA administrators were not aware of any recently organized, comprehensive attempt to document services or otherwise identify the needs of elders in the community. Quite the contrary, the competitive environment discouraged collaboration. Even among the five CMA agencies, to some degree they guarded their data and financial information because they often found themselves as rivals rather than partners, particularly when it came to vying for funding such as grants and contracts.

They agreed that a comprehensive needs assessment should be conducted, while recognizing the important barrier of the potentially high costs. There were other questions: How would this work? Who had staff, time, and funds to devote to this? What exactly is being assessed? If we do an assessment, then what? With no simple solutions, the administrators agreed that they had been very successful at bringing up more questions than answers. As the hardy group of administrators began to tire and feel more frustration than movement, they began to set out requirements for an assessment. First, each of their agencies needed to commit to being flexible and expedite the process in whatever way possible, individually and collectively. Second, someone needed to take the lead in tapping resources outside the CMA structure. Finally, before embarking on the project, they needed to deliberate thoughtfully on its potential pitfalls and benefits.

To reach out to other resources, the CMA administrators decided to create a separate ad hoc coalition, composed initially of the five CMA agencies, which would carry out the community needs assessment. Jane was asked to invite the director of the Regional Planning Institute (RPI) to join the coalition. RPI, a nonprofit agency, provided community planning and technical services, such as grant writing and fund development, and had worked very closely with several of the CMA agencies. RPI's participation, reasoned the CMA administrators, would lend credibility and expertise to the needs assessment. Jane and Lee were appointed as the two-person steering committee of the newly created "Brookfield Coalition: Aging in the Twenty-first Century." Jane, in turn, asked Lee to serve as the coalition project director. To expedite the development of the coalition, its inaugural meeting was scheduled two weeks down the road.

Lee left the CMA administrators' meeting tired but exhilarated about the direction the CMA meetings had taken and with the knowledge that there were a lot of hurdles to jump in the next two weeks. Driving home, she thought about the months to come and slowly realized that the stakes were potentially very high. This project could profoundly influence the course of local service delivery for the elders in Brookfield, not to mention the viability of the Center for Senior Services and, of course, her own position there.

FROM IDEAS TO ACTION:
LET'S PUT ON A SHOW!

Lee and Jane moved rapidly to get the needs assessment project up and running. First, Jane quickly gained the commitment of Sharon Nowakowski, director of the Regional Planning Institute, to help. With Sharon's consultation, they began to synthesize what the CMA agency administrators and direct practitioners had said; to identify the initial issues to resolve; and to puzzle out the shape, process, timing, and funding of the needs assessment. Sharon wanted to approach the Mid-State Aging Agency for funding: "We've got a common goal here, to improve community support systems for elders. I know they've been stretched about a mile wide and a millimeter thick, but this is one way we might be able to get some support from them. And, if they do help, they can say they've got at least a toehold in this project." Lee argued, "Our Mid-State Aging Agency is committed to funding direct services. I think we'll be hard-pressed to get them to accept a needs assessment as direct service. Maybe we can connect the assessment with their planning year activities."

As they deliberated further, Lee and Sharon found themselves struggling with the political complexities of interagency relationships deriving directly from the funding issues raised at the CMA administrators' meeting. If the Mid-State Aging Agency was to fund the needs assessment, should the money be channeled through the coalition as an entity, one of the coalition member agencies, or should they figure out another option? Although the Mid-State Aging Agency had not been an active player in the Brookfield network of services for elders, each of the coalition agencies (i.e., the five CMA agencies and RPI) had received some funding from it. Because of their focus on services for elders, the center had a history of receiving a fair amount of Mid-State Aging Agency funding for several years. The other agencies typically received small grants, primarily subsidies for supplemental staff for programs that included some elders. Concerned about the appearance of conflict of interest and the potential of angering the other coalition agencies, Lee and Sharon went to Jane, as director of the center, for advice. Jane replied, "We're all in the same little boat with Mid-State. They've had funding cuts too. If we apply on behalf of the coalition, then we have more headaches to work through in setting up accounting mechanisms and all that jazz. The Mid-State folks know us best here at the center; and, if they can fund us, we'll get the money more quickly than with any of our other options. Let's float the balloon and see what happens."

Lee and Sharon drafted the proposal for the community needs assessment, using the center as the grantee. The proposal included .5 FTE funding for Lee, as coalition project director, and technical support for data collection and analysis. The proposal outlined a three-part assessment design of compiling demographic information, determining the status of the service-delivery network for elders and identifying the current needs of Brookfield elders, and developing a five-year projection of future needs and services. As envisioned, the design relied on existing census information and agency records, such as client profiles, services, utilization patterns, and fee structures. The design also called for collecting information from service providers and consumer focus groups.

At the first coalition meeting, held as scheduled a short two weeks following the CMA quarterly administrators' meeting, Lee, Sharon, and Jane presented the proposed assessment design and the Mid-State Aging Agency proposal. Coalition members endorsed the needs assessment strategy and the plan to obtain grant funding from the Mid-State Aging Agency. Some questions were raised about whether the coalition should be the sponsor of the funding request, but there was general agreement that using the center would satisfy Mid-State Aging Agency's funding guidelines as long as Mid-State could move past its direct-service criteria. As the final order of business at the meeting, members struggled over setting a deadline for finishing the needs assessment project. Because time to influence future funding from Federation for Community Giving and other leveraged resources was rapidly diminishing, they reluctantly set an eight-month completion date.

IMPLEMENTING THE ASSESSMENT: THE LONG, FULL HAUL

Over the next eight months, the needs assessment project took on a life of its own. When the Mid-State Aging Agency proposal was approved, Lee gratefully announced to Jane and Sharon, "Now, we're official." Lee and Sharon had not waited for the funding to work on the three critical parts of the needs assessment. First, demographic data were compiled using the resources of the RPI. Sharon had access to census information and city and county statistical databases. The summary reports included county, city, zip code, and some census-tract-level data. The final profile of the elderly population included functional status, community areas where elders were concentrated, poverty levels, and unmet needs including the adequacy of transportation and other public services.

Second, the assessment strategy called for surveying agencies that served the elderly population. Feeling heavily pressured by the project deadline, Lee drew first on the time of other center staff and, later, used temporary help hired through the Mid-State Aging Agency grant. For the survey, local agency representatives were interviewed by telephone about the types and characteristics of clients served, definition of services, fee scales, and waiting lists. Agency representatives were asked to identify other agencies that they worked with regularly, as well as gaps or barriers in service delivery. As information regarding other agencies became available, these newly identified agencies were snowballed into the survey.

The third project component called for conducting focus groups of "representative senior service consumers" to determine what social services they used, what needs were not being met, what problems seniors encountered, projected future needs, and how satisfied seniors were with the services they received. Lee and Sharon soon found that the focus groups were easier to plan than to carry out. Getting access to "representative senior service consumers" proved to be extremely difficult for the other coalition member agencies. As Lee said, "It's not that the other agencies don't want to help or that seniors don't want to talk about issues, it's more a matter of finding captive audiences, and we are just not having any luck." As time continued to pass, Lee arranged for five focus groups of seniors via the center's social and educational programs.

In addition to the three major assessment components, the project included a plan for local agencies to meet to address the status of services for elders, identify potential remedies, and expand the service network. Lee and Sharon decided that the best forum for achieving this kind of agency interaction would be a workshop featuring a panel of agencies providing senior services. The workshop was held with three months remaining before the needs assessment deadline; agencies contacted for the service-delivery survey were invited. Lee was excited about the positive response to the workshop, with more than 60 percent of the invited agencies sending representatives. Although much of the workshop's focus was on identifying crucial issues, such as access to transportation and other public services, home care services, health and medical care, long-term care alternatives, and income subsidies, Lee heard a recurrent, underlying theme: "We are in a competitive, individual survival-mode environment; can we realistically overcome this to pull together a truly comprehensive solution?"

Two months before the deadline, Lee, fondly remembering when she didn't work 85-hour weeks, pulled together the preliminary results of the demographic analysis, agency survey, focus groups, and agency workshop. The findings supported the coalition's initial assumptions that Brookfield's elders had dramatic, increasing needs, and the resources to care for them were sadly insufficient.

ARE WE THERE YET?

From Lee's perspective, the coalition meeting at which she reported the preliminary results proved to be a watershed. Relieved to have the bulk of the project behind her, she began her comments confidently: "We now have a comprehensive analysis of our community and the data to support it." As coalition members digested her presentation, however, the course of action that had once seemed so clear grew more and more fuzzy. Coalition members offered a variety of tentative ideas about how to proceed, but no consensus emerged. Lee's sense of accomplishment dissolved as the extent of the dilemma became obvious. One member noted in frustration, "The next step seems to be figuring out the next step." To Lee's relief, another coalition member suggested that they revisit the original purpose of the needs assessment. Where, for example, was the input of city government, civic leaders, the corporate community, and major funding agencies? Although Lee agreed that these key stakeholder groups should be part of the process, she also had an uneasy feeling that some of the coalition members were as interested in engaging particular power brokers for their individual agency interests as they were in completing a comprehensive, community-based assessment.

Based on this discussion, coalition members decided to extend the project deadline one month and hold a public forum as the last major step in the needs assessment. With intensive, round-the-clock work on Lee's part, Jane's continuing redirection of center resources toward the project, and help from Sharon and some of the coalition members, the public meeting was hurriedly planned and held.

More than 50 people attended the "Strengthening Our Commitment to Seniors" public forum, held at the centrally located Brookfield high school. Representatives of a variety of service organizations came, including civic and religious organizations; the Brookfield City Council and other elected officials; public services; funding agencies, including the Mid-State Aging Agency and Federation for Community Giving; National Senior Citizens' Association; local senior citizens groups; and other human service agencies. Lee wasn't sure whether concern for the elders, the power of information and resources represented by the presenters and participants, or other factors influenced the turnout, but she was pleased with the community support and cooperation that the participants seemed to bring. At the forum, Lee, Sharon, and Jane presented summaries of the needs assessment data collected to that point. Then, the participants split into groups in which they were asked to identify and prioritize critical needs and issues to be resolved.

From Lee's perspective, the forum ended on a highly successful note. When the groups of participants reconvened as a whole, overall feedback was positive. The small-group sessions produced some immediate results. For example, representatives of two agencies who had been in the same group agreed to keep working together to improve adult day service programming.

Buoyed by the community response and the reality that the needs assessment project had met its deadline, the coalition meeting following the forum was upbeat. As they assessed the project and its outcomes, coalition members reflected on their hopes: That, in addition to broadening the data collected for the needs assessment project, the project would educate the Brookfield community about the needs of elders; develop communitywide participation in elder care issues; and, potentially, evolve into an active, long-term, community-based initiative that would continue to plan for the future needs of Brookfield elders.

Whereas the full effect of the coalition's efforts could not be immediately known, some consequences were apparent. The two agencies that had agreed to continue to work together as a result of their experience at the forum had already had a first meeting. Jane reported that a few agencies represented at the forum had subsequently augmented services for elders in the community. For example, a church in a neighborhood with a high proportion of low-income elders established an emergency fund for rent and utilities relief. The Brookfield Public Transit Authority had begun to review its routes near areas that had a high density of elders. The Federation for Community Giving had announced plans to establish a blue-ribbon commission to study aging issues and had allocated $35,000 for a consultant to assist with the study. Oddly enough, no coalition member agency had yet been asked to participate on the commission.

As the coalition meeting ended and Lee stood to leave, she reflected about all that had happened since that first Center for Senior Services management team meeting less than a year ago. As she left the room, Lee concluded, with mixed feelings of tired satisfaction, relief, and uncertainty, that the jury was still out on just what had been accomplished through the intense, rapid, complex assessment project just completed.

DISCUSSION QUESTIONS

Defining Community

1. How have Lee and her colleagues defined community?

2. What theoretical perspectives would you use to define community in this case?

Participatory Processes and Actors

1. Where on the continuum of stakeholder participation do the actors in this case study fall? Have necessary stakeholders been included in timely and appropriate ways?

2. How might Lee and her colleagues have better engaged the target population (elders) in the Brookfield community? Are the voices of elders heard in this needs assessment process? Why or why not?

3. How do you think the preexisting relationships among the CMA organizations affected the process used to gather community-based involvement, support, and information from the community? What were the power dynamics?

4. In what ways did the influence of future funding in Brookfield overtly and covertly affect the efforts of the coalition?

5. In the wake of the Federation for Community Giving's renewed attention to aging issues, what should the coalition do to strengthen its position or the position of the coalition members?

6. What is the role of the *aging* network in this case, and to what extent does Mid-State Aging Agency have a power base?

Community Needs Assessment Tools and Techniques

1. To what degree did Lee and the coalition create an adequate community needs assessment process and product? What were the driving and restraining forces in their efforts?

2. Did Lee and the coalition accomplish what they set out to do? What information from the case study and theoretical background material supports your opinion?

3. Identify strategies, other than the creation of an ad hoc coalition, that might be undertaken by the center to address the problems of their elderly clients. What methods (tools and techniques) could be used to carry out these strategies?

2

HATE CRIMES LEGISLATION

Legislative Advocacy for the GLBT Community

D. VERONICA CREECH, STEPHEN P. WERNET,
and JEFF WUNROW

On October 11, 1998, Matthew Shepard, 22, an openly gay college student, was brutally beaten, tortured, tied to a fence and left to die in Laramie, Wyoming. This tragedy became a triggering event for the country to focus on the public safety of an oppressed group—members of the gay, lesbian, bisexual, and transgender (GLBT) community. In the months that followed, former President Clinton referred to Shepard's murder in the State of the Union address, and "The Hate Crimes Prevention Act (HCPA) [became] part of the Clinton administration's attempt to strengthen antidiscrimination laws. Although defeated in 1999, the bill would have given the Justice Department more power to prosecute hate crimes across jurisdictions; including crimes linked to gender, disability, and sexual orientation" (Karger & Stoesz, 2002, p. 87). Although hate crimes legislation did not become part of national law, advocates within various states continued to push for policy change within their jurisdictions. This case documents the struggle in one state to pass hate crimes legislation following Matthew Shepard's death.

The events of this case focus on the debate surrounding the public safety of the community, specific to sexual orientation. If the United States enacts laws to protect citizens based on race, age, religion, sex, and national origin, why is it so contentious for states to pass legislation that protects a population that is repeatedly harassed, abused, and killed due to their differences? Is it possible that only some people define this as a problem? What are the necessary and sufficient conditions needed to ensure that a public good is institutionalized in law for an oppressed population? Reflected here is the ongoing, ever-present debate of private good versus public good, especially as applied to the protection of the rights of an oppressed minority group, that is, the GLBT community.

THEORETICAL AND PRACTICE PERSPECTIVES

In this case, three themes for social work macro practice emerge. First, understanding a target population and the problems they are facing becomes critically important. The target population is persons with sexual orientations different from others in the dominant society. Second, defining and analyzing the problem from the perspectives of the target population, but also from the perspectives of those in power, is necessary in order to move toward change. Third, the dynamics among coalition members and others who advocate for change must be carefully balanced, as illustrated by two policy entrepreneurs and an unlikely network coalition pushing legislation through a very narrow policy window.

Understanding the Target Population

Gathering information and locating available data are critical to identifying the extent of any problem. The Federal Bureau of Investigation (FBI) reports widespread anti-gay and lesbian violence, and the National Center for Victims of Crimes indicates even higher numbers of hate crimes against gays (Karger & Stoesz, 2002, p. 87). The National Gay Lesbian Task Force states:

> *Hate violence targeting gay, lesbian, bisexual, and transgender people remains a daily reality. Hate crimes under-reporting and under-documentation combined with pervasive homophobia existing within law enforcement often result in many hate crimes remaining invisible and not prosecuted. State governments can play a major role in addressing such hate crimes by enacting favorable legislation providing for data collection of motivated hate crimes and/or providing for enhanced criminal penalties for hate crimes perpetrators. Such laws send a powerful message that the state will not tolerate crimes motivated by bigotry. At the same time, some states have attempted to pass unfavorable hate crimes bills that intentionally exclude people (http//www.ngltf.org/).*

The journey of the GLBT community to receive equal protection has similarities with the experiences of people who have fought for racial desegregation, access for disabled persons, or funding for art education (Wyszomirki, 1997). In each of these examples, there have been forces that have tried to deny a segment of a population group resources that traditionally have been seen as public goods. In addition each group will have unique experiences, depending on how they are viewed by others within the larger society. Even the names used to refer to groups of people are social constructions that hold great symbolic meaning. Understanding the meaning of difference for the target population becomes critical to pursuing change (Rosenblum & Travis, 2000).

Since problems affect people, change efforts must reflect an understanding of the people affected (Netting, Kettner, & McMurtry, 2004). Therefore, it is important to locate resources that provide an understanding of the population group served. As a start, readers might find the following books helpful: *Not Just a Passing Phase: Social Work with Gay, Lesbian, and Bisexual People* (Appleby & Anastas, 1998), *Social Work with Lesbians, Gays, and Bisexuals: A Strengths Perspective* (van Wormer, Wells, & Boes, 2000), or *Foundations of Social Work Practice with Lesbian and Gay Persons* (Mallon, 1998). A historical view of cultural competence with gay and lesbian persons of color is provided in the Walters, Longres, Han, and Icard book (2003).

Defining and Analyzing the Problem

By definition an issue implies disagreement among various constituencies (Netting et al., 2004), and there are multiple issues in this case: How to define hate crime, who should be protected by policy, and how to go about addressing the problem. A policy window opens when the time is right for a new issue to be raised and support gathered so that the issue moves successfully onto the policy agenda (Jansson, 2003; Kingdon, 1995). Policy windows can be predictable, such as the annual renewal of a funded program, or unpredictable, such as an opportunity opened by a cataclysmic event. Policy windows do not stay open long, as with the annual budget debate in a legislature, and open infrequently, but can result in major public policy changes. The process of opening a policy window involves three converging streams: (1) discovering and defining a problem, (2) developing and advocating feasible solutions, and (3) gaining a set of supportive political forces. Timing is not only important—sometimes it is everything (Jansson, 2003; Sink & Stowers, 1989).

Triggering mechanisms are unforeseen events that are chief among the factors important to creating a favorable policy environment (Cobb & Elder, 1983). Triggering mechanisms can be classified as internal (financial audit, change of staff) or external (environmental, tragic event) devices. Sometimes, triggering events are cataclysmic. Linked dynamically with the action of a policy entrepreneur, a triggering mechanism can be a potent and fortuitous event. Triggering mechanisms can be general or specific. A general trigger has enduring usefulness for a coalition that seeks to move its issue onto the policy agenda. A specific trigger, in contrast, has a time-limited utility before it loses its potency and potential as a catalyst. In the case that follows, the Matthew Shepard murder was a potent catalyst.

Since timing is important, advocates must be prepared to assess the situation at hand and identify exactly what the problem is. In this case, there is little disagreement that what happened to Matthew Shepard was a criminal act, a violent crime, and completely unacceptable behavior. However, the difficulty in defining the problem is that it is complicated by the intent of the perpetrators to do harm not only to a person but to what that person represents—a gay male. The symbolic nature of this type of crime is a statement going beyond the violence done to an individual; it is a projection of hate onto an entire population group. It sends a message about difference and the unwillingness of some to accept differences. Analyzing the problem, therefore, is much more complicated than simply saying that this murder was a crime. Analyzing the problem requires thinking through why such crimes occur, what messages are being conveyed, and how the social construction of difference can incite violence (Rosenblum & Travis, 2000).

Dynamics among Coalition Members

Policy entrepreneurs, as described by Kingdon (1995), are people willing to invest their resources (e.g., time, energy, reputation, money) in the hope of a future return. That return might come in the form of policies of which they approve, satisfaction from participation, or even personal aggrandizement in the form of job security or career promotion (Sink & Stowers, 1989). Further, social workers and other policy entrepreneurs can help open policy windows by joining solutions with problems, anticipating softening and opposition, and capitalizing on a triggering mechanism (Sink & Stowers, 1989). The policy entrepreneur's role is important and difficult to perform. In this case, the policy entrepreneurs are a state representative, an executive director of the nonprofit (501 © 3 and 501 © 4) organization, and an MSW student intern.

In the political process, it is essential to build coalitions. When addressing contentious and unpopular issues, broad coalitions are essential for legislative success. The coalition that forms for the purpose of influencing a policy agenda must have considerable resources, expertise, contacts, and leadership in the political process (Jansson, 2003; Karger & Stoesz, 2002; Sink & Stowers, 1989). The members must agree on what problem is being targeted and articulate its definition, participate in its analysis, and determine how to use that information in the change process. In this case, the network coalition that formed over a short seven months had an array of elements that prodded government to adopt an innovative and aggressive approach to the identified problem.

Coalitions operate according to a pattern of exchange relationships and form for different reasons: (1) to allocate authority or resources (an enabling coalition), (2) to cooperatively produce services (a functional coalition), and (3) to promote norms and values (a normative coalition)—see, for example, Bailey and Koney (2000) or Sink (1987). The coalition in this case could be described as a normative coalition that tried to promote norms and values that reflected the needs of the GLBT community (Roberts-DeGennaro, 1987). To fully explore the potential for coalition-building, the reader may want to access the Web site for the National Gay and Lesbian Task Force (www.ngltf. org). For guidance about how coalitions can advocate for legislative change, see *Social Work Advocacy* (Schneider & Lester, 2000) and *Advocacy in the Human Services* (Ezell, 2000).

REFERENCES

Appleby, G. A., & Anastas, J. W. (1998). *Not just a passing phase: Social work with gay, lesbian, and bisexual people.* New York: Columbia University Press.

Bailey, D., & Koney, K. M. (2000). *Creating and maintaining strategic alliances: From affiliations to consolidations.* Thousand Oaks, CA: Sage.

Cobb, R., & Elder, C. (1983). *Participation in American politics: The dynamics of agenda-building.* Baltimore: John Hopkins University Press.

Ezell, M. (2001). *Advocacy in the human services.* Belmont, CA: Brooks/Cole.

Jansson, B. S. (2003). *Becoming an effective policy advocate: From policy practice to social justice.* Pacific Grove, CA: Brooks/Cole.

Karger, H. J., & Stoesz, D. (2002). *American social welfare policy: A pluralist approach* (4th ed.). Boston: Allyn and Bacon.

Kingdon, J. (1995). *Agendas, alternative, and public policies.* New York: Longman.

Mallon, G. (Ed.) (1998). *Foundations of social work practice with lesbian and gay persons.* New York: The Haworth Press.

National Gay Lesbian Task Force Web site—http://www.ngltf.org/.

Netting, F. E., Kettner, P. M., & McMurtry, S. L. (2004). *Social work macro practice* (3rd ed.). Boston: Allyn and Bacon.

Roberts-DeGennaro, M. (1987). Patterns of exchange relationships in building a coalition. *Administration in Social Work, 11,* 59–67.

Rosenblum, K. E., & Travis, T-M. C. (2000). *The meaning of difference: American construction of race, sex and gender, social class, and sexual orientation* (2nd ed.). Boston: McGraw-Hill.

Schneider, R. L., & Lester, L. (2001). *Social work advocacy.* Belmont, CA: Brooks/Cole.

Sink, D. W., & Stowers, G. (1989). Coalitions and their effect on the urban policy agenda. *Administration in Social Work, 13*(2), 83–98.

Sink, D. (1987). Success and failure in voluntary community networks. *New England Journal of Human Services, 7,* 25–30.

van Wormer, K., Wells, J., & Boes, M. (2000). *Social work with lesbians, gays, and bisexuals: A strengths perspective.* Boston: Allyn and Bacon.

Walters, K. L., Longres, J. F., Han, C-S., & Icard, L. D. (2003). Cultural competence with gay and lesbian persons of color. In D. Lum (Ed.), *Culturally competent practice: A framework for understanding diverse groups and justice issues* (2nd ed.). Pacific Grove, CA: Brooks/Cole.

Wyszomirski, M. J. (1997). Through the policy window: The context of culture policy. *Arts Education Policy Review, 98*(5), 9.

THE CASE

HATE CRIMES LEGISLATION

James Hedgerow returned rejuvenated from a much-anticipated vacation ready to start a new week at the St. Louis-based organization, Privacy Rights of Missourians (PROMO). Formerly known as the Privacy Rights and Education Project, this organization had begun its grassroots lobbying work after its founding in 1986. James mused over how far the organization had come, remembering his involvement years earlier.

One part of the organization's mission in the 1980s was to address hate crimes, which at that time was a topic of national discussion. The organization partnered with a diverse coalition of supporters to draft inclusive hate crimes legislation. After intensive lobbying for the legislation, a moment came when it was clear that if sexual orientation was deleted from the bill, it would pass. Sexual orientation was cut and the Ethnic Intimidation Act, which included race, color, religion, and national origin as protected groups, passed.

James remembered how Janet Reno had mandated all US District Attorneys to establish a hate crimes task force in the 1990s. Under the Clinton administration, GLBT issues came up in various arenas, including the hotly debated topic of gays serving in the military. The regional Task Force that included St. Louis involved the U.S. District Attorneys from Eastern Missouri and Southern Illinois, community groups, civil rights advocates, law enforcement officials, and prosecutors. As a part of the local Task Force, this organization was in a position to reach a broad spectrum of nontraditional partners.

James was now the executive director of PROMO, the nonprofit voice for lesbian, gay, bisexual and transgender rights in Missouri's state capital. PROMO's primary focus is to protect and expand the rights of lesbian, gay, bisexual, and transgender Missourians. On his way to work, James had been thinking about all he does at PROMO—seeing that all program activities get carried out successfully; raising money to cover the budget; running the office; providing field supervision for interns; overseeing communications with board and committee members, volunteers, community groups, and allies. He smiled to himself realizing that advocacy is hard work, but he could think of no other work that brought him as much personal satisfaction as knowing that his efforts were bigger than himself and that his work at PROMO was helping to improve the lives of others.

TRAGEDY AND IMMEDIATE RESPONSE

His feelings of rejuvenation were jolted into reality and quickly replaced with urgency and overwhelming sadness. Shortly after walking into his office, James learned about a young college student having been brutally beaten and left for dead in Laramie, Wyoming. Later James recalled the moment he learned of the event: "I remembered being out of town for several days away from the news. I didn't hear about this until a few days after it happened. Someone called the office and said, 'What are you going to do?' I didn't know about what until I checked my email. I was stunned, then incredibly angry. All my energies focused on contacting our board members."

Rallying immediate support and response was critical in providing a place for the community, gay and straight, to mourn such a tragic loss. Always running on a shoestring budget and understaffed, James turned to the new social work intern, Mary, to collaborate with community organizations to organize an event to help the local community join together in an effort so as not to feel isolated or helpless following such a terrifying event. James then turned his attention to the political community.

Mary shared with James her hesitancy in taking on such an important project as her first assignment as an intern. They talked about Mary's hesitancy and fears. He believed that she could do a good job with a little encouragement and support and knew that she was comfortable working with the GLBT community because she had asked for this placement as her first choice. Seeing James's confidence in her and feeling strongly about the death of Matthew Shepard, Mary used social work knowledge and skills to begin planning and organizing an event. She remembered from her social work classes that the best people to plan an event are the people the event is created to serve. Given this, Mary immediately began calling members of the community and PROMO volunteers to help her brainstorm ideas about organizing a memorial event. She found herself almost in a counseling role, listening to the concerns, hearing the anger and sadness in people's voices, realizing that many of the people with whom she talked were taking this as a personal affront to their sexual identities. One idea that emerged more than once as a memorial was a candlelight vigil.

After these very moving interactions, Mary was totally committed to her task. Next, she contacted the owners of a local coffee shop where many members of the GLBT community regularly meet to socialize. They discussed hosting a candlelight vigil. The shop owners were very pleased that Mary contacted them because they wanted to do something in the community but were not sure how to start. The coffee shop had been filled with people who had come together to support one another, to share their feelings, and to just be in one another's presence at this sad time.

Working collaboratively, PROMO, the coffee shop owners, other GLBT community supporters, and more than 450 people showed their outrage and grief over the tragedy by attending the vigil. James found the attendance to be amazing given there had been only two days to plan and organize the event. Mary was proud and emotionally moved to see her first assignment with PROMO materialize. With such attendance, James and Mary knew the death of Matthew Shepard had personally touched the lives of many people. The vigil was seen as a public statement, and soon James received phone calls from a state senator and a state representative, both members of the Democratic Party and both of whom were saying, "This is horrible! What can we do to prevent this in Missouri?"

GETTING STARTED (LEGISLATION AND OUTREACH)

With the political leadership already coming forward, James looked to his own organization to begin the policy work that lay ahead. Being a seasoned policy entrepreneur, he knew they had only seven months to organize, educate, and lobby if a bill was to be introduced and voted on in the upcoming session. He started with PROMO's Legislative Committee whose top priority at that point was the state's Civil Rights Bill. However, in the wake of Matthew

Shepard's death and with the political support in Jefferson City, the Legislative Committee shifted its priority and began working on a draft Hate Crimes Bill. This all-volunteer group met on a regular basis to plan PROMO's legislative strategy and to advise the executive director on carrying out legislative plans. Some members were attorneys and others were professionals with a strong interest in policy issues.

Following the vigil, Mary worked with the Legislative Committee in a support role, attending committee meetings, recording meeting notes, tracking legislation, and researching requested information when needed. The Legislative Committee reviewed existing Missouri legislation to see if any other groups were not covered under existing laws. After reading the legislation, the committee decided to include not only sexual orientation but also gender and disability—two very common categories often included in legislation but not in Missouri's laws. The committee had considered adding age but determined existing laws against adult abuse and child abuse were already quite strong and decided it was unnecessary.

They decided to propose adding new categories to an existing Missouri law rather than introduce new legislation. This would be an amendment rather than an entirely new bill, which seemed to be an effective approach. The major issue for the committee was how to define sexual orientation. After looking at examples from other states, they used wording from Minnesota's Civil Rights Law. The Legislative Committee completed its work in two months, in time for the state senator, who had connected with them earlier, to file the bill in the Senate in January 1999. The senator also contacted the representative who had stepped forward after the vigil and reached agreement leading to a companion bill to be introduced in the House. At this point, Mary wondered about this major step—filing legislation.

Sam, an attorney on the committee, who often spoke in technical terms, explained:

> When a bill is filed, the process includes the legislation being drafted by someone in the legislature's research office, then being released to the House as what is called a blue back because three copies of the bill with a blue cover page are provided. Cosponsors sign their names and district numbers to all three cover pages and then they are submitted to the Speaker of the House and printed. In the Senate, they are called yellow backs because the cover pages are yellow.

Mary found Bob's reply somewhat boring and mechanical, but she realized there might not be much one could do to add excitement to such a process. She also speculated that until she had participated in the process, it would continue to feel very unfamiliar.

James was focused on the often tentative and cautious work with the religious community. Sometimes communities of faith use their doctrine to support anti-gay legislation. However, just before PROMO started its outreach to the religious community, the Interfaith Partnership of Metro St. Louis endorsed a resolution calling on states to pass Hate Crimes legislation. Such a resolution from such an influential and powerful body in Missouri could not have come at a better time. The mission of the Interfaith Partnership was "to provide a timely voice and visible presence of the religious community by bringing together people of faith for dialogue and celebration; to communicate what is happening in social ministry; and to identify needs and to stimulate responses."

Understanding the conservative culture in Missouri and capitalizing on the release of the Interfaith Partnership's resolution, PROMO created packets of information about the legislation and about the support from different faith groups. PROMO activists worked closely with United Methodist leaders, knowing they were very supportive of social justice legislation based on official statements and declarations made by the United Methodist Church both nationally and locally.

NEXT STEPS (LOBBYING AND GRASSROOTS EFFORTS)

With the legislation drafted and filed in the Senate, and with strong support from religious communities, PROMO members turned their attention to lobbying at the capitol and to grassroots organizing. James began calling their work "a zigzag approach to policy change." With Mary's help, one day James was in Jefferson City talking to individual legislators, and the next day he was in St. Louis documenting the story of a gay man who was harassed by a truck full of men when he left a gay bar. A few days later James was back in Jefferson City securing votes from legislators, then in Kansas City talking about the bill to a group of faith-based social workers. At the state capitol he was ferreting out who opposed the hate crimes legislation; in the community, Mary was working to launch a Equality Begins at Home program—a week-long national project to draw attention to state and local efforts toward GLBT equality and to identify the problem of hate crimes as a public issue.

Continuing their zigzag efforts, one day James was in Jefferson City learning how to convert legislators who were opposed to the legislation; another day Mary was working in the community with law enforcement members of the original Hate Crimes Task Force to capitalize on their support in order to overcome objections from legislators. Some days they were both educating representatives on the importance of the hate crimes legislation; other days they were coalescing the religious community's support, making sure they were still onboard.

STRATEGY (POLITICAL AND GRASSROOTS)

While PROMO's zigzag lobbying and grassroots efforts continued, strategy was being implemented in the community as well as at the state capitol. In the community, PROMO and supporters used the Interfaith Partnership's resolution as a leveraging tool in approaching churches to introduce themselves and to open dialogue. Once inside the doors, PROMO could point to the resolution signed by their church's leader in order to continue the conversation.

Mary was with James at the capitol in January when the legislation to amend the hate crimes law was concurrently introduced in the Senate and the House. The first hearing was in the Senate; following the hearing, the committee chair, a powerful rural Democrat, combined the Hate Crimes Amendment bill with three other bills that were all sponsored by Republicans. James commented to Mary, "Combining the bills is ingenious because it forces Republicans to consider either voting against their own bills or supporting the hate crimes bill." Later, when looking back at the events, Mary understood the *ingeniousness* in the move because, as James predicted, one Republican sponsor voted for the whole package, while another Republican voted against his own legislation because he opposed the Hate Crimes Law amendment.

Political and grassroots strategists joined forces with a powerful statewide rally on the steps of the capitol on March 21 as part of the Equality Begins at Home project which was organized by the National Gay and Lesbian Task Force and the Federation of Statewide Lesbian, Gay, Bisexual, and Transgender Advocacy Organizations. PROMO and coalition partners organized the rally that more than 250 people attended. Participants included political allies as well as community collaborators. The state treasurer delivered the keynote address prior to announcing his run for governor. His coming out in favor of amending the hate crimes law was an important step toward credibility because he was the first statewide elected official to support PROMO's efforts. Collaborators attending included a representative from the National Organization for Women, a representative from a disability rights organization, and nationally recognized activists and leaders.

The maneuvering between supporters and opponents heated up in March. A gay Kansas City autoworker took a copy of the bill to the United Auto Workers local union for endorsement. The UAW endorsed the legislation, authorizing their lobbyist to support the bill. At the same time, it was learned that the bill had not been placed on the calendar for Senate debate.

When the UAW lobbyist learned this, he spoke with the president pro tem of the Senate, whom the UAW had supported in the past. Within three days of their conversation, the bill was on the calendar for the full Missouri Senate's consideration and vote.

A significant moment came when one senator offered an amendment regarding transgender language. The original definition was ". . . or having a self-image or identity not traditionally associated with one's biological maleness or femaleness." He felt that definition was too obscure and proposed changing it to ". . . not traditionally associated with one's gender." Given that this senator was a very conservative rural Republican, some felt his tactic was not intended to be helpful but was instead a stall tactic. Yet, it was agreed that this was not a point worth picking a fight over, especially if it meant this senator might support the bill. However, the language was adopted, and the process moved on.

By early April, the bill that encompassed the four legislative matters previously combined passed the Senate with a bipartisan 20 to 14 vote. This was the first time in history that a chamber of the General Assembly voted to protect Missouri's lesbian, gay, bisexual, and transgender community.

ANTICIPATING AND RESPONDING TO HURDLES

Meanwhile, in the House of Representatives, the Committee on Civil and Criminal Law held hearings on hate crimes. The opposition from the conservative right included a lobbyist expressing concern over the inclusion of disability, saying she had yet to see a workable definition of disability. A state representative from Columbia, the only member in the legislature who uses a wheelchair, answered, "Well, I think I have one."

Later during the same hearing, a Republican representative from St. Charles County shared a story about his father being a National Guardsman during integration in Mississippi. He talked about how his father escorted black students into the schools during that time. Although this representative was known for his conservative views, he was an early and faithful supporter of the hates crimes legislation. In fact, he was the tiebreaking vote in committee not once, but on two separate occasions.

Going into the month of May, the Speaker of the House took a personal interest in the legislation. He delayed the legislation while waiting for the Senate to concur with a version of another, unrelated bill that he supported. The Speaker did this not because he opposed it, but because he was using it as leverage (political horse trading) to secure passage of an unrelated bill he supported. That conflict was resolved and the Hate Crimes Bill moved up on the House calendar.

ALL EFFORTS CULMINATE

Lobbying, grassroots efforts, strategy, and political maneuvering continued in early May and into the last hours of the session in mid-May. Hate crimes legislation had not been debated yet in the House. James shared with Mary that he hoped they could find a vehicle to which they could attach the bill. Unfamiliar with this process, Mary asked James to explain this: "In this situation, a vehicle is a bill that other language can be amended onto. Attaching language to another bill is standard strategy at the end of a session. Supporters need a bill to attach to because it's feared the legislation is not going to be heard and would die and not get to the floor for a vote."

PROMO held meetings with legislative allies to get the "lay of the land," which included finding out which legislators were supporting the bill, which ones were wavering on the bill, and who was available to help lobby the wavering representatives. James enlisted 10 of the strongest allies to help with the final floor vote. He gave them each a list of eight legislators to make sure that they could be contacted when it came time to vote. The Wednesday before the session ended efforts intensified. The chief sponsor of the bill, a Democrat, went to the Speaker of the Democratic Leadership Caucus and said this was an important amendment, urging the Speaker to have it attached to a bill. The Speaker agreed to attach the proposed hate crimes amendment language to a larger crime bill that was being debated.

The larger crime bill was debated on the floor for 45 minutes during which a conservative Republican from suburban St. Louis offered an amendment that would entirely repeal the existing Hate Crimes law, leaving no protection for anyone. Since the new legislation PROMO sought was in the form of a proposed amendment to the existing Hate Crimes law, many people did not want to jeopardize the existing law, given its importance and the high price paid to enact it in the first place.

Wednesday's heated debate continued through Friday and mounted with intensity as the session was nearing its 6:00 PM deadline. The larger crime bill was now unwieldy and unfocused, and Republican senators tried to start a filibuster against the bill, but they were outmaneuvered by the Democratic majority floor leader.

Supporters of hate crimes policy change did not find rest in the last few hours of the session. James spoke with one representative who was quick in realizing that the bill that had already been passed by the Senate might offer hope. Other lobbyists joined James and this representative as they strategized on how to move consideration of the Senate bill ahead of others. Some behind-the-scenes logrolling occurred, and with only 15 minutes left in the session, the approved Senate bill was brought up for brief debate. Before the vote was called, many Republicans realized that a bill that they especially wanted passed in this session was next on the agenda. Republicans knew if they were going to get a vote on the next bill, they would have to let this one go. A vote was called for. After votes were tallied, the outcome was 85 votes in favor of passage, 3 more than needed to pass! The chamber erupted into applause; the chief aide to the Speaker jumped out of his chair and the media applauded. James found the climatic ending very inspiring and Mary watched with great excitement. She was already thinking of how she was going to use this field experience in her paper on problem identification and analysis for her macro practice course. Overwhelmed by the process and the eventual successful outcome, James found refuge in the quiet office of an ally who was a Democratic state representative from St. Louis county; the first thing he did was to share the victory by telephoning everyone who served on PROMO's Legislative Committee.

DISCUSSION QUESTIONS

Understanding the Target Population

1. Social workers help to educate individuals about how to advocate for themselves. What involvement did members of the GLBT community have during this case?

2. Would it have been appropriate for a member of the GLBT community to address the media in support of this legislation? Why or why not?

3. How did the Matthew Shepard murder serve as a triggering event for the mobilization of the community? How does this crime reflect a set of broader societal attitudes about difference and how might those attitudes impact the GLBT community?

4. What resources does the social work literature provide for the profession in understanding the target population?

Defining and Analyzing the Problem

1. How would you define the problem that this hate crimes legislation is addressing?

2. In analyzing the problem, what types of data and information would you gather if you were James and Mary? What controversies do you expect to encounter in the analysis process and why?

3. How might different ways of analyzing the problem produce different approaches to problem resolution? What would you want to know in order to adequately define and analyze the problem?

Dynamics among Coalition Members

1. How would you describe the coalition that formed to advocate for passage of the Hate Crimes Bill? What type of coalition is it? How does including language about gender and disability, in addition to sexual orientation, change the dynamics?

2. For a new professional, what are the risks involved in vocalizing support for the passage of controversial legislation? What are the risks involved if you do not vocalize your support?

3. The social work profession promotes inclusion and tolerance of diversity. However, if you personally opposed the passage of hate crimes legislation, how would you confront personal/professional conflict? How would you balance the two in your professional social work practice?

3

THE UNDERGROUND ADVOCATES

Legislative Advocacy for and with Service Users with Disabilities

STEPHEN FRENCH GILSON

THEORETICAL AND PRACTICE PERSPECTIVES

This case describes how a coalition of service users and state bureaucrats developed. Often, these two groups are at odds. Service users tend to organize to work for change within an existing system, whereas bureaucrats tend to work to maintain the status quo and prevent uncontrolled change from occurring. In the case at hand, however, the issue of service user or consumer-directed personal assistance services for people with disabilities is so compelling that everyone wants to "do the right thing."

The issue of service user, or consumer direction of attendant services, reflects a critical ideological and philosophical change in thinking related to the shift in provision of health and social services from institutionally situated to community-based. Additionally, a second ideological shift has occurred because of the primacy of economics in the domain of services and supports for disabled individuals. The notion of disabled individuals as objects of charity and in need of "help" is replaced by the characterization of these individuals as informed purchasers of goods and services. This shift in both ideology and practice has co-occurred with a shift from individuals having services determined for them by professionals to the individual disabled person determining the needed and desired services.

Work within the legislative process requires advocates to carefully consider and select from a range of alternative strategies and tactics before acting. As suggested by Netting, Kettner, and McMurtry, "tactic selection tests the professional judgment of the change agent, particularly in how to approach the target system" (2004). The relationship between the change agent and the target will influence the selection of strategy and accompanying tactics. This is not a static process since the social worker must remain flexible to choose among the tactics as the situation changes, selecting from the continuum of tactical categories: collaboration—campaign—contest (Netting et al., 2004).

Consistent with the definitions of the terms *strategy* and *tactics* as used by Netting et al. (2004), the overall effort (strategy) of the work of the "underground" advocates in this case was designed to bring about the development of service user- or consumer-directed personal assistance services (PAS) for persons with disabilities, and the specific techniques and behaviors (tactics) that the advocates used with the target system(s) were selected to ensure accomplishment of the strategy to have PAS adopted by the target system(s).

Ability to engage in the legislative process increases the chances of success for the bureaucrat who works in an advocacy role. It may seem altruistic or professional to stay above the political fray, but as in this case, it is in the political process that critical decisions are made that have a direct and consequential impact on the lives of individuals, families, and communities. Competency in legislative activities as well as policy and regulation development increases the possibilities for success in the change process. For a more in-depth discussion of tactic selection and an examination of related skills needed by social workers, we refer the reader to Jansson's *Becoming an Effective Policy Advocate* (2003) and Haynes and Mickelson's *Affecting Change* (2002).

Many social work macro practitioners are employed with state and federal government programs and engage in legislative activity—a positive and legitimate function. The trick is to work for change within the confines of the rules of the governmental unit in which they are employed. For a classic overview of the role and behaviors of the bureaucrat, see Anthony Downs, *Inside Bureaucracy* (1967), an old but very useful interpretation pointing out the multitude of motivations and constraints influencing the operation of government bureaus. For an understanding of the potential for change leadership of both the civil servant and the politically appointed federal official, see Berkowitz, *Mr. Social Security* (1995), a biography of Wilbur Cohen who was closely connected with the Social Security system for more than 40 years beginning with its creation in 1934; Birnbaum and Murray's *Showdown at Gucci Gulch* (1987) is an interesting presentation of the relationships between lobbyists and legislators as is Birnbaum's *The Lobbyists* (1992); and Weatherford's *Tribes of the Hill* (1981) is also useful. Of interest for this case is Weatherford's chapter, "Battling Guerrillas and Swatting Gadflies," which provides an insight into working the process "outside the lines." For an alternative view of how to frame these encounters in other than war metaphors, see Tannen (1998).

This case is not the usual coalition-building situation in which independent agencies coalesce. Rather, it features bureaucrat change agents who join together with two informed, concerned individuals and with potential users of a new service. The situation calls for obtaining service user involvement since additional forces working for change are required to counter the opposing forces. Two interesting questions arise: Is there an organization of people with disabilities already in existence that is capable of advocating for the specific service needs of personal assistance service users? If not, should there be one, or should the players in the case, primarily bureaucrats, organize and advocate alone to have the legislation passed? An additional question arises: Might an ongoing consumer advocacy organization develop out of the coalition effort as a secondary benefit of the effort?

Bureaucrats can be sensitive to the needs of service users, but there are still large power differences between service users and bureaucrats. This is not a coalition of equals—at least not at this point—and it points out the long-term need to empower service users, using a strengths perspective and approach (see, e.g., Saleeby, 1996).

Mizrahi and Rosenthal (2001), in their identification of the *dynamic tensions* that commonly characterize coalitions, provide a useful framework for assessing the conflicts as well as the cooperation that emerges in working with such groups. They discuss coalitions as "complex organizations of organizations" (pp. 178–179) and identify five tensions that exist within them: (1) the cooperation–conflict dynamic, (2) mixed loyalties–dual commitments, (3) autonomy versus accountability, (4) means to accomplish a specific social change goal versus a model of sustained interorganizational coordination, and (5) unity and diversity. Haynes and Mickelson (2002) write about techniques and strategies that are useful for influencing the political process and effecting legislative change. They provide a framework of organizing that is compatible with and expands on the observations of Mizrahi and Rosenthal (2001).

As the case illustrates, coalitions offer many strengths for bringing about change, including increasing the forces for change, establishing the legitimacy of consumer needs, and greater service user participation through consumer-led organizations. Ultimately, consumers may be able to initiate change efforts and lead legislative advocacy efforts. Then, the change-oriented bureaucrats will have established and achieved a major process-oriented system change in addition to having the immediate issue at hand settled successfully.

REFERENCES

ADAPT. (n.d.). A community-based alternative to nursing homes and institutions for people with disabilities. Centers for Medicare and Medicaid Services, retrieved online on July 15, 2002, at www.ADAPT.org.

Berkowitz, E. D. (1995). *Mr. Social Security: The life of Wilbur J. Cohen.* Lawrence: University Press of Kansas.

Birnbaum, J. (1992). *The lobbyists: How influence peddlers get their way in Washington.* New York: Times Books.

Birnbaum, J., & Murray, A. (1987). *Showdown at Gucci Gulch.* New York: Vintage Books.

Centers for Medicare and Medicaid Services. (n.d.). Details of Executive Order 13217. Retrieved online on July 15, 2002, at http://www.cms.hhs.gov/newfreedom/ec061801.asp.

Downs, A. (1967). *Inside bureaucracy.* Boston: Little, Brown.

Haynes, K. S., & Mickelson, J. S. (2002). *Affecting change: Social workers in the political arena* (5th ed.). New York: Longman.

Health Care Financing Administration (HCFA). (1991, August). *Home and Community-Based Waivers—Guidelines—No. 3: State Medicaid Manual.* HCFA Publication 45-4, 4440; Transmittal No. 54 [CD-ROM]. Citation from: Medicare and Medicaid Guide, Commerce Clearing House CD-ROM and online for Windows; Network Version 3.00 K.

Jansson, B. S. (2003). *Becoming an effective policy advocate: From policy practice to social justice* (4th ed.). Pacific Grove, CA: Brooks/Cole.

Mizrahi, T., & Rosenthal, B. (2001). Managing dynamic tensions. In J. E. Tropman, J. L. Erlich, & J. Rothman (Eds.), *Tactics and techniques of community intervention* (2nd ed.). (pp. 178–183). Itasca, IL: F. E. Peacock.

Netting, F. E., Kettner, P. M., & McMurtry, S. L. (2004). *Social work macro practice* (3rd ed.). New York: Longman.

Saleeby, D. (1996). The strengths perspective in social work practice: Extensions and cautions. *Social Work, 41*(3), 296–305.

Tannen, D. (1998). *The argument culture.* New York: Random House.

Weatherford, J. M. (1981). *Tribes on the hill.* New York: Rawson, Wade.

THE CASE

THE UNDERGROUND ADVOCATES

BACKGROUND

We were feeling very confident, sitting in the House of Delegates Hearing Room at the state legislature that December afternoon. At that point, except for Janet, the other five of us were principally observers, but all of our roles were to alter radically as the proceedings developed. We would soon become active participants, the people that we would fondly dub "underground advocates."

The PAS Project Team

Janet, the project director, had worked for almost 20 years in state public and private nonprofit sector arenas. She knew well what worked in advocating with public officials and how to develop politically feasible strategies in advocating for change. Currently, she was the director of the newly established Personal Assistance Services Project Team, a program established to change the approach to obtaining and directing personal assistance services (PAS) for people with disabilities. The PAS Project was to develop a public awareness and understanding of the role that service user- or consumer-directed PAS could play in the lives of persons with disabilities, as well as address concerns arising from the more traditional long-term care community. Janet took the position with the project knowing full well that she would be spending a great deal of time educating home care agency directors and health care program administrators about consumer-directed PAS. She also knew that service user-directed PAS was much more than care services, it was about a philosophical approach to service delivery and was connected to the principals of empowerment, self-determination, and choice. One of Janet's goals was to help develop a partnership between users of PAS, those people Janet considered "service users," and the agencies and organizations that were established to provide and pay for services for those service users. Janet knew that educating other agency directors and public policy makers might be difficult, but she certainly did not expect that the most difficult person to educate just might be her own boss, the director of her agency—the state Department of Human Services. But more on that later.

Frank, a service user advisory board member, taught on the school of social work faculty at the local university. His interest in disabilities was both professional and very personal, having sustained a major injury that necessitated his using forearm crutches for mobility. His passion for advocacy was known throughout the community and he had gained a reputation for being a person who could navigate around structural and psychological barriers. Frank first became a user of PAS following the accident that led to his disability. Initially, his needs involved some difficulty with some of his Instrumental Activities of Daily Living (IADLs), such as shopping for meals and meal preparation, as well as with some of his Activities of Daily Living (ADLs), such as bathing and dressing. As he adjusted to his disability and sought accommodations, his need for assistance with IADLs lessened, but he still required assistance with some ADLs.

Ann, as a program and administrative consultant, brought a unique package of skills, talents, and experiences to the group. Having grown up with a brother with a disability (polio), Ann was well versed in many of the experiences and consequences faced by people with disabilities and their families. Added to her "life experience" was an educational background that provided her with further insights into the physical and psychosocial issues that are common to people with disabilities. Ann held degrees in physical therapy and in social work. Prior to beginning work with the PAS Project, Ann's nearly 20 years of work in disability health and social services work included working at a rehabilitation facility for youngsters with orthopedic disabilities, setting up a case management program for individuals with developmental disabilities, providing behavioral support consultation to community-based disability services, as well as working with a consumer-directed PAS program in another state. Ann considered herself a macro social worker, with a background in direct services to individuals and their families, and her interest focused on program development, policy formulation, and systems change.

Kevin had quite a following in the disability community. As the nursing consultant on the team, he was considered the expert on the development of consumer-directed PAS. Like Janet and Ann, Kevin had an extensive background in disability services work, having worked in a variety of settings, institutional-based as well as community-based. His short period of work in an institution for individuals with developmental disabilities convinced him that community-based living, work, and recreational opportunities offered the only true chance for self-determination and empowerment for individuals with disabilities. Kevin's research for his doctoral dissertation focused on the development of PAS options, including funding supports for those services.

Kate had spent much of her professional life combining her creative artistic energy with her interest of involving people with disabilities in the visual arts. Although not employed with the PAS Project, she played a critical role within the group, both as an individual skilled in conflict resolution and as Janet's long-term companion. Because of her employment as a secretary in another part of the Department of Human Services, Kate needed to regularly evaluate the potential impact of her association with us on her career. However, because she was so consumer-focused, when the question of possible personal costs was raised, she reminded us of our responsibility to the people with disabilities who would benefit from an expanded personal assistance services program. Kate was the quietest of the group, but clearly actively involved, providing reasoned advice and support. Her talents as an artist would come into considerable use when we began to use promotional buttons as a part of our awareness campaign.

Jack, like Kevin, was a staff member to the PAS Project. Although no one would believe it because of his bearlike appearance, Jack tended to be quiet and perhaps a little shy. This shyness was clearly not a sign of lack of commitment, as he brought to the group a sense of tenacity and humor as we began to encounter barriers in our identification of and work on service user-

or consumer-directed PAS legislative issues. Jack had spent several years working in disability services, with experience in both direct work and administrative and supervisory roles. He was relatively new to the PAS Project, having transferred from another rehabilitation agency during a period of state workforce reductions. Jack's status as the new kid on the block did not lessen his enthusiasm for the program that we were going to propose, nor did it interfere with his making a commitment in helping to assure that service user-directed PAS got to the people who desired and needed the program. Jack had a presence that was indeed formidable.

The PAS Project

The PAS Project was established as an innovative state response to Section 1915(c) of the Social Security Act (the Act), which authorizes the Secretary of Health and Human Services to waive certain Medicaid statutory requirements enabling states to cover a broad range of home- and community-based services as an alternative to institutionalization. This provision, also known as Medicaid Waiver, was added to the Act as part of P.L. 97-35, OBRA (Omnibus Budget Reconciliation Act) of 1981, and as "amended by P.L. 99-272, COBRA (Consolidated Omnibus Budget Reconciliation Act) of 1985; P.L. 99-509, OBRA 1986; P.L. 100-203, OBRA 1987; P.L. 100-60, the Medicare Catastrophic Coverage Act of 1988; P.L. 100-647, the Technical and Miscellaneous Revenue Act; and P.L. 101-508, OBRA 1990." The focus on home- and community-based services continued with P.L. 105-33, the Balanced Budget Act (BBA) of 1997; the July 1999 Supreme Court decision in *Olmstead v. L. C.* (http://www.cms.hhs.gov/olmstead/, July 15, 2002); and June 18, 2001, Executive Order No. 13217—Community-Based Alternatives for Individuals with Disabilities (ADAPT, Centers for Medicare and Medicaid Services, n.d.).

"Prior to P.L. 97-35, the Medicaid program provided little coverage for long-term care services in a noninstitutional setting, but offered full or partial coverage for such care in an institution" (Home and Community-Based Waivers—Guidelines, 1991, p. 1). The decision to extend to people with disabilities and to elders home- and community-based services that, previous to this legislation, they could only receive in an institution was liberating to the individual but required a difficult transition for a system of health care service delivery largely founded on an institutional basis. The intent of these changes on a federal level was to allow individual states to develop programs to meet the needs of citizens.

An important consideration regarding the efforts of this state-based activity was the related legislative advocacy work that was taking place at the federal level. Legislation, such as Medicaid Community Attendant Services and Support Act (MiCASSA), is pending. If passed, the bill would advance self-determination and autonomy of individuals by creating a national program of community-based attendant services and supports for all people who are considered to be legitimately disabled within the definition of the law. Of particular note for our work was the focus on the increase in control over services and thus living locations that would be afforded to individuals with legitimate disabilities who currently reside in institutions (ADAPT, n.d.).

Initially, it seemed logical to many to have the home- and community-based services continue to involve agency oversight and direction. For most states, home- and community-based services were called personal assistance services. PAS included assistance with ADLs, such as eating, bathing, dressing, bladder and bowel requirements, and IADLs, such as assistance with food preparation, medication management, and community safety skills.

Agency-directed PAS was only the beginning. Increasingly individuals with disabilities, and advocacy groups for people with disabilities and elderly persons began to focus on an approach to services that would allow individuals to recruit, train, and manage their own services. The move from agency-directed home- and community-based services to service user-directed ones began when our state legislature passed a joint House and Senate Resolution requesting the Department of Human Services to evaluate the feasibility and advisability of amending our existing Elderly and Disabled Medicaid Waiver to allow individuals who require assistance with personal care activities the option to hire and manage their own personal attendants.

Like a number of PAS Projects in other states, our project was administratively located within our state's Department of Human Services. Other projects were attached, for example, to Departments of Medical Assistance Services, Departments of Health, or Departments of Rehabilitative Services.

At the basis of our PAS Project was a vigorous service user–professional relationship. We took pride in our work together to push for systems change for persons with disabilities and their families. It was this systems-level change that brought us together in the Hearing Room at the State House of Delegates.

Preparation for the Hearing

The issue at hand was that we needed to present information that would assist the Disability Services Committee to recommend to the entire state legislature as to whether to amend the current Medicaid Waiver. Our data and the input of service users clearly supported a new option allowing users to direct PAS services. We had spent the last few months preparing for this day. Our interpretation of our responsibilities from the previously enacted legislation was that we needed to identify personal assistance services problems and issues and to develop solutions to those problems. This new Medicaid Waiver option, allowing people with disabilities and elders the option of a service user- or consumer-directed model of services, supports the values of personal independence, dignity, and control over one's life. Kevin updated his original research comparing the components of personal assistance services in other states, research on the skills, and the capabilities an individual would need to best utilize a service user-directed approach versus an agency-directed approach, and developed a model for our state that incorporated the successes of the others.

After careful consideration of financial and political factors viewed in the context of our commitment to the principles of self-determination and empowerment, we were convinced that a model offering the option of user direction would best meet the needs of service users. In addition, we thought the model would be politically salable, would maximize public resources, and would allow participation by older individuals and persons with disabilities in all aspects of community living. The initial set of recommendations regarding specific aspects of the design of home- and community-based services included the following provisions: (1) a user-directed services option should be offered to individuals who are 18 years of age and older, without a significant cognitive impairment and able to communicate sufficiently to hire, train, and provide instruction regarding their needs to attendant staff; (2) community agencies, such as providers of home health, personal care, and centers for independent living, should serve as the fiscal agents for user-directed services; (3) the service user should be advised of the availability of the option of user-directed services at the point of preadmission screening, as well as at subsequent points of reevaluation of needs; (4) a single point of agency entry for home- and community-based services; (5) services should be available when and as needed by the user; (6) the service user-directed model should include training for the user in the recruiting, hiring, and managing processes of his or her services; (7) attendants in the service user-directed model should be a minimum age of 18 years, have an ability to read and write, perform basic math skills, be willing to submit to a criminal record check and have had an introduction to the philosophy of consumer-directed services; (8) as a physical extension of the service user's body, the attendant should be able to provide at the user's direction, any service needed without restriction; and (9) there must be quality-control mechanisms built into the program, including user evaluation of services.

We were at today's hearing to support the extension of this option of user-directed services to individuals under provisions of the Medicaid Waiver program. Because we were new to this business of legislative advocacy, we enlisted the expertise of a consultant, James, who had decades of experience in working in state government at all levels and who had an ongoing professional relationship with a number of key legislators. James, though remaining in the background during the legislative session, taught us many skills and strategies that would be critical as we worked to have the legislation move forward to authorize user-directed PAS. We were able to obtain James's expertise through a preexisting "personal services contract" that was not specific about why we needed him. A personal services contract sets a spending limit under a specified dollar amount allowing a state agency to bring in a consultant for time-limited projects without a time-consuming procurement procedure of obtaining bids from multiple sources. We had to be very careful in using James as a consultant because agency funds cannot be used for lobbying activities. Public employees in our state were not allowed to initiate any contact with legislators, nor could any funds be paid to registered lobbyists. We were safe in using James because, although he was on a first-name basis with many of the legislators and knew them well from previous state employment, he was neither a registered lobbyist nor a current state employee.

The Hearing

We were prepared, or thought we were, for what would occur that day. We had our supporting data compiled into folders that had been distributed to all of the members of the special legislative Disability Services Committee that was meeting in the Hearing Room. The Disability Services Committee, whose members were appointed by the governor, had been in existence for seven years. Its chair was the lieutenant governor who at the time of the hearing was from the political party opposing the governor's party. The Disability Services Committee had been established by legislation and was given the authority to create its own agenda based on citizen input. Members of this special committee were expected to determine and prioritize the bills and budget amendments that they, as state senators and delegates, would introduce during the legislative session each January.

Janet was standing alone at the podium summarizing the written materials that were in front of the committee members.

> *We are before you today, seeking your support for the development of an option of user-directed personal assistance services under our current Medicaid Waiver based Personal Assistance Services program. We have conducted national research of various types of personal assistance programs, including that currently available in our state, albeit on a limited basis, to individuals with physical disabilities and the elderly. As you are aware, we offer the option, under a non-Medicaid financed program, of both service user-managed and agency-managed services to some individuals. Although elements of each of these models can be intertwined, individually they have unique features that require careful analysis.*
>
> *An agency-managed personal assistance program involves a system of service provision that connects several individual attendants with several elderly and disabled persons. A service user-managed, or consumer-directed, personal assistance services program involves specific attendant or atten-*

dants providing services to a specific individual, at that individual's direction and guidance.

Our user-directed services program was developed as a pilot or trial program. Its success is clear and without question. Home- and community-based services reduce costs to the state and to third-party insurance programs, while enhancing the overall quality of services and level of satisfaction for those services on the part of the individual. Of the approaches to providing attendant care, the service user-directed model gives the most benefits, responsibility, independence, self-reliance, and life satisfaction. Home- and community-based services are also economically sound, reducing costs for services and thereby increasing the numbers of individuals who may be served without increasing the overall dollars spent. If we examine national averages, for every one aging or disabled person housed in a nursing home, the average annual cost is $40,784, while the average annual cost of providing Medicaid Personal Care to an individual is $9,692.

After careful consideration of all the issues involved, we are recommending that the option of a Medicaid Waiver based service user- or consumer–directed model best meets the needs of all persons with disabilities and their families in our state. We are recommending that the pilot program of providing the option of user-directed home- and community-based personal assistance services to the elderly and disabled be made permanent and that it be expanded to all those eligible under the existing program guidelines. We believe that this can be done safely, with full respect for the individual, while also assuring that programmatic safeguards be built in that protect the individual in the event of the absence, loss, or diminution, or impairment of cognitive function.

Thank you for your consideration of our proposal.

Never had she been so eloquent in her presentation of issues that supported the development of user-directed services that could expand the options of community living for so many people with so many types of disabilities. It was clear that this model offers the opportunity to have people discharged to the community from nursing homes, state hospitals, and state developmental disability centers. The committee members listened very carefully and began asking questions. More than one of them expressed how impressed they were with the data presented. They began to talk excitedly among themselves regarding how they, as a body, could propose the legislation, determine who would be chief patron, and what strategies could be used.

All of a sudden, the director of our state agency, who directly supervises Janet, rose and made his way to the podium. Positioning himself in front of the microphone, he asked to be recognized by the chairperson of the committee. The agency director began by stating, "I think we need to wait because we have not studied this issue enough. I ask that you not put forward legislation for the user-directed personal assistance services option of our Medicaid Waiver."

The hearing room became deathly quiet. Everyone, committee members and those of us in the audience, turned to each other with a look of disbelief on their faces. There was not a person in the room who did not know that this was a boss pulling the plug on his own staff who had just been successful in generating legislative interest in a new program.

Finally, after a moment had passed, Yvonne, director of the Department of Human Rights, a state agency that also serves people with disabilities, asked to be recognized and urged the committee to move forward in spite of what her fellow state agency director had just said. But it was clear that the lines had been drawn. A "we" and "they" had emerged. The "they" included the agency director, his boss, the secretary of Health and Human Resources Programs who was a member of the governor's cabinet, and numerous agency employees. As for the "we," we had no more supporters than when the meeting began because committee members were confused, and, although they cautiously agreed to support the development of a service user-directed PAS program, it was not clear what would happen in the one-and-one-half months prior to the opening of the legislative session.

In the past, legislation put forward by the committee always came with a recommendation and support from the corresponding state agency. Now here was the service user-directed PAS program, which was to be sponsored by the Disability Services Committee, without the endorsement of the agency director or apparently of the governor's cabinet secretary who oversees all disability-related agencies.

The PAS Team Regroups

Frank, stung by the comments of the agency director, in a not too muffled voice when leaving the Hearing Room, exclaimed: "Where does he come off talking against service user-directed PAS? He claims that he wants our ideas and that he listens to us, but then talks against the program. I guess he'll support 'our ideas' so long as they are 'his ideas.' He may have an impairment, but that does not make him understand the needs of disabled people!" As we met later that night and the next day, Frank's feelings of betrayal began to shift to distrust of the director. This change was not necessarily bad because it also forced Frank to begin to take seriously the need to strategize and to plan for change.

Although Janet appeared to Frank to be taken aback by her bosses' lack of support at the hearing, rather than saying something negative said, "I didn't see that one coming. I guess I will just need to work harder and be better prepared next time. I sent him the information ahead of time, I informed him about what we intended to do. Maybe he thought that if he could make me look bad, he would look good." Knowing the details of personal assistance services programs, Kevin just shook his head, and said, "I don't think that is it. This guy is not informed on what it is like for many people with disabilities. Instead of thinking that he knows what people need or are capable of, he should be asking and listening. Look, we are here for the long haul. We were here before our director, and we will be here after him. For him, being the director of a human services agency is just a job. For us, our work is about people and disability, and rights and access to the types of services they are asking for and want."

Ann, ever the one to see beyond the immediate crisis to the future said, "Heck, he is only one person. We just need to be smarter and begin to turn to the strengths of our work, disabled people. We've got to get disabled people involved. The disability community knows our director is no ally." Kate, after sitting quietly for some time, said, "The better we do, the worse he will appear. This is not about trying to get him, it is about us working to make sure folks can get what they want and need." Jack noted, "He was just trying to show that he is in charge. If he can act like 'the boss,' he thinks that people will know he is in charge. And if he can show that he has control over this, then he thinks that other people will let him control them and their programs." Frank, not willing to let this go quite yet, said, "For me, this is about whether I am going to let some professional bureaucrat control my life. Well, let's get this straight. I am tired of professionals thinking they know what is best for me. As a disabled man, I think I know who is the expert on the issues that affect me and my life, *me!*"

After the Disability Services Committee meeting, we regrouped and began to strategize how to get persons with disabilities involved, facilitating the voice of our service users. It was very apparent that, except for Frank, who worked at the university, paid staff of the PAS Project were the ones principally making the case for what service users needed, and not the users themselves. There had been few in the audience who could have spoken directly from personal experience as to the need; in fact, no service users had spoken at the hearing. We had not yet figured out how to maximize consumer representation, voices that can be much louder and less cautious than those of state employees.

Janet suggested, "We should encourage the strongest public speakers to be our spokespersons. In this way, we could increase the impact of the testimony. After all, it will be difficult for legislators to look into the faces of people with disabilities and then vote 'No' on the bill."

After thinking about Janet's comment, Kevin noted, "When our state Disability Bill of Rights was reauthorized in 1995, the disability organizations were encouraged to have individuals with disabilities take on a greater role in our legislative processes. We can use this 'encouragement' to justify using money from our PAS Project's budget to pay for necessary accommodations, such as transportation and sign language interpreters, so that these spokespersons can participate in public hearings."

"I can rewrite our informational reports and fact sheets in a style that makes them easier to read and follow. We also need to work on getting the fact sheets out to as many people and groups in the disability community as possible," said Ann. "Kevin and Jack, I am going to need help in making sure that all of the information materials that we distribute are in alternate or accessible format."

Without any hesitation, Jack replied, "Ann, just give me a computer disk with the informational reports, the fact sheets, as well as anything that you think is important on it, and I will take care of translating them into large print, Braille, and audiotape and make duplicate disk copies. I don't think that we should wait until we are asked for them; we need to make sure that we always take our reports and fact sheets to any meetings in accessible format."

Seeing a place for her talents, Kate reminded us that she had a background in art and design. "I can make up 'Support PAS' buttons. We can pass them out and ask people to wear them at all public legislative hearings dealing with personal assistance services." Individuals wearing these buttons were to become known by sight and even by name to a number of key legislators.

WHAT THE UNDERGROUND
ADVOCATES LEARNED

Ever the pragmatist, Ann sat down and began to sketch out a strategy of contacts, making sure that we sought support from both political parties and senators as well as delegates. Ann said, "Let's make a list of contacts with names, telephone numbers, fax numbers, office numbers, and addresses. We should talk with a couple of the committee members we know and get their suggestions. But let's not leave James out of this. After all, he knows the system much better than we do. We are just learning it, but he has been doing it."

So we decided to push for legislation this year that would establish the service user- or consumer-directed PAS program for conversion of waiver services for 35 people, and to spend the time between this session and the next working on converting services for an additional 75 people. We learned a great deal about legislative change and about the power of underground advocacy. We want to be clear in stating that no agency rules or state policies were broken by our underground tactics. We were not seditious or insubordinate, but we were very calculating at being at the right place at the right time and in inviting potential customers of service user-directed PAS to speak for themselves. In the end, a bill was passed, policies established, and an outcome was achieved at a time when we were told at every level of state government, "You can't do this!" There is no doubt that we worked very hard and had many ups and downs along the way; we had two great achievements. First, we were successful in securing legislative authority that created the structure for the operation of the expanded PAS. Second, we emerged from the process with a profound realization that without the strong voices of the individuals with disabilities and their caregivers, the system does not change.

The following year we were back at the table, now with insights gained from our legislative success the previous year. It is important to note that the "we" this time was not the original underground advocacy team. Rather, an expanded "we" was comprised of a cross-disability coalition of disabled individuals from around the state, family members, and nondisabled allies. Janet, Ann, Kevin, Kate, and Jack were still around but were clearly in technical assistance roles. Frank took on an expanded role. As a disabled person who was not employed by the PAS Project, he could continue to help lead the way in passing on the lessons learned the previous year; with a sense of confidence that comes from learning and being successful, Frank was able to adopt a more public activist role. As is often the case with systems change and bureaucracies, the "they" were still there. Because often bureaucrats and political appointees seem to move from position to position within an agency, or from agency to agency, this time the "they" were a similar, but different, group of individuals. Unlike many agency directors and gubernatorial appointees who would come and go, Frank's disability played a role in ensuring that he would remain there. After all, legislative changes such as these have a very direct and real impact on his life and on the lives of others with disabilities.

DISCUSSION QUESTIONS

Understanding the Problem

1. How would you define the problem(s) identified by the Underground Advocates in this case? How would you state the problem so that *others* could clearly comprehend what you are wanting to do?

2. In preparing for change, what might the coalition have done *before* the hearing to identify and analyze the problem? How would this process assist members of an advocacy coalition in preparing to respond to unanticipated consequences?

3. What opportunities, conditions, needs, and issues should be considered in building and forming a coalition between bureaucrats and service users? In what ways do the bureaucrats in this case behave as you would expect? In what ways did they behave in ways you would not have expected?

Understanding the Population

1. Where would you go to gather literature about service user- or consumer-directed personal assistance services for persons with disabilities?

2. What theoretical frameworks would you use to better understand this population group?

3. Why is it important for the coalition for disability issues to have a person with a disability as spokesperson? Are there certain circumstances when a person without a disability should be the spokesperson? How would you include diverse voices and perspectives in articulating and understanding the identified problem(s)?

Organizing for Change

1. What potential conflicts might be expected by bureaucrats who want to gain the support of state legislators?

2. How might a paid lobbyist be used in representing a service user coalition before legislators? In what areas might a lobbyist have greater influence than a disabled constituent?

3. If you were Janet and all of your planned change efforts had failed, and the legislation did not gain support from any legislator to introduce it, what would you have done? How would you go about redefining and re-analyzing the problem so that your coalition would be more successful in the future?

4

THE GUATEMALAN
STOVE PROJECT

MELISSA L. ABELL

THEORETICAL AND PRACTICE PERSPECTIVES

The following case illustrates some of the complexities of community practice within a framework of sustainable development. A social worker from the United States, Teresa Kanter, travels to a poor community of indigenous people in Guatemala. Impressed with the work of a parish church that has embarked on a plan of sustainable development, she becomes involved with the community over an extended period of time. Eventually, Teresa becomes involved in the identification and analysis of a community problem that adversely affects the health of families and the environment. Teresa attempts to initiate a project to provide a safer, fuel-efficient alternative to the open-air fires used for cooking in homes. Along the way, however, she encounters some resistance in the community and her own cultural biases. Several themes emerge: (1) the definition of sustainable development and what it entails, (2) ideas about gender roles in a patriarchal society, and (3) cultural competency requirements for macro practitioners.

Sustainable Development

There is considerable emphasis on the economic growth of developing nations. For example, the gross domestic product (GDP)—a measure that captures the production of all goods and services within the country—has increased in Guatemala over the past 20 years. However, economic growth has not been accompanied by improvements in the social well-being of many individuals and the environment of the community (Cobb, 1995; Midgley, 1995). This imbalance results in "distorted" development (Midgley, 1995, pp. 73–74). Further complicating the process of sustainable development in Latin America is vast inequality. Guatemala is among the top five countries in the world in terms of unequal distribution of wealth (UNDP, 2001). Wealth is so skewed that national statistics do not accurately reflect the state of economic and social well-being for most indigenous Guatemalans who are among the poorest citizens. Social indicators reflective of health and education are not improving for most indigenous Guatemalans in spite of increases in GDP (The World Bank, 2001).

In 1987, the World Commission on Environment and Development (WCED, also called the Brundtland Commission) defined sustainable development as "development that meets the needs of the present without compromising the ability of future generations to meet their own needs" (p. 43). This definition of sustainable development is, however, ambiguous. Many believe that the WCED definition fails to address the social welfare needs of individuals and the environmental issues of communities (Brown, 1991; Estes, 1993; Midgley, 1995; Pandey, 1998).

The definition of sustainable development should encompass the concept of social development. Social development approaches involve community residents in the development of community goals, implementation of interventions, and understanding the costs and benefits of development projects (Pandey, 1998). Inherent in the concept of social development is the concern with human dignity, justice, and the equitable distribution of resources (Midgley, 1995). Such approaches to sustainable development must be ecologically friendly and involve community members. Any improvements, such as roads, buildings, and other infrastructures, should be constructed of local resources and, as much as possible, avoid the infusion of additional outside resources (Brown, 1991).

Gender Roles in a Patriarchal Society

Teresa Kanter discovered that understanding gender roles and their significance is particularly important to facilitating the implementation of the stove project in this rural setting. Kemp states it this way: "As a key determinant of social power, gender (defined here as sexual difference that is socially organized or constructed) is deeply implicated in the ways in which environments are constituted and experienced by women and by men" (2001, p. 8). Because the identified problem directly impacts women, male community leaders may be reluctant to allocate scarce local resources to it. Women play critical roles in rural Latin American family life, and their roles are clearly defined as caregivers. They are expected to be subservient to the men in the household who occupy positions of authority.

As a result of their prescribed roles in family and community, women face unique health hazards in their environment that are different than those faced by men (Kettel, 1996). The women in this case work primarily within the home; if they become ill, it is likely as a result of the health hazards within that setting (Young, 1997). Women and children are more likely than men to be adversely affected by the smoke and flames of in-house, open-air fires. Consequently, men may fail to realize the full health benefits of the stove project because their interests lie instead on the economic benefits of paid jobs within the community and the preservation of the forests. For a provocative analysis of the global implications of gender and home-based work, see Prugl (1999) and Folbre (2001).

Not only is gender an important consideration, but the layering of racial and gender identities within a given society increases the complexity of understanding the needs of any population group. Baca Zinn and Thornton Dill emphasize the importance of racial and class differences as "primary organizing principles in a society which locates and positions groups within that society's opportunity structures" (1997, p. 24). This leads to the third theme with which Teresa must struggle—the necessity of having cultural competency.

Cultural Competency

Although Teresa, a social worker from the United States, was sensitive to cultural differences and the importance of maintaining the cultural integrity of any intervention, she was not ready for the extreme poverty and deprivation she witnessed in a developing country. Her enthusiasm for wanting to improve the lives of families had to be tempered with the realization that she was within a community that holds traditional Mayan values and prefers technological improvements that support those values. The Mayan culture is based on a very simple agrarian way of life with a focus on religion, community, and family life. It also reflects a patriarchal society. Teresa came to appreciate that Mayan people have expertise and knowledge that she does not have. It was important that she learn from her Mayan friends the best ways to become involved within their community in a manner consistent with their values and goals so that it would be sustainable. Cultural competence is derived from an understanding that people of different cultures have their unique approaches to "helping" that, in part, defines their perceptions of identity (Harper & Lantz, 1996). Teresa began not only to understand these cultural differences but to apply them.

A model of social development emphasizes the need for collaboration with community members and a sensitivity to local cultural values (Midgley, 1995). Many individuals and organizations from the developed world, including government agencies, churches, and nongovernmental organizations (NGOs), seek to assist communities in the developing world. Often, those who want to help bring with them a sense of technological, financial, and intellectual superiority and ideas that reflect the culture of the developed world. The consequences of their actions can result in development that does not reflect local customs, is not environmentally friendly, and is simply not sustainable because of the use of equipment and technology that is not readily available in the region.

REFERENCES

Abell, J. D. (1997). Peace in Guatemala? The story of San Lucas Toliman. In J. Brauer & W. G. Gissy (Eds.), *The economics of conflict and peace*. Brookfield, VT: Ashgate Publishing.

Baca Zinn, M., & Thornton Dill, B. (1997). Theorizing differences from multiracial feminism. In M. Baca Zinn, P. Hondagneu-Sotelo, & M. Messner (Eds.), *Through the prism of difference: Readings on sex and gender* (pp. 23–29). Boston: Allyn and Bacon.

Bread for the World. (1990). *Hunger 1990*. Washington, DC: Institute on Hunger and Development.

Brown, L. D. (1991). Bridging organizations and sustainable development. *Human Relations, 44*(8), 807–831.

Cobb, J. B. (1995). Toward a just and sustainable economic order. *Journal of Social Issues, 51*(4), 83–100.

Estes, R. J. (1993). Toward sustainable development: From theory to praxis. *Social Development Issues, 15*(3), 1–29.

Folbre, N. (2001). *The invisible heart: Economics and family values*. New York: New Press.

Harper, K. V., & Lantz, J. (1996). *Cross-cultural practice: Social work with diverse populations*. Chicago: Lyceum Books.

Jonas, S. (1991). The battle for Guatemala: Rebels, death squads, and U.S. power. Latin American Perspectives Series, No. 5. Boulder: Westview Press.

Kemp, S. P. (2001). Environment through a gendered lens: From person-in-environment to woman-in environment. *Affilia, 16*(1), 7–30.

Kettel, B. (1996). Women, health and the environment. *Social Science Medicine, 42*(10), 1367–1379.

Midgley, J. (1995). *Social development: The development perspective in social welfare*. London: Sage.

Pandey, S. (1998). Women, environment, and sustainable development. *International Social Work, 41*(3), 339–355.

Prugl, E. (1999). *The global construction of gender: Home-based work in the political economy of the twentieth century.* New York: Columbia University Press.

United Nations Development Programme (UNDP). (2001). *Human Development Report: Making new technologies work for human development.* Oxford: Oxford University Press.

World Bank. (2001). *World development indicators.* Washington, DC: The International Bank for Reconstruction and Development.

World Bank. (1995). World Development Report. New York: Oxford University Press.

World Commission on Environment and Development (WCED). (1987). *Our common future.* Oxford: Oxford University Press.

Young, I. M. (1997). House and home: Feminist variations on a theme. In I. M. Young. *Intersecting voices: Dilemmas of gender, political philosophy, and policy* (pp. 134–164). Princeton, NJ: Princeton University Press.

THE CASE

THE GUATEMALAN STOVE PROJECT

The crowing of the roosters signified daylight breaking over the mountain. Teresa Kanter pulled the pillow over her head to shut out the cacophony of roosters, dogs, and cars that had become a familiar part of her morning. Her dog, Alistair, wandered over to her bed and licked her face, letting Teresa know that he was ready to go for their morning walk. Within minutes Teresa was walking Alistair through the rutted streets of Santo Andreas, a community of about 40,000 people largely of Mayan descent—the Cackchikel peoples—indigenous people whose ancestry dates back to 700 AD. The bright sunshine and warm temperature enhanced her mood. The aromas of the community coming to life were upon her; the open wood fires used in most Mayan households for cooking, fresh ground corn to be used in tortillas, and coffee from the parish church.

As she walked she reflected on the turbulent history of this community. Although Santo Andreas is located in the heart of one of the most fertile coffee-producing regions in Guatemala, there is a shortage of arable land. Like other indigenous peoples in Guatemala, the people of Santo Andreas have been systematically removed, through disease, enslavement, and exploitation, from the lands of their ancestors since the Spanish conquest in the sixteenth century. Since that time land has been increasingly concentrated in the hands of a ruling oligarchy and powerful agribusinesses, many from the United States. Land shortages have created social, economic, and political problems. When an attempt was made to redistribute the land to many of the indigenous people by Guatemalan president Jacobo Arbenz in 1952, the US government supported a military coup that brought down the Arbenz regime and restored the land to the Guatemalan oligarchy and powerful US corporations such as United Fruit.

Stripped of everything but the ability to endure endless hardship working on the plantations for the landed elite while receiving negligible wages, many indigenous people found themselves embroiled in a battle for survival. They took up arms in the form of a guerilla insurgency (Abell, 1997). The government's response to the guerilla movement was quick and violent. A 30-year civil war ensued whereby thousands of Mayan people were violently repressed by the Guatemalan military, and many indigenous communities experienced sweeping massacres until the end of the war in 1996. As one of those communities, the people of Santo Andreas experienced terror, extreme poverty, and violence at the hands of the Guatemalan military. Even though a fragile peace was negotiated in 1996, for the most part the Mayan people remain landless and among the poorest people in Guatemala.

To people from North America, the residents of Santo Andreas appear quite poor. Their homes are simple structures with dirt floors and corrugated tin roofs. Most have communal sources of water and limited access to electricity. Their vacation time is nonexistent. They work from sunup until sundown. Leisure time, usually on Sunday afternoons, is spent with family and friends in the central plaza of town. Few have luxuries such as cable television, VCRs, telephones, computers, electronic mail, DVDs, cell phones, or any of the other technological devices that North Americans use to make their lives so much "better."

The benefits of industrialization have not been realized by most of the people of Guatemala. The human development index (HDI) that ranks all UN member countries in terms of health, education, and economics places Guatemala lowest of all Latin American countries, with the exception of Haiti (UNDP, 2001). Even so, most human development indicators fail to account for the differences between the indigenous people and the middle and upper classes of Guatemala (Jonas, 1999). There is vast inequality in Guatemala where 2 percent of the people own 80 percent of the land (Bread for the World, 1990) and the richest 10 percent receive nearly half of all income (World Development Report, 1995). Adult literacy is 68 percent in Guatemala, but most indigenous people are illiterate (UNDP, 2001). Unemployment rates in Santo

Andreas are more than 50 percent. Overall poverty in Guatemala is nearly 60 percent (UNDP, 2001).

In the face of industrialization and expanding globalization, the Mayan people have retained much of their native culture. Historically, their way of life—culturally, spiritually, and economically—has been agrarian. Land is the primary natural resource in Guatemala. The volcanoes that formed this small country have endowed it with fertile soil. The climate permits a year-round growing season. As a result, agriculture is the principal way to make a living. Using only simple tools, few farm animals, their hands and their backs, the Mayan people have been and continue to be successful farmers.

THE RAMON FAMILY

Teresa grew up in and still resides in Michigan. She became involved in Santo Andreas three years ago as the result of an ecumenical mission project organized through her church. From the beginning, she was impressed with the economic development efforts of several US priests who, with the backing of a Catholic diocese in the United States, had come to Santo Andreas in the late 1960s to establish a parish church and move the community toward a model of sustainable economic development. Now she spends her summers working there when she has time off from her job as a school social worker. She has even learned rudimentary Spanish so that she can now engage in basic dialog with most of the residents. The majority of Mayans speak a tribal language so Spanish is a second language for them as well.

As a social worker, Teresa was most interested in the way in which the priests utilized the idea of self-determination and built on individual strengths and cultural values to resolve economic and political problems throughout the turmoil of the civil war into the present. Local men comprise the "committee"—members of the indigenous community employed by the parish who manage the myriad projects that occur in Santo Andreas. They are the leaders of the coffee project, the water project, the health clinic, the reforestation project, and other programs designed to foster the community's economic and social development. Committee members meet weekly with the parish priests to discuss the progress on their respective projects, identify funding and labor issues, and examine other community needs.

Teresa and other volunteers from across North America and Europe visit Santo Andreas throughout the year to assist the community leaders on these projects. Many of the volunteers come to Santo Andreas as part of their churches' mission projects, but others come as long-term volunteers without the support of a church or other community organization. News of the Catholic church's mission in Santo Andreas has spread throughout North

America as a result of fund-raising efforts by the parish priests in the United States over the past 30 years.

The priests from the parish church in this largely Catholic community raise funds through their sponsoring Catholic diocese in the United States, other North American Protestant and Catholic churches, nonprofit volunteer organizations, and individuals to facilitate programs that are economically and environmentally sustainable. Their philosophy is to keep the construction simple so that it can be accomplished locally. Rather than bring in laborers and craft workers from outside the community to build schools, health clinics, and water projects, the Santo Andreas men are trained and hired to do the work. Most of the construction materials for the projects are produced within Santo Andreas; for example, cement blocks used in the construction of the health clinic, schools, and other buildings are made locally using sand, cement, gravel, water, and manual presses. This results in employment for those who procure the materials and those who are able to fabricate the blocks from the materials. For the most part, the wages paid to local workers remain within the local economy. Some of the finest coffee in the world is grown in the mountains of Guatemala. In Santo Andreas they have a small coffee export project whereby coffee is grown, roasted, and shipped for a fair market price to a variety of churches and small distributors in the United States. The beans are handpicked, sorted, and roasted manually in what is a labor-intensive process, but one that ensures that the product is of excellent quality. These are only two examples of the myriad ways in which the community uses local labor to create jobs that pay a living wage.

During Teresa's second visit to Santo Andreas, she met the Ramon family who lived in a village outside of Santo Andreas. She was fascinated by this family's work ethic and lifestyle. Juan Ramon leaves his home early in the morning, before 6:00 AM to begin his journey to a large coffee plantation where he works as a day laborer making 20 quetzales per day, about $2.50 US dollars. After a long day of planting or harvesting the crops on the plantation, he returns home, but he does not rest. In the daylight that remains, he collects the firewood that is used to prepare the family's meals the next day. This means that he will traverse steep hillsides near his village to cut small trees and haul the firewood, which weighs about 100 pounds, home on his back. Then, Juan will tend his family's small garden. Unlike many indigenous families, the Ramons are lucky and have a small plot of land near their home on which they can grow squash and beans to supplement their diet.

Juan's wife, Lucia, rises at 5:00 AM to begin the meal preparations for her family. She is young, only 21 years old, and has four children under the age of five. Her first task is to build a fire. Her stove is constructed of a piece of tin supported by four wooden legs rising about four feet off of the dirt floor in the small room that she calls her kitchen. Lucia carefully arranges the pieces of firewood in a triangle on the tin surface before lighting it. Over this fire, she grills corn tortillas and warms squash and beans that sustain the family throughout the day.

The fire is both a blessing and a curse. Without it, the young mother would not be able to cook the corn tortillas that provide the family's sustenance. However, the open-air stove also threatens the health and well-being of this young family and the community. The arms of the young mother are burned and scarred from reaching across the fire to turn the tortillas. She and her children suffer from frequent respiratory infections, and their eyes are red from the ongoing exposure to the heavy smoke in their dwellings. Cooking pots rest precariously on the small pieces of firewood and many children in the community have been seriously burned, and some subsequently disabled, from the boiling contents of pots that fall. The smoke from open-air fires in all of the homes in the community pollutes the air, and a good deal of wood is needed to sustain the daily fire. Cutting the wood is not only a physical hardship on the men who collect it but also results in massive deforestation of their environment.

WOMEN'S GROUPS

Through the encounter with the Ramon family and her other experiences in Santo Andreas, Teresa noticed that there might be ways to more fully involve women in the development of the community. Teresa spoke with Lucia Ramon and some of her friends about the possibility of convening an informal open-ended group for women to discuss issues of importance to them. Lucia agreed to be a co-leader of the group. By posting notices in the church and through word of mouth, 12 women met at the church to talk with Teresa and Lucia about their family, health, and social and economic concerns. It seemed to Teresa that the issue of most concern was the health of their children. Even when the discussion was directed toward jobs, wages, and family concerns, the focus of the dialog ultimately was on the way these issues affected their children. Because children in this community are often sick, health-related issues were prominent. This outcome was not surprising to Teresa, or to Lucia, but neither was sure about how to act.

The roosters awoke Teresa early in the morning after the fifth meeting of the women's group. She was having trouble sleeping anyway. The group was growing; there were 16 women who attended yesterday, yet there seemed to be no discussion of how the women might begin to improve the health of their children. Her time in Santo Andreas was growing short—she was due to return to the States early the next week. It was apparent to Teresa that the open-air fires were contributing in many ways to the poor health of children as well as their parents. On this morning as she was walking Alistair, she began to think about ways in which she could introduce the idea of a basic modern stove to this community. She struggled with the question of how to move the community toward more modern technologies that might promote the health of the residents, improve the environment of the community, and increase family leisure time, yet be affordable, use available fuel, and foster sustainable development. All of this seemed to Teresa to be a major challenge.

TERESA GOES HOME

As she had done in the past, on her return to the United States, Teresa made a presentation about her visit to Santo Andreas to the members of her church. This time, however, she focused her presentation on the problem of the fires. She explained that any solution to the open-air fires should be consistent with the idea of sustainable development. That is, it would need to be a product utilizing local labor and resources to enhance the economic development of the community, and it needed to be a simple idea.

Afterwards, a member of the congregation, Jim Lefferds, indicated to Teresa that, as an engineer, developing the plan for such a stove held great appeal. Jim and Teresa met over the course of several months and together they gathered information from international organizations and developed a blueprint for stoves that would be inexpensive to build, would use firewood efficiently, and could be built with materials available locally. Stoves would be constructed of cement blocks, which Teresa knew were already produced locally, and put together by mortar. Stovepipes could be molded out of cement. The only thing that they needed from outside the community was the stove top. The design called for a flat piece of iron with removable plates called *plancha*. These could be purchased in Guatemala City. Although the design was simple and efficient, the materials for the stove would still cost money. Teresa had to take her plan to the next phase—fund-raising.

She and Jim presented their plans for the stoves to the members of the church. They discussed a number of ideas to raise funds to build the stoves and during their discussion Teresa had an idea. When she visits Santo Andreas in the summer, she could return to Michigan with coffee from the project in Santo Andreas to sell in small stores, co-ops, and churches. Not only would this provide additional US outlets for the coffee, but it would provide seed money for the "stove project." Other church members indicated that they could help by distributing the coffee through friends and other church congregations.

Feeling excited about this prospect, she called the parish priests in Santo Andreas to seek their support. Although they were encouraging, they expressed concern that the stove project might not be embraced by the indigenous Mayan people. They suggested that she meet with the men from the community who comprised the local committee about her idea and ways to initiate it. Teresa felt downhearted. She knew the stove would improve the quality of life for the women and children in this community, but now she had to "sell" the idea to the community leaders. To make matters worse, she had not even discussed it with the women in her group. What if they didn't like it? Reluctantly, Teresa had to postpone her plans until her next visit to Santo Andreas the following summer. In the meantime, she researched the import regulations on coffee and continued to explore fund-raising alternatives. With the help of Jim Lefferds, she refined her stove project presentation to ensure that it would be clear and appeal to their interests. She would be ready to meet with the committee on her return to Santo Andreas.

RETURN TO SANTO ANDREAS

Traveling from the airport in Guatemala City with Timo, the driver from Santo Andreas sent by the parish church to pick her up and bring her to the mountain community, Teresa felt mixed emotions. As usual, she was happy to return to this beautiful country and the convivial surroundings of the parish and the community. And, she always felt somewhat nervous as her experienced driver daringly negotiated the narrow two-lane highways that wound through the mountains. More than this, however, she was worried about how her plan would be received by the community. She felt sure that Lucia would be supportive, but would they be able to convince the committee and other families of the utility of the stove?

After settling into her modest room, she set off to find Lucia. They had a warm reunion, and Teresa, in her simple Spanish, explained her idea about the stove. Teresa drew a picture of the stove for Lucia as she and Jim Lefferds had designed it, and they even marked off a place on the dirt floor where the stove might best be placed in her home. Lucia was excited by the prospect of the plan, yet she had many questions. Who would build the stoves? How could families pay for it? Would the stove work as well as the open fires? Teresa tried to respond as best she could, and Lucia worked with Teresa to modify her planned presentation on the stove project for the next meeting of the women's group. Lucia had continued to convene the women's group that had been started last summer and interest was growing. Nearly twenty-five women were meeting regularly now.

Teresa and Lucia prepared large, colorful drawings of the plan for the stove. They talked about the prospect of raising funds in the United States to help families pay for the stove. She admitted that she had not worked out all of the details, but was anxious to obtain their thoughts about the project. To her delight, the women expressed strong support, although they had many of the same questions that Lucia raised with regard to costs and the utility of the stove for their traditional cooking style. Nevertheless, as mothers well-versed in the adverse health outcomes as a result of the open-air fires, they were anxious to try something new that might improve the health of their families.

Now, Teresa needed to present her idea to the committee. The Mayan culture is patriarchal—men make the decisions for their families and lead the community. Since the war, however, the prestige of women had increased. Some women participated as guerillas in fighting against the government military forces. Many others became family and community leaders when the men were absent. Nevertheless, Teresa, knowing the local culture, was concerned that the male community leaders might not recognize the importance of this and simply dismiss it as a "women's issue." Teresa appealed to the women in the group for their thoughts about how to present the idea.

Monday morning is the usual committee meeting time. They gather at the parish church to talk with the priests and provide updates on the various projects of which they are leaders. Teresa met with the parish priests and asked for permission to attend that meeting and make a presentation. Teresa, Lucia, and Angela, a woman from the women's group whose young daughter had been badly burned from the open-air fire stoves, practiced their presentation. Lucia and Maria would start the presentation with a description of the problems with the open-air fires, then recount personal stories of children they knew who were burned when the contents of a hot pot balanced precariously on the firewood tipped over and spilled, of the respiratory infections in adults and children, and of the times they burned their own arms as they worked over the very hot fires. Next, Teresa would present their drawing of the stove. The women were nervous going into the presentation.

Members of the committee listened politely to their presentation. Afterwards, several expressed skepticism about the feasibility of the project. Their concerns were centered around funding the stoves; finding a skilled person to manage the building project; and, to a lesser extent, ensuring that the materials could be easily acquired within the community. In a time of scarce resources when larger projects, such as the coffee project, the reforestation project, and the water project, were in need of money and skilled labor, they were reluctant to consider funneling both into a small project, the benefits of which were perhaps less apparent than those of the other projects.

Conversely, several committee members endorsed the idea. Although they were cognizant of the feasibility issues discussed by others, they also noted the many advantages the stove project offered for their families and community. The stoves were designed to better the health of their families; and the project would employ a few local laborers, use local materials, and hopefully would diminish the destruction of the valuable forests. Teresa was relieved to see that several of the men saw this as a community issue and not simply a women's issue that could be easily dismissed. However, all community leaders, both those who were supportive and those who expressed skepticism, were less hopeful about funding the project. They also were reluctant to assign a skilled laborer from one of the larger projects to manage the stove project. After much debate in which both sides agreed that the stove project was worthwhile, the priests offered funds to pay the salary of one laborer to initiate the project. Impulsively, Teresa offered to donate the materials for the first stove.

IMPLEMENTATION OF THE STOVE PROJECT

Teresa was awakened by fireworks, which are as popular in Santo Andreas as they are in much of Latin America. This was a holiday in Santo Andreas. In celebration, people were setting off fireworks at 5:00 AM as they got up to start their day. There would be no further sleep this morning, so she got up to walk Alistair who was still asleep beside her bed. As she walked, she worried. So far, her tactics were working. She probably should have done things differently, such as obtaining approval from the community members before engaging in the planning and stove design, but, in the end, she was able to secure the support of both men and women in this indigenous community. She wondered if she had been appropriate in volunteering to pay for the first stove, but she quickly chided herself for second-guessing. Now, however, the rubber hit the road. Who was going to implement the stove project? Even though she had worked on the stove design with Jim, she didn't feel as though she had the skills to construct such a stove. And how was the project going to be funded? Would selling the coffee in the United States raise enough money to buy the building materials? She decided that she needed to meet with the parish priests to see what advice they might be able to offer.

The priests knew of a 16-year-old Mayan man, José, who might be the perfect candidate for leading the project. José, explained the priests, was the head of his family of five. He was responsible for the care of his mother and four younger siblings because his father died two years ago. José had been working on the parish reforestation project since that time. The project manager had remarked on José's strong work ethic, intelligence, and organizational skills; the stove project might be a perfect opportunity for him to assume greater job responsibility. The parish priests would continue to pay him the salary that he received from the reforestation project to manage the stove project, so any funds needed for the stove project would only need to be used for materials. Initially, José would work alone to build the stoves.

That was all well and good, and Teresa was grateful for the support of the parish, but still there remained the thorny issue of actually constructing a stove. Teresa felt uncertain about José's ability to manage the project given his young age. The following Monday, during the meeting of the committee, José came to the church. Teresa met him there and brought along the stove drawings to show him. José examined the drawings with great intensity. He appeared confident in his ability to construct the stove based on the blueprint that had been translated into Spanish and used the metric system with which he was familiar. Teresa was optimistic, yet harbored some doubts about the ability of a 16-year-old with limited education to construct something as complex as a stove solely from a blueprint and a drawing.

Teresa talked with Lucia about her concerns. The Ramons knew José to be a fine young man, but they could not reassure Teresa about his ability. They did agree to have a test stove built in their home. She contacted José, and arranged to meet with him at the Ramons' house to plan the construction of the first stove.

The First Stove

Although the roosters crowing outside of Teresa's room from 4:00 until 5:00 AM diminished her sleep, it did not lessen her excitement. This was the big day. José, Lucia, Juan, and she were going to begin building the first stove. This morning on her walk with Alistair she revisited the ideas in her mind for building the stove that she had already gone over a thousand times. They picked up the materials that they had ordered—cement blocks, cement mix, string, tape measure, and stovepipe—yesterday at the local hardware store in Santo Andreas. The cement blocks and stovepipe had been molded locally. A shovel, hoe, pick axe, sand, water, and trowel were available at Lucia's home. They only needed the *plancha* that she and José would pick up in Guatemala City tomorrow.

When she arrived at the Ramons' she found José digging up sand in their small yard. Asking what she could do to help, he gave her a shovel and invited her to dig. They dug the sand, then sifted it to remove larger stones and trash. They mixed the sand with the cement purchased at the hardware store and water. This mixture would be used to bind the cement blocks that were to comprise the bulk of the stove. First, however, José wanted to make a smooth place in the dirt and lay out a straight rectangle of blocks to form the foundation of the stove. Teresa was quite impressed with this young man's knowledge of construction and his attention to detail in the face of fairly crude building materials and tools. Before the end of the day, Teresa and José had worked together to construct the stove's cement block foundation. The stove was rectangular and the cement blocks would be mounted to form a four-foot high stove with a semi-hollow interior for the firewood. Their work was completed by the end of the week with the attachment of the stovepipe running from the top of the stove through a cutout in the tin roof and the placement of the *plancha* across the top of the blocks that formed the rectangle. On the final day of construction, Teresa wanted to see how the stove worked. Lucia started a fire and prepared her tortillas on top of the *plancha*. Juan and José thought they tasted as good as before.

WHERE TO GO FROM HERE?

At the next meeting of the women's group, Lucia and Teresa reported on the stove project. Lucia suggested that there were some minor problems to be worked out with the construction, such as improving the draw on the stovepipe to further reduce the smoke and increasing heat to the back burners of the *plancha*. For the most part, however, she was quite pleased about the diminished smoke in her home, and more important, she was less fearful about her children being burned. The women were anxious to see the stove, so the meeting moved to the Ramons' home. Many women in the group became excited about the prospect of having a stove built in their modest homes. Teresa expressed her concerns about funding future stoves. Although the stoves were fairly inexpensive by US standards, they were still beyond the means of most of the Mayans. She then shared with the women her plans, to be coordinated through the parish church and the diocese in the United States, to export the local project's coffee, which she would sell to friends, churches, and local co-ops in Michigan. Teresa made it clear that this was only a beginning. More money would be needed to ensure that every family who wanted a stove could have one.

Maria, a quiet young woman who had been attending the group since its inception, spoke to the group. She knew that the beautiful, labor-intense weavings done by the Mayan women brought very little income to their families when sold in Santo Andreas. She also knew, however, that volunteers from churches across North America visit the parish in Santo Andreas regularly. She suggested that perhaps an appeal could be made to the parish church volunteers to return home to the States and sell the weavings there in hopes of obtaining a higher price. The funds from the weavings could be used to build stoves. Those women who contributed weavings would be the first to have stoves. Teresa liked Maria's idea, but was concerned that not all families would be able to participate, hence some still might not be able to have a stove. The women's group decided it was now up to them to address this so that other means of earning money could be found and all families wanting to participate could do so.

DISCUSSION QUESTIONS

Sustainable Development

1. What do *you* think that "sustainable development" is, and how does this concept fit with the case you have just read?

2. How do you think that sustainable development in Santo Andreas differs from sustainable development within a U.S. community with which you

are familiar? How would this difference influence how you would approach problem identification and analysis?

3. What is the problem that Teresa identifies? Would your definition have been the same as hers? Why or why not?

4. Do you think the stove project will continue? What would you do next?

Gender Roles

1. If you were Teresa, how would you begin to understand gender roles within this community? With whom would you talk? What would you observe?

2. What resources would be helpful to Teresa in fully understanding the population group with whom she is working? Are there theories or frameworks that she might use?

Cultural Competency

1. Are there instances within the case when *you* think Teresa could have been more culturally sensitive? How might she have handled these situations differently?

2. How does one develop cultural competency skills? Why are they important to develop, and what difference might they make?

THE COMMUNITY AS
THE ARENA OF CHANGE

In the previous part, there were a number of communities represented. Some communities were place-related such as the Guatemalan village in which the stove project began or the locality in which a needs assessment process for elderly citizens was beginning. Other communities had broader boundaries, including the bonds that transcended local geographical places and linked advocates with the interests of special population groups.

In this part, we focus on the community as an arena of change. In the pages that follow, three major themes emerge. The first is community as a concept, with its many different meanings and operationalizations. Social workers will have different views of what community means, but it is particularly important to capture the views of persons who comprise those communities and who face the problems that have been identified. The second theme is participation in democratic processes. Both individuals and organizations are participants in the decision-making processes of a democratic society. How does one create inclusion in a diverse society with a multitude of competing interests and issues, and still take action? The third issue is the role of the practitioner in working with and in a community. The contemporary practice arena is varied and requires a range of skills that at times may be in conflict with each other. These practice skills tend to focus on expertise and organizing. The tension is frequently between the expert who is pushing a quick resolution or solution to an issue, and the organizer allowing the slow, democratic, participatory process to unfold and having the group's preferred solution to an issue evolve.

Each of the four cases is set in classic practice situations with contemporary twists. "The Reverend and Me" focuses on faith-based organizations that have always been centers of community resources but are now being called on to help Temporary Assistance for Needy Families (TANF) recipients. "Riverton" depicts an attempt to build a sustainable, regenerating community that balances a multiplicity of issues. "The Native Hawaiian Children's Center" demonstrates how difficult it is to balance community needs with staff expertise so that services can truly be targeted to address community needs. "Lindblom County" focuses on diversity and inclusion of excluded groups in the social planning process.

Across these cases, the role of the practitioner is varied. For example, in "The Reverend and Me," the community practitioner works in and with indigenous communities. He must be sensitive to the needs of the community, the potential impact of white institutions on minority communities, and the need to facilitate development of indigenous leadership within the community. This balancing of multiple agendas typifies community practice. It is practice in the middle—between a variety of issues and groups that may be antagonistic toward each other.

The community practitioner walks a line between two arenas of practice. On the one hand, she or he is called to be an expert on technical or content issues and is usually an employee of an organization that makes its own demands. This practice aspect requires expertise and proficiency in such things as needs assessment, instrument development, program design, and budgeting. On the other hand, the community practitioner is called on to be an expert on group work and group processes. This aspect requires expertise in group dynamics, conflict resolution, negotiation, and political organizing. The challenge to the community practitioner is to mix and phase these skills with the community's work and stage of development as a cohesive entity.

In "The Reverend and Me," the main character moves slowly, gets to know the reverend, and waits for the opportunity to arise rather than prematurely forcing anything to occur. Yet, this case (unlike the ones in Part II) flows into the implementation phase in which new issues arise. In "Riverton" and "Lindblom County," the workers are attempting to build, rebuild, and sustain a sense of community that they hope will engage a range of subgroups into the problem-solving work they face. These cases demonstrate the oscillation between technical expertise and group process work that is required of contemporary community practice, and this process is the primary focus of "The Native Hawaiian Children's Center."

As one reads the cases, one sees the concept of community played out in each case. Addressing needs and problems as a community brings greater resources to the work. Building a community that can competently and continually renew itself is the goal of the community practitioner: The challenge is identifying and coalescing the various members thereby creating and defining community.

5

THE REVEREND AND ME

Faith Communities and Public Welfare

ROBERT WINEBURG

THEORETICAL AND PRACTICE PERSPECTIVES

"The Reverend and Me" is a community practice case that reflects the importance of interpersonal relationships and trust in making change happen. It also places community practice and change squarely in the policy arena, and thus has relevance for understanding the tension between various policy perspectives. The themes highlighted in this case are (1) perspectives on social welfare as reflected in community practice, (2) the role of faith communities in the provision of welfare services, and (3) the use of indigenous leaders in community work.

The classical and authoritative work of Wilensky and Lebeaux (1958) shaped the underpinnings of welfare policy development until the 1980s. Their distinction between residual and institutional perspectives of social welfare drew the lines between conservative and liberal thinking about the nature of human beings in relationship to the marketplace.

The residual perspective is based on the premise that people's needs are met in three ways: through individual efforts, through family support, and by success in the marketplace. Respectively, these are the most important sources of independence and self-sufficiency. When there is a breakdown in any of these structures, like an individual bout with depression, a family's self-sufficiency threatened by the death of a bread winner, or a recession causing unexpected unemployment, welfare is seen as an emergency and temporary institution.

People are only expected to use this help in a crisis. Human service workers who provide help let the recipients know that help is temporary and not to expect more assistance once the family or the economic system starts to work properly. Because of its residual, temporary, and substitute characteristics, there is always the stigma of being "on the dole, or being a charity case," lurking in the minds of the recipient and the giver (Wilensky & Lebeaux, 1958). This was also the view traditionally held by conservative thinkers and a perspective that had lost favor with the public from the New Deal to the 1980s. In the last 20 years, however, a residual view of social welfare has made a resurgence and now underscores the reasoning behind the Personal Responsibility and Work Opportunity Act of 1996, commonly referred to as "welfare reform."

Like the residual view, an institutional perspective assumes that an individual is connected to large and intertwined systems and subsystems that include the individual, family, and economic system. However, this perspective recognizes that at any given time, people are both members of family systems and the global village. Some of the forces that keep them from mastering their fate in the family, community, or world are often beyond their control. In order for the individual and the society to function with a degree of dignity and stability, society sets up permanent ways to achieve, or institutionalizes, a balance between individual and social needs. This perspective implies no stigma, no emergency, no abnormalcy. Social welfare becomes accepted as a proper, legitimate function of modern industrial society in helping individuals achieve self-fulfillment, whereas the complexity of modern life is recognized and enhanced through institutionalized services. The change in the language of the new welfare reform from Aid to Families with Dependent Children (AFDC) to Temporary Assistance to Needy Families (TANF), and its accompanying five-year lifetime limit on federal assistance, reflects a shift away from the institutional to the residual perspective. Welfare is no longer permanent, but is temporary assistance to needy families.

In the case that follows, these two perspectives emerge in conversations between the Reverend Calbert Richmond and his social work colleague. They discuss residual and institutional perspectives of social welfare and literally bring these differing views into the local community arena.

A second theme that emerges in this case is the role of religious or faith-based communities in the provision of social welfare services in local communities. This case highlights one congregation's recent efforts to engage in social welfare provision, yet it is important to note that the relationships between religious and human service communities predate the profession of social work. The helping professions in the United States were influenced by a long history of religious traditions (see, e.g., Chambers, 1985; Loewenberg, 1988; Lohmann, 1992; Marty, 1980). Today, these relationships are being reexamined in light of the push for less government, more decentralized decision making, and privatization of services. With this push have come questions surrounding the role of the voluntary sector, secular and religious. These questions form a backdrop for this case.

Calls for the religious community to become increasingly involved in welfare reform, dating from the Reagan administration, are rooted in the residual perspective. There is a major assumption that people who fail in the marketplace and slide into poverty do so because of a lack of moral strength. It is also assumed that, if they cannot help themselves, or their families cannot help them out of their moral and impoverished bind, then the local church can both address the moral cause and help with the concrete provision of services until those in need are able to find their own way. In either instance, the solution for an individual's personal or economic demise is logically found through one's association with a faith community.

The case begins prior to President Bush's establishment of the White House Office of Faith-Based and Community Initiatives (White House, 2001), yet exemplifies the types of efforts promoted by this Office. The Welfare Reform Liaison Project that is described in this case became the *first faith-based* Community Action Agency in the United States (McGlaughlin, 2002). There are a thousand of these community action agencies nationally, and most evolved from the Way on Poverty initiative of the Lyndon Johnson era. When the opportunity became available to apply for the designation of the county's Community Service Block Designee, the persons involved in this case were a little nervous about partnering with government, but felt that they had an organizing base within the neighborhoods and in small churches. Within four years, the agency evolved out of a small emergency assistance ministry of a local church to an award-winning welfare-to-work training program that has placed more than 75 percent of its students in employment, becoming much more than a welfare-to-work program while remaining a nonprofit organization closely affiliated with its parent church.

The extensive involvement of the religious community in social service provision through both congregations and religious affiliate is well documented (Cnaan, 1999; Hodgkinson, Weitzman, Kirsh, Norga, & Gorski, 1993; Netting, 1984; Wineburg, 2001). There is a renewed research interest in the role played by religious communities in social welfare provision today. For the reader who wants more in-depth reading in this area, a number of articles are available (e.g., Chaves & Tsitsos, 2001; Cnaan & Boddie, 2002; Smith & Sosin, 2001).

Last, a theme that permeates this case is the importance of indigenous leaders in community work. Readers will discover how professionals with different perspectives on social welfare begin to trust one another and work together collaboratively. The inevitable tensions inherent in this relationship-building process are discussed in the community practice literature (Hardina, 2002) as well as the importance of ethnic-sensitive practice (Delgado, 2000).

REFERENCES

Chambers, C. A. (1985). The historical roots of the voluntary sector. In G. A. Tobin (Ed.), *Social planning and human service delivery in the voluntary sector* (pp. 3–28). Westport, CT: Greenwood Press.

Chaves, M., & Tsitsos, W. (2001). Congregations and social services: What they do, how they do it, and with whom. *Nonprofit and Voluntary Sector Quarterly, 30*(4), 660–683.

Cnaan, R. A. (1999). *The newer deal: Social work and religion in partnership.* New York: Columbia University Press.

Cnaan, R. A., & Boddie, S. C. (2001). Charitable choice and faith-based welfare: A call for social work. *Social Work, 47*(3), 224–235.

Delgado, M. (2000). *Community social work practice in an urban context.* New York: Oxford University Press.

Hardina, D. (2002). *Analytical skills for community organization practice.* New York: Columbia University Press.

Hodgkinson, V., Weitzman, M., Kirsh, A., Norga, S. A., & Gorski, H. A. (1993). *From belief to commitment: The activities and finances of religious congregations in the United States: Findings from a national survey.* Washington, DC: Independent Sector.

Loewenberg, F. M. (1988). *Religion and social work practice in contemporary American society.* New York: Columbia University Press.

Lohmann, R. (1992). *The commons: New perspectives on nonprofit organizations and voluntary action.* San Francisco: Jossey-Bass.

Marty, M. E. (1980). Social service: Godly or godless. *Social Service Review, 54,* 463–481.

McLaughlin, N. H. (2002, February 14). *Church gets grant lost by Jones—The Welfare Reform Liaison Project: An outreach of Mount Zion Baptist Church on Alamance Church Road.* Greensboro, NC: *Greensboro News* records, B1.

Netting, F. E. (1984). Church-related agencies and social welfare. *Social Service Review, 58*(3), 404–420.

Smith, S. R., & Sosin, M. R. (2001). The varieties of faith-related agencies. *Public Administration Review, 61*(6), 651–670.

White House. (2001). Rallying the armies of compassion—online at http://www.whitehouse.gov/news/reports/faithbased.html.

Wilensky, H. L., & Lebeaux, C. (1958). *Industrial society and social welfare: The impact of industrialization, supply and organization of social welfare services in the United States.* New York: Russell Sage Foundation.

Wineburg, B. (2001). *A limited partnership: The politics of religion, welfare, and social service.* New York: Columbia University Press.

THE CASE

THE REVEREND AND ME

Some of the most profound and often heated policy and social service issues get discussed in the men's locker room at Hillslide College where I play basketball three days a week. I refer to it as the low-testosterone game, a game for men in their 40s and 50s where, unlike the younger men's game at Hillslide, friendship is more important than winning. There is one woman in her 50s who plays regularly. Yet, as liberal as Hillslide is on some issues, the locker rooms are still separate. On some days there is probably more energy pumped into the political discussion before and after the game than what is exerted on the basketball court. It takes a lot more to move old bodies up and down a 90-by 50-foot slab of wood for 75 minutes than it does for them to bandy their political opinions recklessly for 15 minutes—which they often do routinely and effortlessly. It was here that I met the Reverend Calbert Richmond, associate minister of Mt. Massada Baptist Church, a licensed and soon to be ordained minister. He also serves as the first director of the Welfare Reform Liaison Project, a new nonprofit corporation established by Mt. Massada to help welfare recipients find and keep employment and to work with small African American churches in building the capacity to help welfare recipients.

There are several reasons why my relationship with Reverend Richmond is special and has implications well beyond the development of a lovely friendship between a Jewish social work planner and an African American Baptist minister. First, Reverend Richmond is what I call a link player. He is a young man of 37 and a former college basketball star who increasingly plays in the low-testosterone game. He doesn't have to play in the game with the older players. He is one of the best players out there, even among the 24-year-old men who still think that scouts from the National Basketball Association are watching. As such, they play with free-wheeling abandonment and individual purpose. Reverend Richmond links well to either game, acting as the elder statesman and arbitrator in the young men's game, and cheerleader in the older folks' game. The young men's games, interestingly, sound much like the political arguments that we older fellows have in the locker room before and after our game. Reverend Richmond is making a transition both on the basketball court and in life.

Statistically speaking, Reverend Richmond should not have made it to college, let alone earned a degree in management in 1984 and a master's degree in theology in 1997. He was one of four kids who lived with his divorced mother. In 1968, when his mother was 25, she had a stroke and the family lived off her $240-a-month disability check, and that was about it. According to Reverend Richmond, in those days, they did not push for child support from the father. As he says, "We were so po [poor] that we couldn't afford the other 'o' and the 'r.' " The college coaches wanted him to major in leisure studies to make sure his grades were good enough to maintain his sports eligibility. In other words, he was a "notch" in the career gunbelt of some college coach.

But Reverend Richmond is a true athlete and understood that to win in the game of life, like sports, three things are important: preparation, preparation, and preparation. Instead of leisure studies, he chose business. Reality came four years later. "I realized I had no more basketball eligibility, no NBA contract, and a year and a half of academic requirements left to graduate. I quickly became a man. I returned to school by way of guaranteed student loans, a work-study job, an academic scholarship, a 1:30 A.M. to 6:30 A.M. job at UPS unloading trucks, and a summer job at a basketball camp. My grades suffered because sometimes I was so tired from working and studying that I dozed off in class." A year and a half later, he earned his business degree. Now, he is a very successful sales representative for a large trucking firm, besides being an associate minister. So what would make this successful man want to give up a business career, seek ordination, and run a program to help welfare mothers develop the skills to maintain employment?

A vision! Silly as it may sound to a rational planner like myself, larger but unmeasurable purposes often dwell behind the motivations of clergy and many social workers too. I have often thought some social workers were secular evangelists looking for their ministry without the trappings of religion. Who else but the "other worldly types" or masochists would want to wallow day in and day out in life's social sanitation, only to come back each day for more wallowing if there weren't more to it than money? Reverend Richmond had a vision. His real purpose in life was to do more than sell contracts for the delivery of packages all over the country. He did not want a sales job until the day he, like one of his packages, was shipped off to his final destination. He saw himself living a life devoted to helping the less fortunate, plain and simple. Interestingly, he chose the most important social policy issue in 60 years on which to hang his new hat, even though he knew very little about welfare, welfare reform, social service delivery, and the people who receive services.

Although we knew each other from the games, we did not develop a relationship until one day I asked him what he was writing his master's thesis about which turned out to be titled, *Some Black Churches Response to the 1996 Welfare Reform Bill*. I thought to myself, "How interesting." Since the early 1980s, I have increasingly focused my attention and work with community groups on the role the religious community plays in service development as government budget cuts cause more voluntary service provision and a corresponding reconfiguration of relationships in the service-delivery systems locally among public, private, and sectarian service providers.

While Reverend Richmond was focusing his energies on becoming a high school basketball star in Charleston, South Carolina, in 1976, I was organizing a town meeting on welfare reform in Utica, New York, as part of then President Carter's attempts at fixing the welfare system. The Carter team came to Albany where our community practice class from Syracuse University attended the meeting. We were so disgruntled with the way it was handled that we organized a "real" town meeting and with some old-fashioned convincing, the Carter folks made another trip to upstate New York. I have been studying the subject and working with local organizations around this issue ever since.

I began to wonder if this conversation was a coincidence or fate, and tried not only to make sense out of it, but wondered as well what I might do next. As I tried to grasp the larger meaning out of what was happening, I remembered my college philosophy professor talking about St. Augustine's notion of free will versus predestination. He stood on the chair as if he were a higher being and said that God, according to St. Augustine, took a snapshot of all the human and natural events from the beginning to the end of time. That was predestination!

He stepped down from the chair and looked us in the eye. He then said convincingly that according to Augustine, even though God knows the outcome of all events, it is one's free will to choose how to act in every situation that gives each human life its unique flavor and life itself its great character. I never quite got that concept down until I found myself more intricately involved with Reverend Richmond. First, I found myself talking to him about welfare reform. Next, I was talking to him about the role the religious community will play in this new policy locally. Finally, and most interestingly, I found myself helping him develop a nonprofit corporation through which his church could make its contribution to help people move from welfare to work. In a flash, my destiny passed before my eyes—in a locker room no less. My philosophy teacher did not say when and where life's choices would hit one between the eyes, nor did he say whether one would blink. It was our choice, according to Augustine.

Here it is, 1999 and for the last four years, the entire human service community has been focusing on welfare reform and increasingly on the role the religious community would play in that new configuration. I just show up regularly for basketball. Because I chose to follow my nose in locker-room political discussions, I now find myself working with the largest African American church in my hometown, helping it conceptualize how it will respond to what will undoubtedly become an increasing set of demands by both individuals seeking help and the community asking where is the church and the charity? Oy!

Initially, my friend Reverend Richmond's idea of a Welfare Reform Liaison Project was rooted solidly in the residual perspective. A man who was so "po" (poor) as a kid that "they couldn't afford the 'o' or 'r' " was convinced that his good fortune was due to his mother's unconditional love, never quitting, the grace of God, and power of prayer. He said that some of the welfare recipients are lazy women who study how to beat the system, and they needed a dose of hard work and old-time religion to solve their impoverishment. When a 48-year-old, balding, Jewish, basketball has-been drives down the lane and looks up to see the 37-year-old Reverend Calbert Richmond, all 6 feet 3 inches, 225 plus pounds of him, trying to block his shot, mercy never comes into the reverend's eyes. That man cuts no one any slack in basketball. You either pass the ball off quickly, throw up a prayer, or get the ball put right in your face—nothing more and nothing less. No charity.

So in the political and theological discussions of welfare reform, I showed no mercy either. I asked Reverend Richmond, "Would Jesus be as tough on those women as you are?" After all, a woman who works 40 hours a week at the minimum wage of $5.35 per hour only makes $956 a month before taxes and Social Security are taken out of her check—hardly a living wage to raise a family in this day and age. Reverend Richmond was very contemplative. So, after thinking about it for a while, he said in a disbelieving tone, "My company spends close to half that much in an evening wining and dining a new business client, but we would never spend money on poor people that way." I responded, "When you think about it, putting 1.5 million women in the labor force in good economic times at such low wages enables companies like yours to wine and dine their clients lavishly because their low-end workers are eating cake." No charity for the reverend!

For the next three weeks, our locker-room chats, especially from his end, had the same caution that I have when I drive down the lane only to see him standing there ready to block a shot without mercy. Then one day he asked me if I would work with his church in developing a nonprofit organization—one of my specialties. I got the feeling then that Reverend Richmond was ready to entertain a more systemic way of looking at things. I told him that I'd be honored, thinking to myself how lucky I am to be invited on the inside of a church's efforts to be a community servant. Our friendship has now expanded from the locker room into a working relationship in program development and community practice.

The growth of poverty and the problems facing the elderly and working poor, from the Reagan and Bush years straight through the good economic times of the Clinton years, had already affected local services. Due to cutbacks in other programs between 1988 and 1997, the nine years the church kept statistics, Reverend Richmond's church distributed $379,000 to help people with food, rent, transportation, prescription drugs, child care, and the like. That does not take into account the numerous onsite programs the church offered, nor the countless volunteer hours used to administer such programs. That's just the cash outlay. Surprisingly, 75 percent of the people who received help were not members of Mt. Massada. Thus, in 1997, after a good look at the data, and my full support, Mt. Massada decided to develop a nonprofit corporation to handle, in a systematic way, what will be exponential demands on the church.

While ideas of the political and religious right were dominating the public discourse even to the point of shaping Reverend Richmond's view, something else very important was taking place. The increasing demands throughout the Reagan era affected Mt. Massada to the point where Reverend Richmond and his senior pastor knew that the new welfare reform would increasingly turn their congregation into a multiservice social service agency if they did not do something to respond.

Without any urging from the religious community, this county's welfare reform plan, the one that had to be submitted to the state, called for closer ties with the religious community. The plan's second priority recommendation in category 3 on page 16—*Staying Off Welfare After Going to Work*—seeks to "Recruit civic organizations, *faith communities* [my emphasis], and service organizations to serve as mentors to Work First (North Carolina's Welfare Program) participants." One does not have to be a nuclear physicist to know that this means that public officials are going to rely heavily on the faith community.

As a social work organizer and community educator involved in one of the most profound service changes in years, my mission was simple: to help a community institution address an important social problem in a well-planned and honest way. My training in community organization 25 years ago was grounded in the idea that the organizer helped communities and organizations build the capacity to help themselves. My challenge with Reverend Richmond was that he had missionary zeal, yet his understanding of what needed to be done to develop a spin-off organization, which is on the one hand legally independent of his church yet linked with it spiritually and concretely with resources, did not match his zeal. Not only did he need a crash course on organization development, but he also needed one in welfare politics; social services in the community; and a home study course in program planning, budgeting, and resource development. With those requirements satisfied, he could then move on to learning the skills of legitimizing his efforts by building community linkages in the least obtrusive manner. Quite a task? Not really. We worked together weekly—me learning as much as I could about what his church wanted to do; both of us studied the new welfare reform; and together, like two well-schooled basketball players, we prepared, prepared, and prepared a solid organizational game plan.

Reverend Richmond brings no bad habits, nor the battle scars of years in the social service trenches, to the table. What a wonderful opportunity to plan appropriately. The public system of services is confused, and poor women are unnecessarily getting clobbered. So good planning and community education to set the record straight about the plight of poor women is the root work for systemic coherence and long-term policy change. The faith community is expected to help, but, in this tumult, it must understand that organizations with resources can now sit at the table and shape the moral environment of the community because in the real world of social service politics, those with gold shape the rules.

Reverend Richmond's zeal, business acumen, and basketball prowess were the assets he needed for me to "meet the client where he was at" and empower him to move his organization and community to where it ought to be. In basketball, business, program development, and life, the requirements for success rest solidly on three principles: preparation, preparation, and preparation. As a former basketball star Reverend Richmond knows that the big games are won after hours of preparation.

The Welfare Reform Liaison Project had its first board meeting several weeks ago, and although I was there in spirit, phase one of my job was complete. It would have been paternalistic if I oversaw the meeting. After a year of weekly planning meetings and some times three in a week, Reverend Richmond was ready. At his bequest, I gave him a pregame pep talk and two reading assignments on how to run a board meeting. Reverend Richmond had done his work and was ready to go it alone.

He ran a very successful meeting. His 30-page, detailed, two-year program and budget plan, which was carefully put together, was adopted by the board of directors, and represented the community and the skills needed to move ahead with this organization. One of his most knowledgeable and sensitive board members is a recent social work graduate and former welfare recipient. With her at the leadership table, all will learn about the complexities and struggles poor women face in their attempts to climb out of poverty. Reverend Richmond was chosen as the first executive director of the Welfare Reform Liaison Project; an interim board president was selected and will preside until a permanent president is chosen.

I recently facilitated the most interesting board retreat that I have ever done. Over the years, I have facilitated quite a few. I combined the presentation on "Welfare Reform, the Religious Community, and Community Practice" for our MSW students with the Welfare Reform Liaison Project's board of directors. It was held in the Sanctuary of Mt. Massada Baptist Church, which has donated office space, secretarial support, and director's salary for the Welfare Reform Liaison Project. I told Reverend Richmond that my fee for this session was that he had to introduce me as the best short, balding, Jewish, low-testosterone basketball player he's ever played against. He did. After all, it was my respect for his tremendous basketball knowledge, his respect for my community practice knowledge, and both of our concern for the plight of the less fortunate that makes our working together such a pleasure.

One thing has remained constant, Reverend Richmond and I play ball together and commiserate daily about basketball, family, social policy, and the practice matters facing both the thriving and survival of his organization. We are friends. Yet, I quite often feel like a yoyo with a cell phone—in his agency—then back to the university for class, out again working with his staff, and back to a faculty meeting. All of this is laced with calls back and forth. It's the routine, and I can't imagine being in a better space. In our more contemplative moments, however, he would call it predestination, and I would call it free will. In any event, the future is now.

DISCUSSION QUESTIONS

Perspectives on Social Welfare as Reflected in Community Practice

1. How do the residual and institutional perspectives of social welfare emerge in this case?

2. What are the difficulties and strengths in a unified approach to service integration?

The Role of Faith Communities in the Provision of Welfare Services

1. What role should religious congregations in local communities assume for responding to social welfare needs?

2. Given the principle of separation of church and state, what issues and value dilemmas emerge when faith communities take active roles in social service provision? As a social worker, how would you deal with these issues and dilemmas?

Working with Indigenous Leaders and Communities

1. What role(s) should a professional assume in working with an indigenous community and/or its leadership?

2. How can social workers be sensitive to diversity issues when they are working with different religious groups, different racial groups, or other types of differences?

6

RIVERTON

Envisioning a Sustainable Community

JONATHAN SCHERCH

In this case, the large minority segment of an urban community faces an array of serious social, economic, and environmental conditions. Although these conditions are viewed as a threat to the welfare of all of the residents, special attention is given to the implications experienced by the community youth. Increasing incidents of delinquent behavior, drug and alcohol abuse, inadequate employment and after-school programming, and decreased funding for social services have evoked concerns across the community. These issues, coupled with regional economic transitions; environmental threats to the quality of the water, air, and land; and perceived political indifference, have created an atmosphere of distress and uncertainty. Current community leaders fear that if nothing is done, the next generation of residents and leaders will be unprepared to competently act on behalf of themselves, their families, and their community. Accordingly, the case reveals several emergent themes: (1) the use of ecological systems theory (EST) as a framework for conceptualizing the origin of the social, economic, and environmental issues challenging the sustainable integrity of the community; (2) the gathering of community resources around a proposed sustainable community development initiative; (3) relevant implications for macro practice with an emphasis on developing a multidisciplinary base of knowledge and technical skills; and (4) the problem of inadequate representation of interests and perspectives of a minority community within the larger urban community.

THEORETICAL AND PRACTICE PERSPECTIVES

First, the reader will find that the use of an EST framework can be helpful toward conceptualizing this type of complex scenario. Germain and Gitterman's (1980) discussion of the *ecological perspective* states that such a perspective provides "an adaptive, evolutionary view of human beings in constant interchange with all elements of their environment" (p. 5). This interchange affords continual reciprocal adaptation between humans and their social and physical environments; they affect and are affected by the quality of these environments. The beleaguered state of the social and environmental systems represented in this case study has had a negative impact on "all who function within them, whether the system is a family, a school, a geriatric facility, or a redwood forest" (Germain & Gitterman, 1980, p. 5). For additional information and examples, readers are encouraged to review McNair's (1996) discussion of EST toward the development of a generic ecological community practice model, and Tester's (1994) provocative examination of EST as an element of the social work profession's grand theoretical traditions.

The case also introduces the reader to an evolving sustainable community development initiative, the Youth and Community Empowerment Program (YCEP). In short, sustainable community development, according to Kline (1997), recognizes and supports people's evolving sense of well-being—including a sense of belonging, place, worth, safety, and a sense of connection with nature. What results is a community's capability to provide goods and services that meet people's needs according to both their own definition, and to limits imposed by the ecological integrity of natural systems (Kline, 1997). On this point, the reader is encouraged to consider how the community residents attempt to negotiate such needs within and among themselves according to their memories of times past, observations about the present, and visions for the future.

Also present within the scenario is a rising current of impatience for social, economic, and environmental justice. Indeed, the initiative may reflect such concerns as evidence that privilege and exploitation are linked to the overall health and welfare of the immediate East Riverton community. Hofrichter (1993) notes "environmental injustices result, in part, from a lack of political power, and they affect the entire fabric of social life" (p. 4).

Thus, by citing personal observations and experiences as metaphors for unresolved issues of injustice, the sustainable community development initiative seems to provide a vehicle and voice to this constituency. Readers interested in these themes should refer to the work of Holmes (1997) and Roseland (1994, 1998) who, among others, discuss concepts of sustainability and justice as inherently linked—a relevant and salient viewpoint for the macro practitioner to consider.

With EST and sustainable community development themes in mind, the case also offers implicit commentary on what an effective macro practitioner ought to know and be able to do. As recent social work literature points out, the complex and multidimensional nature of the case study scenario calls attention to the need for practitioners to develop knowledge, skills, and sensibilities that would enable them to competently assess and respond to current social, economic, political, technological, and environmental contexts of social issues (Abdullah, 1999; Rogge, 1994; Shubert, 1994; Weil, 1996). Thus, for example, readers may discover where and how the case study scenario implicates the need for workers to possess interdisciplinary knowledge (across the social and natural sciences, and humanities) and technical skills (e.g., proficiency with various types of computer software, Geographical Information System [GIS] programs, etc.), as Register (2002) suggests, to both comprehend and acknowledge a community's web of strengths as well as weaknesses.

Also, from reading the case, readers may find value in having practice experience with diverse populations and settings, and in developing competency at assessing complex situations and articulating results in terms understandable to those in need of, or ultimately affected by, such information. For additional information, readers may find the following organizations and references useful: Sustainable Social Work Mandala (www.blarg.net/~tn2wa), Living Planet Network (www.ecocity.com), Global Ecovillage Network (www.gaia.org), The Natural Step (www.naturalstep.org), and Environmental Justice Resource Center (www.ejrc.cau.edu).

REFERENCES

Abdullah, S. (1999). *Creating a world that works for all.* San Francisco: Berrett-Koehler Publishers.

Germain, C. B., & Gitterman, A. (1980). *The life model of social work practice.* New York: Columbia University Press.

Hofrichter, R. (1993). *Toxic struggles: The theory and practice of environmental justice* (p. 4). Stony Creek, CT: New Society.

Holmes, H. (1997). Just and sustainable communities. In R. D. Bullard & G. S. Johnson (Eds.), *Just transportation: Dismantling race and class barriers to mobility* (pp. 22–32). Stoney Creek, CT: New Society.

Kline, E. (1997). Sustainable community indicators: How to measure progress. In M. Roseland (Ed.), *Eco-city dimensions: Healthy communities, healthy planet* (pp. 153–166). Philadelphia: New Society.

McNair, R. (1996). Theory for practice in social work: The example of ecological community practice. *Journal of Community Practice, 3*(3/4), 181–202.

Register, R. (2002). *Ecocities: Building cities in balance with nature* (pp. 229–258). Berkeley, CA: Berkeley Hills Books.

Rogge, M. E. (1994). Field education for environmental hazards: Expanding the person-in-environment fit. In M. D. Hoff & J. G. McNutt (Eds.), *The global environmental crisis: Implications for social welfare and social work* (pp. 258–276). Brookfield, VT: Avebury.

Roseland, M. (1994). Ecological planning for sustainable communities. In D. Aberley (Ed.), *Futures by design: The practice of ecological planning* (pp. 77–78). Philadelphia: New Society Press.

Roseland, M. (1998). *Toward sustainable communities: Resources for citizens and their governments.* Stoney Creek, CT: New Society.

Shubert, J. G. (1994). Case studies in community organizing around environmental threats. In M. D. Hoff & J. G. McNutt (Eds.), *The global environmental crisis: Implications for social welfare and social work* (pp. 240–257). Brookfield, VT: Avebury.

Tester, F. J. (1994). In an age of ecology: Limits to voluntarism and traditional theory in social work practice. In M. D. Hoff & J. G. McNutt (Eds.), *The global environmental crisis: Implications for social welfare and social work* (pp. 75–99). Brookfield, VT: Avebury.

Weil, M. O. (1996). Community building: Building community practice. *Social Work, 41*(5), 485.

THE CASE

RIVERTON: A HOME PLACE IN DISTRESS

BACKGROUND

Despite signs of economic productivity and costly community development initiatives, the social, economic, and environmental future of the southeastern city of Riverton and inhabitants remains uncertain. As its name implies, Riverton developed from, and is dependent on, the southeastern flowing Cooper

River that bisects the city geographically, demographically, and industrially. To the west of the river lie the results of the past 12 years of investment and development: 25,000 new homes (averaging $150,000 each); new roads and highway widening projects; eight miles of strip shopping centers; 12 grocery stores (open 24 hours) owned by three absentee companies; two privately owned shopping malls; and three golf courses.

Since 1985, the city recorded population growth from 235,000 to 425,000. Such growth is largely attributed to availability of jobs as local industries prosper from the "Mayor's Matrix," an economic policy initiative coined by the previous two-term mayor of Riverton. The Mayor's Matrix refers to a three-dimensional economic development equation involving (1) industrial access to inexpensive resources of water and hydro-generated electricity; (2) a continuously available semiskilled workforce; and (3) a low-tax, growth-oriented economic atmosphere. With the application of the Mayor's Matrix, Riverton witnessed tremendous westward urbanization. Urban expansion was characterized by the rapid development of corporate industrial parks, conversion of large tracts of farmland into housing subdivisions, drain and fill mitigation plans for wetlands, and modernization of the Trappe Dam Hydro-electric facility on the Cooper. The daily *Riverton Journal* newspaper frequently proclaims the prosperous achievements of the Mayor's Matrix policy in action, citing the policy as a timely and appropriate means of encouraging ethics of hard work and familial responsibility. Nonetheless, the policy is not without critics.

Critics charge that the Mayor's Matrix emerged with minimal analysis and public participation and, moreover, that the coverage provided by the *Riverton Journal* has largely served the interests of the political and corporate beneficiaries of the policy. As a result, critics contend that public perception of the popularity of the Mayor's Matrix is misguided, contributing to polarized political debate—typically involving only the camps of liberal and conservative partisans, narrow and shallow in content and a poor representation of various public views and interpretations.

Whether the popularity of the Mayor's Matrix be real or perceived, any talk of deviating from this policy pathway is considered politically dangerous. The current mayor learned this lesson during his expensive and close election campaign that many believe resulted from his suggestions of policy reform. More specifically, during his campaign, the mayor observed that "not everyone in Riverton is partaking in the benefits of my predecessor's economic policies. Indeed, at times I question whether the metaphor of a *gap*, believed to exist between the rich and poor, might be better characterized as a *river.*" Some interpret the mayor's commentary as a reference to the Riverton neighborhoods east of the Cooper River, known as East Riverton, that have experienced serious social, economic, and environmental problems in recent years.

organization
collaboration

Checking the Bioregional Pulse of Riverton

In view of the swirling debate around the Mayor's Matrix, a volunteer group comprised of Riverton citizens, researchers, students, business owners, and community leaders and organizers initiated a research project designed to examine the state of the bioregion where Riverton lies. The group was able to secure financial and administrative support for the project from a local nonprofit organization well known for research of national and international sustainable community development initiatives. The rationale for the study was threefold: (1) to provide a research-based body of knowledge for current information about the holistic health of the bioregion (without fear of political or economic sanctions); (2) to bring together members of the larger bioregional community as a diverse group representing various disciplines, professions, ecumenical communities, political affiliations, and cultures; and (3) to use the product of the research to inform debate over current and future policy initiatives.

The widely read *State of the Bioregion Report* (the Report) revealed serious social, economic, and environmental implications resulting from the Mayor's Matrix that, according to the authors, were heretofore not widely known or regarded. Indeed, with increasing frequency and fervor, demands are being made for community leaders to address perceived social, economic, and environmental injustices viewed to be root causes of East Riverton's decline in contrast to West Riverton's growth and resulting prosperity. The following sections summarize the findings of the Report related to the effects of the Mayor's Matrix.

Life on the East Side of the River

The Report revealed that, like all other families living in Riverton, those in the low-income, predominantly African American East Riverton community were directly affected by and largely dependent on regional socioeconomic trends. However, historically low-income producing jobs, such as unskilled factory work, positions within the hospitality service sector, and/or government labor positions, have inequitably and negatively impacted the economic stability of the East Riverton families. By extension, the prevalence of low-wage jobs affected the nature and quality of public institutional programs such as health care services, public education, law enforcement, and youth recreation programs and facilities. Thus, risks of familial disintegration appear to have intensified proportionately with the trends in economic development and declining access to quality social services and resources.

Many who live in the East Riverton community argue that the Mayor's Matrix created a three-dimensional bind composed of (1) a growing low-wage earning, underemployed workforce; (2) an increased dependency of the poor on expensive, environmentally unfriendly, and/or nonlocally produced resources for daily living (RDLs) such as convenience store or fast foods and utility grid energy products; and (3) a phenomenon commonly referred to as "brain drain"—the bright inner-city youth and adult leaders migrate away from East Riverton in the face of these, and other undesirable, conditions. Thus, the bind has created a socioeconomic scenario in which economically disenfranchised members of the community are forced to participate in an inequitable, unsustainable economic system in order to acquire resources for survival—resources involving activities that exploit and ultimately perpetuate their disadvantaged status.

Moreover, with the brain-drain phenomenon, community tasks of learning, adopting, and adapting more suitable and sustainable living practices are made more difficult. Though the implications of this phenomenon are not yet well understood, many believe that the health and welfare of the community are dependent, in part, on the retention of the community's "indigenous sons and daughters."

Impact on Youth, Families, and the Community-at-Large

Community trends in underemployment were illuminated in the Report. The research indicated an increase in the availability of jobs within the Riverton city limits (good news for those monitoring the unemployment roles), although many jobs, especially in East Riverton, were found to afford only minimum-wage earnings and offer workers limited or no health insurance benefits—factors that created an employed, though at-risk workforce (bad news for proponents of time-limited "welfare-to-workfare" programs). Moreover, according to the Report, crimes and violence have risen in the East Riverton community, associated by many with increased statistics in juvenile delinquency and gang-related offenses. Citing data gleaned from personal interviews, the authors of the Report indicated that many East Riverton residents view these problems as outgrowths of limited educational, recreational, and entrepreneurial opportunities for youth. Life on the street, as it were, offers rewards of affiliation and money that, for youth "across town," might be more easily accessible and satisfactorily attained via regular school and community programs.

Compounding the problems of East Riverton youth are the conditions faced by many of their families. The Report cited evidence of familial disintegration, increased reports of domestic violence, drug and alcohol addictions, spousal separations and divorce, and associated challenges presented to single-parent-headed households with dependents that have all but overrun the local social service system. Like many social welfare agencies elsewhere, where imbalances exist between the numbers of people, the diversity of their needs, and the limited resources available, the relationship between the resident and the welfare office worker was reported to be plagued by frustrations experienced on both sides of the desk.

In addition to the inadequacies of the social welfare system, the Report identified a wide range of environmental issues adversely affecting the health of the bioregion, and exacerbating the social problems faced by the East Riverton community. Among many issues, the authors of the Report referred to concerns such as the effects of population growth, resource consumption and waste management trends, threats to flora and fauna, water and air pollution, and industrially contaminated soils. Moreover, the Report showed connections existing between these social and environmental problems. For example, the Report cited the role of the fast-food industry as a significant contributor to trends of rising underemployment, community economic insecurity, and absentee ownership. Related problems included rapid consumption of imported resources (i.e., fuels, foods, and fibers), tremendous waste production and subsequent management and disposal dilemmas (including procedures for identifying and using future solid-waste landfills), and permanent aesthetic changes to the visual character of the bioregion's communities, including East Riverton.

Finally, the Report discussed how the brain-drain phenomenon, and subsequent loss of current and future community leaders, compromised the East Riverton community's ability to effectively mobilize its resources to confront so-called "corporate polluters." The perception existed that corporations abused their power in several ways: employee work conditions (low wages, poor benefits), the environment (discharge of air and water effluents within East Riverton), and local politics (contributions for sweetheart political favors). The lack of effective resource mobilization was also cited as a reason for the city's tendency to invest public resources in westward urban development plans. Consequently, issues affecting the health of East Riverton (i.e., numerous leaking septic and underground storage tanks, hazardous soil contamination, ill-equipped schools and libraries, poorly maintained public parks and recreation facilities, vacant and/or dilapidated commercial buildings, etc.) were deferred to the city's perennial to-do list. Thus, for many residents of East Riverton, reading the Report raised their awareness about the interconnected, systemic nature of these social and environmental issues, as well as the need to find ways of addressing both types of issues simultaneously and sustainably.

RESPONDING TO THE COMMUNITY IN CRISIS

Frustrated by the perceived consequences of the Mayor's Matrix, associated impacts on the community's youth, families, and environment, and the ineffectiveness of existing social services to mitigate the resulting circumstances, many people in the East Riverton community urgently turned to their churches for support and guidance. In the interest of sharing experiences and strengthening relations, church leaders and congregations engaged in focused discussions about their community's problems, with equal emphasis placed on stimulating new approaches for responding to the immediate and future needs of the community. An example of this type of creative activity is the enterprising work of the Reverend Albert Houston and the All Saints Community Church. The following is a brief history of their work.

Community Action Beginning with Discussion

As an outgrowth of recent church discussions about the welfare of the East Riverton community, the All Saints Community Church initiated efforts toward the development of a center for youth and community programs. The programs would eventually evolve into a nonprofit, tax-exempt organization eligible for private grants and public funds. Prior to this initiative, the church made inquiries during regular meetings about how supportive the community would be of the intent to develop a center, and what, if any, ideas it had in mind for its mission and function. The church received broad-based support from the community for the creation of a multipurpose community center. This was an anticipated response given the trust developed with the strong historical roots of the church within their community.

Building on this support, the church, under the leadership of the Reverend Houston, enlisted the participation of community residents around two specific activities. First, the group created a preliminary proposal for the development of a Youth and Community Empowerment Program (YCEP) as a means by which to focus the discussions between the church and community, and to allow for the input of community "stakeholders" in the development and shaping of the program(s). Second, members engaged in correspondence and discussion with local realtors and city government officials in the interest of acquiring low-cost property(s) to house the YCEP program.

Remarkably (or miraculously, as some described it), at the same time, the All Saints Community Church identified and acquired three local residential properties at a reduced cost of $25,000 each. The properties were secured through an agreement with the city of Riverton that the "vitality and productivity of the dilapidated homes and associated properties would be restored for the betterment of the community." Each of the two-story homes were in need of renovations to recover and improve their utility—new roofing, heating and cooling, wiring, and so forth—to increase the real estate value. Taken together, the properties offered a contiguous 2.5 acres of partially wooded land (uncommon to most inner-city settings though somewhat typical for Riverton) with each home suitably oriented for daily southern exposure to the sun.

The church purchased the properties as an investment in the sustainable future of the community whereby, according to Reverend Houston, "community activities can take place that can help to restore the social, economic, and environmental health of our home place." To this end, the church and community saw grand potential in the utility of the properties as the physical infrastructure for programs designed to reach, engage, educate, and inspire the community's youth, and by extension, the larger East Riverton community. Specifically, the church envisioned using the properties in support of a variety of indoor programs. The programs included development of recreational and educational activities for both youth and adults (including computer and Internet resources), counseling and peer-support group programs, administrative offices and storage, and space and facilities for future income-generating entrepreneurial efforts.

The church also viewed the property as a multifaceted resource for the development of outdoor recreational facilities (e.g., playgrounds, basketball courts), programs making use of the grounds for producing fruits, vegetables, and herbs (e.g., community gardening, use of permaculture designs), creating a city sanctuary for various flora and fauna as a way of reconnecting residents and nature, installing various alternative energy technologies both indoors (e.g., efficient lights, passive solar heating) and outdoors (e.g., solar panels, a wind turbine) to model use and benefits.

At a press conference celebrating the acquisition of the properties, Reverend Houston, speaking on behalf of the YCEP Program Development Committee, noted that the center and programs would offer the community

> *An opportunity to improve the quality of life, today and tomorrow, with the integration of traditional community development approaches, along with the use of new technologies, creative entrepreneurial opportunities, and effective educational programs. . . . I have a special interest in looking at new ways of acquiring the resources we need to live well which are reliable, cost-effective, socially and environmentally friendly, and consumer-supported.*

STAKING A CLAIM IN THE FUTURE OF EAST RIVERTON

In keeping with the committee's intent to include stakeholders in the development of the program, a meeting was called to briefly discuss the state of the community and to generate ideas for developing objectives for the YCEP. Those in attendance included several church elders, several young people, a social worker–community organizer, an undergraduate social work student assigned to a local social-change organization, several local business owners, and the district's member of the city council.

After providing a brief historical review of the YCEP initiative, Reverend Houston asked for comments from the audience to solicit its views about the state of the community and how the YCEP could be useful in response. Reverend Houston emphasized the committee's interest in hearing ideas about how the programs of the YCEP could effectively create opportunities for youth and older adults to interact and learn from one another. Mrs. Althea Downing spoke first. A retired seamstress, a life-long resident of the community, and a church elder, Mrs. Downing commented on her perception of how the community has changed over her 77 years of life.

> When I was a girl, there was much to do; none of this idling we see today, with kids hanging out on the corners, looking suspicious. Years ago the street in front of the house was a place for strolling and courting—today, traffic, noise, and drugs have taken over. In my time, we had our fun, Lord knows we did, but we were also busy with our daily chores—tending to the garden, helping with dinner, completing our school lessons, and so on. I feel like if our youth had an opportunity to experience some of what I experienced as a girl, they would learn a lot about life, and how to be proper adults.

On that note, Ms. Violet Jenkins, also a life-long resident and church elder commented:

> I'm not sure if kids today understand how different life was years ago. Back then, there were no 24-hour supermarkets with everything under the sun to choose from year 'round. I'm not sure they understand the difference. I remember, back in the '50s and '60s, we used to go to the market down on Marshall Street for our vegetables, and if we got there late in the morning, we would miss the farmer, or at least the best of his selection for that day. It may be more convenient to go to the local supermarket anytime, but we sure pay the price in many ways. There is no comparison to the quality of their tomatoes and one that is farm-fresh, that's for sure.

Reverend Houston followed these comments by noting that much can be learned from the integration of ways of living more common years ago, with those of our modern mainstream society.

Then, Kim West, MSW, a community organizer working for the local environmental advocacy group, People for Sustainable Communities (PSC), spoke.

> Building on your comment Reverend Houston, I'd like to note that my social work background and my experience in working with PSC has impressed on me the value of learning from, as you say, other ways of living. It strikes me that your comment suggests the same or at least a similar notion. Let me just

say that, without going into great detail here and now, I have some ideas, and perhaps may be able to share them with you and the group later on. I would first like to hear what other people here have to say.

After a few moments, Alan O'Brien—a local community organizer operating a nonprofit recycling program within several inner-city housing projects— rose to speak.

I like what I've heard so far, in that we're not talking in terms of simply how we can solve our problems with more of the same. I like hearing about how different ways of living can be a new approach to consider. That's what my work is all about—getting people to consider what happens to their cans and bottles once they're done with them, and to think before they throw. I, for one, would like to see that kind of thought put to other aspects of people's lives. Like, for instance, energy. I think we could benefit from finding new ways to use our energy more efficiently, and from teaching our kids about how they could someday produce their own electricity from solar panels—for free! That kind of practical knowledge could really make a difference in their lives down the road; kind of what I think Ms. Jenkins was talking about.

With that comment, the meeting began to buzz with smaller discussions about the headline in the newspaper that day highlighting the projected cost increases in electricity, associated with deregulation trends among electrical utilities. In the article, alternative, decentralized, renewable energies (such as solar, wind, and micro-hydro technologies) were referenced as popular among people who desire to be more energy-independent. Many felt that the article was timely considering the nature of the evening's discussion.

The discussion then evolved into comments about prospective goals of the YCEP. The ensuing 35 minutes revealed a variety of participant ideas that were recorded on a flip chart under the heading "The YCEP should be":

- cost-effective and, ideally, should be able to pay for itself, like an entrepreneurial business
- an improvement to the realm of existing social service models and approaches
- educational and recreational for the community's youth (when this was said, several of the youth in the audience said that they would also like to find a way to earn some money from a job that could potentially offer some career-path experience)
- supportive in promoting interactions between the young and old
- helpful in enhancing the quality and accessibility of vital RDLs for the community, ideally from within the community
- a reflection of values of a sustainable community that consider the needs and welfare of both current and future generations

- a vehicle for "growing" competent community leaders to improve East Riverton's representation and influence within and across the public and private sectors

With this list recorded, Reverend Houston asked if there were any additional comments to be heard. Jim Brooks rose to speak.

> *Reverend Houston, my wife and I feel uneasy about the list of goals. In our view, the answer to our community's troubles will not come from anything short of strengthening families and compelling them to take more responsibility for themselves. We both work and are the parents of two teenagers. We feel as though we set a good example of what it means to work hard, spend quality time together, go to church, and help others help themselves. We are concerned that the goals up there (on the flip chart) could have us do more than we should for those in need. We believe that promoting good parenting is a key, along with simply being a good, law-abiding citizen.*

This comment drew both supportive and dissenting remarks from the group. As Reverend Houston motioned to the group for calm, a woman in the back row yelled out:

> *Yeah, that's right, blame the victim and trust the system! Well, I don't want to hear your crying when you get on the receiving end of it all! We are all responsible for getting ourselves into this mess, and so we are all responsible for getting out. Me, I'm a hardworking, single mom, but I'm voting for change—for me, my kids, my church, for everyone.*

Reverend Houston rose to address the group. Speaking at times over heated chatter, he acknowledged that future meetings would likely involve passionate discussion, making the group's work together rich and rewarding though perhaps at times somewhat delicate. He was preparing to adjourn the meeting when councilman Roy Stevens (D) asked for time to address the group. Councilman Stevens indicated his favor for the discussion of the evening, and as chair of the mayor's Community Relations Task Force, commented that the YCEP could qualify for $10,000 of available committee funding if a proposal can reach his desk in the very near future. He indicated that funds are available for groups that can clearly articulate how they would be used as an investment in the sustainability of the community. On this point, he explained:

> *The mayor and city council are cognizant of how the social and environmental issues facing our community not only impact us today, but will also be a detriment to the welfare of future generations. So, it is our intention to use the funds to foster a spirit of innovative problem solving at the grassroots*

level. I encourage you to think boldly and creatively, knowing that we would equally support the unconventional as well as the tried and true. The money may be used for expenses anticipated in the start up and administration of your effort.

At the conclusion of councilman Stevens' comments, Reverend Houston thanked him for his expressed support, and the group for their participation. After setting the next meeting date for two weeks hence, Reverend Houston asked the group to come prepared to offer ideas and recommendations about how these and/or other goals could be achieved. He then adjourned the meeting.

A Challenge at Hand

Aware of the urgency of the issues threatening their community, and with an interest in the availability of city government funds, the church and community are compelled to act. Essentially, their task is to reach consensus on the types of program initiatives to be undertaken, and to describe and prioritize the programs as part of a proposal to councilman Stevens for funding.

DISCUSSION QUESTIONS

1. In what ways does Reverend Houston's role reflect the use of macro practice skills? What would you do if you were in his position? How would you need to prepare?

2. What needs to occur in order for a solid funding proposal to be created and delivered to councilman Stevens? How would you try to facilitate this project?

3. How would you prioritize the tasks with this new group? How, and in what ways, should the proposal reflect the information drawn from the *State of the Bioregion Report*?

4. How might the community's youth be served by the YCEP initiative given their needs and interests? What is the community value of having young people and older adults interact?

5. What might be the next step for the social worker to take in supporting this initiative? Given her sustainable community practice experience, what ideas do you think she has in mind?

6. What would you do to stimulate sustainable community development in East Riverton? What would you consider doing first? What would you need to know in order to do this?

7. What issues of disagreement or conflict might the group need to resolve in order to proceed with the initiative? How could this be done? What is at stake? Is such conflict healthy to the process?

8. How can ecological systems theory be useful to the group in envisioning and developing a healthier future for East Riverton? How does EST relate to sustainable community development?

9. How important is a multidisciplinary base of knowledge and skills to this type of macro practice scenario?

10. What implications result for social work practice and education?

7

THE NATIVE HAWAIIAN CHILDREN'S CENTER

Changing Methods from Casework to Community Practice

ELIZABETH A. MULROY and JON K. MATSUOKA

THEORETICAL AND PRACTICE PERSPECTIVES

In this case, a nonprofit agency devoted to serving orphaned children in Hawaii has recently shifted its methods of intervention from the traditional casework approach to community building. The agency has a central administrative office and 10 free-standing units, or outreach offices, geographically located throughout the state to serve residents on all six of the state's major islands. The case raises a number of themes: (1) the utilization of community building as an agencywide practice method, (2) the tensions that ensue among staff and managers as workers shift from the traditional service-delivery orientation to a community-development approach, and (3) an emphasis on cultural competence reinforced by the principles of community practice with an indigenous population.

In the first theme, management and staff redefined the way they wanted to assist their intended beneficiaries. Instead of relating to children and families on a direct one-to-one basis, the focus shifted to macro systems goals: helping people out of poverty, strengthening informal social support networks, and increasing resources and opportunities within communities. First, what does community-building mean? An underlying assumption is that the "dynamic of community building tends to operate spontaneously in neighborhoods marked by a strong social infrastructure (that is, an extensive grassroots network of churches, schools, banks, businesses, and neighborhood centers) that nourishes and supports the life of the community" (Naparstek & Dooley, 1997a, p. 78). Therefore, community building takes a holistic approach to all the interconnecting issues that people in poverty must deal with to make progress toward economic independence: family and health problems, education and labor-force development, and affordable housing (Naparstek, Dooley, & Smith, 1997; Gibson, Kingsley, & McNeely, 1997; Fabricant & Fisher, 2002). Halpern (1995) suggests that it is necessary to first understand the history and public policy context of persistent poverty and community disinvestment in order to understand the possibilities of community building as an intervention.

Svirdoff (1994) suggests that community building is a weaving together of *people-based strategies*—traditional human service programs with a defined package of services to individuals—with *place-based strategies*—community development that focuses on physical development such as housing, infrastructure, and commercial structures. The convergence of people-based strategies with place-based strategies generates four principles of community building: (1) it is comprehensive and integrative, (2) it takes advantage of new forms of partnerships and collaborations, (3) it targets neighborhoods to enhance resident participation, and (4) it builds on neighborhood assets (Kretzmann & McKnight, 1993; Naparstek & Dooley, 1997b; Mattessich & Monsey, 1997).

The second theme concerns theories of practice that guide employees in the application of their new community orientation (Mulroy & Lauber, 2002). All agency employees are essentially initiating an innovation. According to Smale (1993), the model for managing innovations that introduce new methods of work needs to consider three major issues: (1) the nature of the innovation, (2) the people involved, and (3) the climate or culture of their organization. Questions pertaining to each of these issues need to be posed relative to the Native Hawaiian Children's Center (NHCC). Mulroy and Shay (1997) provide a conceptual piece that documents how an understanding of the theory of a community-building innovation informs practice for social workers who must work across multiple systems simultaneously, perhaps for the first time.

Unlike the traditional top-down service delivery model, community building presents a new set of relationships among: (1) a community worker and a resident who now interact as partners with common community improvement goals; (2) community workers from multiple agencies who serve on interagency teams; and (3) agency executives who share risks and rewards through partnerships, which require a participatory management style (Adams & Nelson, 1995; Hadley, 1993; Smale, 1993; Mulroy, 1997; Mulroy & Shay, 1997).

Constraints to utilizing a community-building approach have been observed in interagency and interpersonal competition for funding, and in the long time frame necessary to reach community-building goals (Gutierrez, GlenMaye, & DeLois, 1995; Mulroy, 1995).

A third theme in this case involves agency and worker commitment to the self-determination of an indigenous people. Ewalt and Mokuau (1995) and Dykeman, Nelson, and Appleton (1995) suggest that social workers must understand and appreciate the cultural characteristics of the population of interest and the context of their oppression. According to Gould (1996), this is not to be confused with the new multiculturalism. Gould argues for "a paradigmatic shift to a framework that informs thinking at a transcultural level rather than a model that merely provides specific strategies for ethno-centric practice" (p. 30). However, when multiple systems and institutions come together to reach community-building goals, conflicting cultures can be anticipated (Matsuoka, Mulroy, & Umemoto, 2002).

REFERENCES

Adams, P., & Nelson, K. (Eds.). (1995). *Reinventing human services: Community and family-centered practice.* New York: Aldine De Gruyter.

Dykeman, C., Nelson, J. R., & Appleton, V. (1995). Building strong working alliances with American Indian families. *Social Work in Education, 17,* 148–158.

Ewalt, P., & Mokuau, N. (1995). Self-determination from a Pacific perspective. *Social Work, 40,* 168–175.

Fabricant, M., & Fisher, R. (2002) *Settlement houses under seige: The struggle to sustain community organizations in New York City.* New York: Columbia University Press.

Gibson, J., Kingsley, T., & McNeely, J. (1997). *Community building: Coming of age.* Baltimore: The Development Training Institute and the Urban Institute.

Gould, K. (1996). The misconstruing of multiculturalism: The Stanford debate and social work. In P. Ewalt, E. Freeman, S. Kirk, & D. Poole (Eds.), *Multicultural issues in social work* (pp. 29–42). Washington, DC: NASW Press.

Gutierrez, L., GlenMaye, L., & DeLois, K. (1995). The organizational context of empowerment practice: Implications for social work administration. *Social Work, 40,* 249–258.

Hadley, R. (1993). Decentralization, integration, and the search for responsive human services. In E. E. Martinez-Brawley & S. A. Delevan (Eds.),

Transferring technology in the personal social services (pp. 31–49). Washington, DC: NASW Press.

Halpern, R. (1995). Neighborhood-based services in low-income neighborhoods: A brief history. In P. Adams & K. Nelson (Eds.), *Reinventing human services* (pp. 19–40). New York: Aldine De Gruyter.

Kretzmann, J., & McKnight, J. (1993). *Building communities from the inside out: A path toward finding and mobilizing a community's assets.* Evanston, IL: Northwestern University Center for Urban Affairs and Policy Research.

Mattessich, P., & Monsey, B. (1997). *Community building: What makes it work?* St. Paul, MN: The Wilder Research Center, Amherst Wilder Foundation.

Matsuoka, J., Mulroy, E., & Umemoto, K. (2002). Conflicting cultures: Linking agency, community, and university in a community-building endeavor. *Social Thought, 21*(2), 12–23.

Mulroy, E. (1995, November). Achieving the systemic neighborhood network: Conflict and cooperation in a nonprofit interorganizational collaboration. Paper presented at the annual meeting of the Association for Research on Nonprofit Organizations and Voluntary Action, Cleveland, OH.

Mulroy, E. (1997). Building a neighborhood network: Interorganizational collaboration to prevent child abuse and neglect. *Social Work, 42*(3), 255–265.

Mulroy, E., & Lauber, H. (2002). Community building in hard times: A postwelfare view from the streets. *Journal of Community Practice, 10*(1), 1–16.

Mulroy, E., & Shay, S. (1997). Nonprofit organizations and innovation: A model of neighborhood-based collaboration to prevent child maltreatment. *Social Work, 42*(5), 515–526.

Naparstek, A., & Dooley, D. (1997a). Community building. In *Encyclopedia of social work,* Supplement 1997 (pp. 77–90). Washington, DC: NASW Press.

Naparstek, A., & Dooley, D. (1997b). Countering urban disinvestment through community building initiatives. *Social Work, 42*(5), 506–514.

Naparstek, A., Dooley, D., & Smith, R. (1997). *Community building in public housing: Ties that bind people and their communities.* Washington, DC: U.S. Housing and Urban Development, Office of Public and Indian Housing, Office of Public Housing Investments, and Office of Urban Revitalization.

Smale, G. (1993). The nature of innovation and community-based practice. In E. E. Martinez-Brawley & S. A. Delevan (Eds.), *Transferring technology in the personal social services* (pp. 14–30). Washington, DC: NASW Press.

Svirdoff, M. (1994). The seeds of urban revival. *The Public Interest, 114,* 82–103.

THE CASE

THE NATIVE HAWAIIAN CHILDREN'S CENTER

INTRODUCTION

As a unit manager at the Native Hawaiian Children's Center (NHCC), Malia Sunn was usually clear and confident about her role in the organization, but as she rose to speak at the agency's first spring training conference, she felt her mouth go dry. She had been asked to participate in a panel called "Growing a Healthy Community: Organizational Change and the Shift to Community Practice." Calvin Kalakawa, NHCC's executive director, had asked her to present because he expected her to inspire other managers and frontline workers with her unit's successes in moving from a traditional casework approach to community building. But as she stood at the podium today, she knew that her unit's shift to community building, while accomplishing many successful projects, had been anything but smooth. The new strategic direction was commendable, but serious issues had emerged that were roadblocks to implementation. How honest and forthright could she really be?

She looked out at the 215 people in front of her and several thoughts intruded into her prepared remarks. She was struck by the visible increase in staff multiculturalism and diversity within this native Hawaiian agency. Malia also noticed the new faces of some university faculty members. NHCC's central management had recently initiated an interorganizational partnership with the University of Hawaii to bring together faculty from urban and regional planning, community extension/economic development, public administration, and social work as a multidisciplinary team to provide technical support to NHCC in its transition to community building. Collaborations were all the vogue, but she wondered if, and how, they were really going to help.

Then, Malia spotted unit-level social workers David Kaniole and Lee Winsome sitting near community workers Marcia Cook and Sam Watanabe. Their faces were lined with strain and tension from a relatively new issue— an agencywide schism between professionalism and paraprofessionalism; traditional casework and indigenous community work—an issue smoldering beneath the surface of the gracious *aloha* spirit in the room.

The Strategic Plan and Organizational Shift

Malia remembered it was three years ago that the organization completed a strategic planning process that redirected agency efforts from individual care to the development of thriving, healthy communities (see Appendix A). All employees were involved in an agencywide environmental scan to examine the economic, political, and social factors posing threats as well as opportunities to clients and to the NHCC. Results of the scan showed that the impact of Hawaii's economic downturn had profoundly affected low-income Hawaiian families who were increasingly unable to meet their basic needs for housing, clothing, food, and child care. Job loss through closure of sugar plantations and related industries left communities with few job opportunities and families with fractured relationships. Simultaneously, a reduction in federal and state government spending on health and human services forced areawide agency downsizing, mergers, and even agency closures that left local communities with fewer support networks to buffer families in these times of increased economic need and family stress.

Staff went directly into the community to find out the needs of native Hawaiians. Residents responded that they wanted the NHCC to do more community-development work and provide visible educational programs.

Leadership for the new strategic direction was set at the top. Calvin Kalakawa, a native Hawaiian and long-time executive director of the NHCC, was seen as a visionary with a leadership style that engendered respect and loyalty among employees and community leaders. With board of trustee support, Calvin carried the banner for community building. He believed that in times of decreasing resources, the agency would have a greater impact by focusing on communities instead of individuals as its target for change. In his opening remarks to attendees at this training conference moments earlier, Calvin said:

> *Our agency is using this opportunity to develop partnerships in supporting the Hawaiian community's investment for having healthy and happy Hawaiian children. It may take the form of economic development so that parents can work; it may take advocacy for housing the homeless; it may take collaborating with others to feed needy families; it will take counseling for some families; and the list continues to grow in the opportunities that communities offer us in supporting their development for a thriving, healthy community.*

Role of Mission

This direction was consistent with NHCC's fundamental theory of intervention that had always acknowledged the vital interconnections between child and family, and family and community. NHCC is the primary beneficiary of a trust established by Hawaii's last reigning monarch for the children of Hawaii eight years before her death in 1917. The mission was "to help orphan and destitute Hawaiian children by providing a safe, nurturing family and a permanent home." Although it considered orphaned Hawaiian children its primary beneficiaries, in 1996, this group constituted 27.9 percent of beneficiaries served. Center resources were also extended to Hawaiian children who were not orphans; to non-Hawaiian children; and to adults, families, and groups. During its more than 50-year existence, NHCC, with 200 employees (including 150 social workers) has served more than 220,000 children, primarily through the provision of traditional child welfare services such as counseling, financial aid, adoptions, and foster care.

IMPACTS OF COMMUNITY BUILDING

Organizational Culture

Community building was viewed as compatible with the organizational culture of NHCC. The concept of *o'hana* (extended family) prevailed over the staff/agency culture (see Appendix A). First, the organizational culture worked to value all personnel so that janitor, clerical staff, receptionist, social worker, and manager felt like stakeholders in the provision of effective services to meet the needs of the Hawaiian community. All 10 unit facilities across the state were strategically located in or in close proximity to Hawaiian communities. Facilities were frequently used as meeting places for a host of other Hawaiian organizations and events.

Second, at the core of organizational culture was the role of spirituality, essential in Hawaiian culture (see Appendix A). Its expression was encouraged in cultural learning and in organizational practices. For example, most meetings, even small staff meetings, began and ended with a prayer, and larger meetings also began or ended with singing traditional songs in the Hawaiian language.

Social worker Lee Winsome welcomed the shift to community building. Lee had worked in the Sand Mountain unit with Malia Sunn for 10 years. Lee believed that she had successfully meshed with the community and the organizational culture. Lee and other unit workers had already assisted local residents, particularly unemployed parents on public assistance, in establishing home businesses through community-based economic development initiatives. These successes increased family income, strengthened family relationships, and added needed resources to the local economy. She had received favorable performance appraisals from her supervisor at her annual reviews. Lee Winsome had lived in Hawaii for 25 years. Born and raised in Wisconsin, she was of Norwegian/Danish heritage and received her MSW from a large university in the Midwest.

Organizational Structure

Malia Sunn anticipated that community building would set the strategic direction for the Sand Mountain unit to be a catalyst for local community development. However, she was frustrated by a lack of autonomy to make critical management decisions in a timely way. The NHCC was a large, hierarchical organization with 10 community-based units spread out on all six major islands in the state. The decision-making structure was centralized. Each month, all 10 unit managers met with central administration managers to make unit-based decisions by consensus. Concerns and needs of each unit were measured and weighed by all managers using criteria that considered the impacts on the whole of the organization. This management practice was consistent with *lokahi*—unity, a value in Hawaiian culture that reflects an emphasis on group relationships and consideration of working together for a common purpose.

Shift to Entrepreneurial Management.   In Malia's experience, the shift to community building required "entrepreneurial management;" that is, the capability of being flexible, making timely decisions, and having an adaptable organizational structure—characteristics thwarted by the hierarchical organizational form inherent at NHCC. For example, two weeks before the spring conference, Sand Mountain community worker Marcia Cook proposed that the unit join an emerging partnership of three respected agencies interested in increasing community-based economic development opportunities for local, low-income, native Hawaiian homesteaders. The partnership would be called *Laulima;* in Hawaiian culture, this means the cooperation of many hands. Bank financing was being packaged to leverage Community Reinvestment Act money with short-term loans. Each agency was asked to donate a staff position to the program. NHCC was asked to fund and staff an outreach and home visiting position. Job requirements included building relationships with families on public assistance who were expected to achieve economic self-sufficiency under the new welfare reform laws (TANF). Technical support would be provided so that heads of households could identify their skills and abilities, and then get help to qualify for *Laulima*-provided financial resources in order to develop and sustain either home-based or community-based micro-enterprise activities. Professional relationships would need to be built with local financial institutions, agencies, and suppliers. Timing was crucial. The next unit managers' meeting, at which she could present her proposal and receive permission for this budget allocation, was three weeks away. Malia needed control of her own budget now—irrespective of what other units within the NHCC needed or wanted—in order to move with this opportunity.

Unit Managers Seek Decentralization.   Nearly all unit managers believed that their units were unique and sought movement toward a decentralized structure. Malia wanted decentralization in order to serve her own area more effectively. She was frustrated by the present lack of autonomy.

The Sand Mountain unit served a large geographic area that had five residential communities within it. The needs of its mostly Hawaiian families and the economic and social conditions in this depressed rural economy posed their own problems, resources, and potential solutions that were different from those units in other locations around the state, particularly those in urbanized areas in and near Honolulu, which had widely diverse populations. Recent immigration from Asia and the Pacific Islands infused Samoans, Tongans, and Filipinos into urban areas to mix with long-term resident populations from Japan, China, the Philippines, Polynesia, and Portugal as well as with native Hawaiians and transplanted mainland whites.

On the Frontlines: Community Building versus Services

NHCC assumed that traditional child welfare services would still be offered across the state, but the emphasis had clearly shifted to a new core focus on community projects and initiatives, cultural and enrichment activities, and family life education (see Appendix B). Even though counseling and other direct services were not going to be eliminated, their importance was clearly diminished with NHCC's new strategic direction. Therefore, since direct services were an increasingly smaller agencywide function, and MSWs performed these functions, the agency decided it no longer needed to hire persons with social work degrees. If professional degrees were necessary at all, the agency considered hiring those with community planning and community-based economic development training, a direction that was consistent with its strategic plan and new core focus (see Appendix B). The personnel category of community worker was then established, and hiring began at the unit level. Recruitment and hiring policies and procedures favored community residents who had firsthand knowledge of local community issues and existing networks of groups and resources. Academic training was not a job requirement.

Unit-level responses to the new strategic direction appeared to depend on the degree to which social workers had to alter their existing practices. Malia observed that the level of readiness for change from casework to community practice corresponded to the roles that social workers were already playing in the community. Some personnel were involved in a variety of community-level activities. She knew that in rural areas like Sand Mountain, some social workers were forced to develop a broader base of skills to address the needs of residents and promote prevention strategies. Those who had been performing multiple roles had a tendency to exert greater leadership in community-building activities. Those who had less experience, by virtue of their previous roles, received on-the-job-training as they were inclined to observe, offer support and input, and engage in a process of mutual learning and confidence building as the process developed.

Attitude Change: Perceiving "Client" as Partner.   The most intractable issue appeared to be resistance among some social workers to shift their perception of a beneficiary from that of "client" to "partner," a core assumption in community building. Malia observed that social workers, such as David Kaniole who had clients that came to him for office appointments, were less inclined to possess a broad repertoire of community-practice skills and were somewhat reticent about venturing out of their units. Working in communities and dealing with groups were novel and sometimes threatening experiences for David.

At a recent unit staff meeting, David Kaniole, a 13-year employee, expressed it this way: "I was trained to be a clinician. Social work means having 'clients' and working on cases. My role is to assess a client's needs and presenting problems, then to help that person change by engaging in therapy or providing other services. This is what I know how to do."

He added, "Community work is too unstructured, too loose for me. Besides, how can I be a partner with a client? I'm the one with the data. I'm the one with the training and expertise." But the nature of practice had changed. All social workers and community workers within NHCC were now required to work *in* the community in partnership with residents and local community-based organizations. Yet there remained a lack of clarity over roles, responsibilities, job titles, and salaries. At the last unit staff meeting, David had asked: "Without the requirement of either academic or professional training, how can community work be considered real social work?"

Even Lee Winsome, who had happily made the transition to community building, could appreciate how David saw his professional identity eroding and their profession marginalized. Were social workers and community workers now of equal status in the organization? Would they receive the same salaries? If so, why bother to spend the time and money to attend college and graduate school? Frontline tension increased and social worker anxiety deepened.

Geography and Cultural Embeddedness

The NHCC considered the shift to community building to be culturally responsive to Hawaii's turbulent history of overthrow and oppression by Western capitalist interests; the process of economic development focusing on land acquisition and development by foreigners had created a unique sociopolitical environment. The systematic conversion of a subsistence economy to one steeped in agribusiness and then tourism placed immense strains on Hawaiian culture and marginalized many communities. In particular, Hawaiians were not inclined to participate in the political and economic process that they found oppressive and inferior to their own systems.

An ideology related to self-determination was in part generated by a mistrust toward outside institutions that took advantage of and misinterpreted situations, leading to victimization of native Hawaiians. Therefore, gaining entry into Hawaiian communities was dubious, especially for outsiders who might not understand cultural protocol, without character references from respected community members. Although the NHCC had very positive relationships with native Hawaiian communities, the agency was mindful of these compelling issues and committed to hire staff who understood and appreciated this context. Establishing the job category of community worker and hiring from the Hawaiian community were regarded as major steps in achieving this critical, strategic goal.

Professional Identity

When Malia spotted the lines of tension on the faces of her staff in the audience, it brought back visions of the most recent staff meeting and a tense encounter between social workers and community workers. The issue was this: Assuming Sand Mountain unit joined the new *Laulima* partnership, what should the NHCC personnel position be called, and what should the job requirements be? Community workers Marcia Cook and Sam Watanabe favored calling it a Family Advocate position, a generic title that clearly conveyed the intended function. However, David Kaniole insisted that it be called Social Worker III to attract experienced professionals. Besides, he hoped the pendulum would eventually shift back to direct practice.

David was worried. If the agency shifted to community building on a permanent basis, would he have to live with this level of uncertainty forever? At first, Sam Watanabe tried to assuage David, saying: "If the position is called a family advocate, then either a community worker or a social worker can fill the position. But under your requirements, David, it will be limited to only people with social work degrees."

Marcia Cook was offended by David's argument, which she felt patronized her and Sam. She shot back, "The most important thing we need is a person with the right attitude; someone who really cares about our people. That doesn't necessarily come with a degree." David retorted, "If community building skills can be learned on the job, then community workers are *not* professionals."

Sam felt that David missed the main point. He said, "The real problems our people face are poverty and oppression. The most important job requirements should be for the person to be a native Hawaiian who is committed to the local community. This position also requires political skills, access to the 'movers and shakers' who can get us the economic resources we need to strengthen the community as a whole."

Lee Winsome was furious. If Sam got his way, Lee, not being native Hawaiian, would be disqualified from applying for a family advocate position, an opportunity she was excited about and felt competent to fill. At first, she found herself in the uncomfortable middle. Her experience with community building to date helped her appreciate Marcia's point that it required a caring attitude and a local commitment. But she had a sense of what David wanted too. Some of the families she had worked with started down the road to self-employment but were short-circuited by episodes of substance abuse, illness of a child or other family member, and domestic violence—including child maltreatment. She believed that these cases require competent assessment skills and knowledge of health and human service resources and state reporting laws—expertise usually learned in a social work curriculum.

Now, feeling rebuffed, yet not wanting to further offend Marcia or Sam either, Lee withdrew and said nothing at all. She sank down into her chair in silence. She couldn't imagine how staff could extricate themselves from this one. Lee wondered silently if David should resign and look for another job as a clinician. The NHCC didn't require that any worker leave because of the transition to community building. Everyone had been promised continued employment if he or she wanted it. But Lee wasn't sure that David and others were interested in assimilating on-the-job training like she had done to get community-building skills. On the other hand, should community building be professionalized at all, and if so, what would that mean?

Lee valued community building and was proud of the work she was doing. However, she wondered if NHCC management had any idea what the impact of the organizationwide shift to community building was having on frontline staff relationships and morale.

Marcia Cook decided that David and Lee just didn't get it. She feared that this schism between professionalism and indigenous community work would sabotage the unit's participation in the *Laulima* partnership, a valuable opportunity that she, a community worker, had brought into the agency. If the NHCC and the unit failed to mobilize itself within the needed time frame, native Hawaiian residents would be the real losers—again.

Malia, who was facilitating the meeting, came up with what she considered to be not only an ingenious idea, but a fair compromise: Why not change all job titles in the unit to Family Advocate? For equity purposes, Family Advocate categories could be designated levels I, II, III, and IV to give credit and incentives for education completed or employment experience. The staff sat there in silence. Then they all seemed to talk at once about identity: either needing to retain the word "community" in a job title or needing to retain the words "social worker." The meeting ended in a standoff.

CONCLUSION

From her view at the podium, Malia was aware of the centrality of Hawaiian culture in this organizational change effort and of its elevated role in community building. She questioned again how the university faculty team could be utilized. Maybe an outside perspective was finally needed. However, Marcia and Sam were already wary of the faculty because none of them was Hawaiian. Sam suspected that faculty—all PhDs educated on the mainland but most with long-time Hawaiian roots—would likely storm in and impose their presumed technical expertise and big theories onto a fragile community-building process.

With such a mixed audience in front of her, Malia hoped that her remarks would be appropriate. The issues of community building and organizational change seem so complex and intertwined. Then she flashed on commonalities she believed existed among those in the room: a deep commitment to the agency's founder; a belief in the founder's vision of the vital connection among a child, its family, the Hawaiian community, and the larger community; and a respect for the self-determination of Hawaiians, their gifts, identity, culture, and rights. Focused at last, Malia Sunn could begin.

DISCUSSION QUESTIONS

1. If NHCC had it to do over again, what steps might management have taken to ensure a smoother transition from the strategic planning stage through to its implementation?
   a. How is community building better than casework as perceived by those social workers who are expected to adopt the new practice?
   b. Which employees experience what losses and gains?
   c. Is the organizational culture receptive to change?
   d. Which aspects of NHCC need to change, and which can be maintained?

2. Can or should community building be professionalized?

3. Can nonindigenous, or nonethnic people—whether faculty, residents, or professionals—*do* community work with indigenous populations?

APPENDIX A

Native Hawaiian Children's Center Organizational Culture

Principles

- We will remain in respectful service to our founder and will carry out her work faithfully.
- We commit to enable Hawaiian orphans to not only survive, but to thrive and to prevent conditions that place them at-risk.

- Recognizing and respecting the gifts of Hawaiians—their cultural strengths, perspectives, choices, aspirations, rights—helps them fulfill their own goals. Cultural translations help them to succeed in both worlds without compromising identity or integrity.
- The founder's beneficiaries live within *'ohana* (family), who live within the larger Hawaiian community, which is part of the whole community. Children's needs, like those of their elders, are not met in isolation, but in and by their communities. Their readiness for the future depends on the willingness and ability of those communities to nurture and prepare them. Therefore, we work to strengthen and encourage *'ohana* and communities, as well as children.
- More people can be served effectively and appropriately when we work collaboratively to coordinate our strategies, our work, and our use of resources with other organizations and institutions, guided by the communities with whom we work.
- Spirituality is essential in Hawaiian culture. We encourage its expression as a common bond that transforms and unites us, though our spiritual choices and understandings may vary.

APPENDIX B
Native Hawaiian Children's Center Strategic Plan

Methods of Achieving Community Building

1. *Community Projects and Initiatives.* Community-based projects that work collaboratively to enhance the social, cultural, health, and economic well-being of the founder's beneficiaries and the families and communities that nurture them.

2. *Cultural and Enrichment Activities.* Planned activities designed to enrich the lives of children, adults, and families by enhancing their knowledge, skills, sense of competency in Hawaiian culture, educational performance, health and wellness, or recreation.

3. *Family Life Education.* Learning opportunities in which individuals share information and skills to better understand issues of community and family life and enhance their self-esteem, personal achievement, and social development.

4. *Individual and Family Strengthening.* Counseling and family assistance to enable parents and caregivers to provide safe, nurturing, and permanent homes for their children.

5. *Permanency Planning.* Counseling, financial assistance, adoption, foster home and *'ohana* care, and legal guardianship services for orphans and other children.

8

LINDBLOM COUNTY

How Diversity Influenced Philanthropic Sufficiency

ROGER A. LOHMANN

THEORETICAL AND PRACTICE PERSPECTIVES

This case is concerned with a number of separate clusters of issues that become intertwined in the course of events. A group of long-time friends find their friendships increasingly tested in the cross-pressures of community and agency responsibilities, and ethnic and gender differences. They form a professional elite that finds itself challenged by an ethnic counterelite, which turns out to have its own internal conflicts involving, not only ethnicity, but populist resentment of professionals and other undercurrents.

These undercurrents impact on and threaten the technical social planning questions of how to increase community philanthropic sufficiency, and how to measure the philanthropic sufficiency of a community within the context of federal and state devolution to a community largely lacking in community-level social planning capacity (Lohmann, 1992).

The Scene: Lindblom County

The events described in this case take place in Lindblom County in the state of Vandalia. Vandalia is a fictitious name for an actual state, although its precise location is somewhat unclear. It could be Maine and share a heavy historic reliance on fishing and timbering; or North Dakota, Wyoming, or Montana, with a local economy built on ranching and mining; or West Virginia, long dependent on coal mining; or Mississippi and reliant on cotton and tenant farming. Or it may be a state of mixed livestock and grain farms somewhere on the great plains. Or its economy might be based on gold, or silver, oil or copper, bauxite or iron ore, and taconite mining. In any case, Lindblom County is one of approximately 50 territorial and governmental subdivisions of Vandalia, with an economy sharply divided between a rapidly expanding higher education system, with Vandalia State University at its apex, and a declining primary industrial base.

Theory

Cindy Stone was a student in a course on rural community planning taught by one of the principals in this case, Dr. Alan Monroe. Through her macro practice field placement at the Lindblom County Family Service agency, she was generally familiar with the events described in this case and wanted to do a paper to discover what the literature on community planning and leadership in rural areas could tell her. In this section of the case study, we briefly examine what Cindy found for her paper.

First of all, Cindy discovered that most of the published work in social work on both community planning and leadership involves large urban and metropolitan areas. She did, however, discover a limited discussion of rural planning issues. Moreover, she found that many of the insights of the urban planning literature were fully applicable to rural areas as well, with suitable adjustments (e.g., to issues of scale and resource limits).

The most fundamental distinction Cindy found was Rothman's tripartite division of community practice into social action, social planning, and locality development (Rothman, 1977, 2001). From what she saw at her United Way placement, Cindy was fairly convinced that the events described in this case were involved at various times in all three activities, but it was usually impossible to tell which was which at any given moment.

Cindy also found that in the late 1960s Robert Morris and Robert Binstock had published a small book highlighting the importance of *feasibility* in community-level social planning (Morris & Binstock, 1966). Dr. Monroe told her that Binstock had been a doctoral student of Edward Banfield in the political science program at Harvard. In the early 1960s, Banfield published an important study on political influence, and his *Politics, Planning and the Public Interest* was the first to raise questions about how well abstract, formal models of the planning process fit with what people actually did in the name of planning (Banfield, 1961; Meyerson & Banfield, 1955).

She noted also that community theory in social work is generally constructed from the assumption that social workers as professional change agents are in the middle between powerless and alienated lower-class clients and influential upper-class community elites. Some very sound conventional advice is offered by one social work text in the following words:

> *[A]n appropriate strategy would be to convince the elite group of the value of the desired policy change and to work with them to achieve it, possibly by getting elected to public office and becoming one of them. You would need to advocate not only why the policy is good, fair, or just, but more importantly, that it would be in the elites' self-interest.* (Haynes & Mickelson, 1997, p. 62)

But in her conversations with her field instructor, Cindy began to wonder aloud what if, as seemed to be the case in Lindblom County, professional change agents already find themselves part of a community leadership elite that becomes sharply divided over issues not immediately related to client needs? Community theory in social work has traditionally been constructed from the standpoint of the existence of a unitary community interest (the common needs and resources of the community) that it is the responsibility of professionals to locate and secure. Yet, what if, as frequently happens in contemporary practice, the actors involved are unable to agree on where that common interest lies?

Germain used the concept of the *competent community* as one that manifests a collective capacity for dealing with the wide-ranging needs and problems in communal life (Germain, 1991, p. 42). She used the definition of community competence set forth by Leonard Cottrell as the ability to collaborate effectively in identifying the problems and needs of the community, achieve a working consensus on goals and priorities, agree on ways and means to implement the agreed-on goals, and collaborate effectively in the required actions (Cottrell, 1976, p. 196). But how are professional change agents to respond when such community competence is not present? And what if efforts to build community problem-solving competence are not only resisted but overturned by powerful actors in the community?

Cindy realized that in the case of contemporary rural communities, efforts to competently solve community problems were occurring in a context in which the federally sponsored planning initiatives of the 1960s had been defunded, often replaced by informal and ad hoc professional collaboratives with little in the way of formal authority or visibility in the community (Lohmann, 1991). She also recognized that the harmonious view of community elites who are ripe for being influenced by professional change agents ultimately stemmed from an earlier era when there was assumed to be a uniform social work interest that was consistent with the best interests of the community (Lohmann, 1992).

One thing Cindy noted was a tendency for some of the discussions of community decision making and its relationships to power and conflict to be carried on at a very abstract level that she wasn't sure she fully comprehended.

Charles Lindblom characterized community decision making in problem solving and policy making as ongoing processes of mutual partisan adjustment in which conflict is inherent (Lindblom, 1965). Benjamin Barber characterized decision making in those cases where we are members of a community held together by the necessity of common judgment and common action as inherently political, and not resolvable by scientific, philosophical, or religious truth (Barber, 1988, p. 14). Such decisions are frequently made by what Herbert Simon called *satisficing*, or selecting the first available alternative that meets the essential requirements of the situation (Simon, 1976). In such cases, according to Lindblom (1965), decisions are made serially (as part of a longer series, with other decisions coming before and after), remedially (in efforts to correct existing problems), and partially (with no expectation that a single decision can fully solve any problem). The overall coherence or rationality of decisions made in this manner comes not from the procedures used to make them, but because they are part of larger strategies.

Cindy, herself, was the first person in her family to attend college, so she was very interested that the same was true of all of the principals in this case. She had learned in her human behavior classes that higher education was one of the principal means to upward mobility, but she knew from her own experience that access to higher education was very unevenly distributed in rural communities (Robbins, Chatterjee, & Canda, 1998, p. 92). It was clear from her readings that the earlier planning literature dealt with a more sophisticated concept of power than simply the ability to access and control resources and people (Robbins et al., 1998, p. 91). Power, she was fairly sure, involved more than the exercise of ability, and also involved elements such as situation, opportunity, opposition, and conflict. Barbara Solomon had defined powerlessness as the inability to manage emotions, skills, knowledge, and/or material resources in a way that effective performance of valued social roles will lead to personal gratification (Solomon, 1976, p. 16). Although she was aware of a huge and growing literature on empowerment, one article that seemed especially relevant to the situation in Lindblom County was about methods of empowering Latinos through the use of groups (Gutierrez & Ortega, 1991). Although she was convinced of the picture of oppression painted by sources like Paolo Freire (1970), like many other upwardly mobile professionals, Cindy was reluctant to see herself or the principals in this case as oppressors. Further, although she had little difficulty seeing the negative effects of oppression on the racial and ethnic minorities of the area, she was genuinely uncertain about what Freire meant by the negative effects of oppression on the oppressors (Freire, 1970).

To Cindy, one thing was clear. Far from the pastoral ideal pictures of rural communities that rural people liked to paint about themselves, there was a lot of conflict in and around the human service community in Lindblom County.

REFERENCES

Banfield, E. (1961). *Political influence.* Glencoe, IL: Free Press.

Barber, B. (1988). *The conquest of politics: Liberal philosophy in democratic times.* Princeton, NJ: Princeton University Press.

Cottrell, L. (1976). The competent community. In B. H. Kaplan, R. N. Wilson, & A. H. Leighton (Eds.), *Further explorations in social psychiatry* (pp. 195–209). New York: Basic Books.

Freire, P. (1970). *Pedagogy of the oppressed.* New York: Seabury Press.

Germain, C. B. (1991). *Human behavior in the social environment: An ecological view.* New York: Columbia University Press.

Gutierrez, L. M., & Ortega, R. (1991). Developing methods to empower Latinos: The importance of groups. *Social Work with Groups, 14*(2), 23–43.

Haynes, K. S., & Mickelson, J. S. (1997). *Affecting change: Social workers in the political arena* (3rd ed.). White Plains, NY: Longman.

Kimmel, S. D. (1997). *Social theory and the "insufficiency" of philanthropic incentive: Towards a public philosophy of nonprofit enterprise,* Occasional Paper #97-5. Indianapolis: Indiana University Center on Philanthropy.

Lindblom, C. E. (1965). *The intelligence of democracy: Decision making through mutual adjustment.* New York: The Free Press.

Lohmann, R. A. (1980). *Breaking even: Financial management in human services.* Philadelphia: Temple University Press.

Lohmann, R. A. (1991). Social planning and problems of old age. In P. Kim (Ed.), *Serving the elderly: Perspectives for practice* (pp. 209–232). New York: Aldine-DeGruyter.

Lohmann, R. A. (1992). The commons: A multidisciplinary approach to nonprofit organizations, voluntary action and philanthropy. *Nonprofit and Voluntary Sector Quarterly, 21*(3), 309–324.

Meyerson, M., & Banfield, E. C. (1955). *Politics, planning, and the public interest: The case of public housing in Chicago.* Glencoe, IL: Free Press.

Morris, R., & Binstock, R. (1966). *Feasible planning for social change.* New York: Columbia University Press.

Robbins, S. P., Chatterjee, P., & Canda, E. R. (1998). *Contemporary human behavior theory: A critical perspective for social work.* Needham Heights, MA: Allyn and Bacon.

Rothman, J. (2001). Approach to community intervention. In J. Rothman, J. L. Erlich, & J. E. Tropman (Eds.), *Strategies for community intervention* (6th ed.), (pp. 27–64). Itasca, IL.: F. E. Peacock.

Rothman, J. (1977). Three models of community organization practice: Their mixing and phasing. In F. Cox, J. L. Erlich, J. Rothman, & J. E. Tropman (Eds.), *Strategies of community organization* (pp. 20–38). Itasca, IL: F. E. Peacock.

Simon, H. A. (1976). *Administrative behavior: A study of decision-making processes in administrative organizations* (3rd ed.). New York: Free Press.

Solomon, B. (1976). *Black empowerment: Social work in oppressed communities.* New York: Columbia University Press.

THE CASE

LINDBLOM COUNTY

BACKGROUND

Nancy Adams put down Cindy's literature review and thought about how completely it applied to the situation in which she and her friends and professional colleagues found themselves at present. "Los Compadres" had been friends since they began the first class in the graduate social work program at Vandalia State University 15 years ago.

On graduation, most of their classmates immediately left Lindblom County for more lucrative urban practices but Nancy, along with Lisa Taylor, Melissa Todd, Andy Miller, Chris Tyler, and Alan Monroe, were all committed to the area and to their ideas of rural practice. Although most of their fellow students in the master's program had been interested in various aspects of therapy, direct practice, and micro practice, Los Compadres were united by their interest in and commitment to administration, policy, and community practice. Like other classmates, Alan had left the area right after graduation, but he left to enter a doctoral program rather than a lucrative urban practice. He returned to the area after three years to join the faculty at Vandalia State and completed his doctorate the following year.

Los Compadres had begun as a study group in graduate school. On graduation, five of the six had continued meeting weekly for lunch, and had formed what they referred to jokingly as the power center of social services in Lindblom County. On completion of his doctorate, Alan joined the others for their weekly "power lunch." They were all conscious of their growing influence in the human services community. Although they wore it lightly, empowerment had become a reality for them. Many of the social workers in Lindblom County had little or no professional training in social work, and they were still the only MSWs among the several dozen executives of small agencies in the county.

The passage of time had, indeed, brought Los Compadres to the forefront of local and regional social services leadership. Without any of them ever intending it, their monthly luncheons had taken on much of the character of a county social services planning committee. There had been a real service planning capacity in the county once (during the 1960s and 1970s), but it was entirely federally funded and disappeared completely in the budget cutbacks associated with the creation of state human service block grants. Since then, agency self-interest had been the sole motive for new service initiatives in the county.

Two years ago, Nancy was named executive director of Lindblom County Family Services. Lisa became CEO of the Lindblom County Community Mental Health Center the following year, and continued to operate a large and successful drug therapy program that she had founded. Melissa was increasingly recognized for her innovative work in directing a local art therapy center that she had founded through an NIH grant. Chris was assistant director for planning for the Lindblom-Chestnut Bi-County United Way and Andy was deputy regional administrator for the Vandalia Commission on Aging. Last year, Alan was tenured, promoted to professor, and named director of the BSW program at Vandalia State.

Nancy and Melissa served together on the advisory committee of the state human services agency. Census data are used in a number of federal funds distribution systems and the group was very aware of the implications of the latest census data. They knew, for example, that the county has a current population of roughly 80,000 with one small city (Wildavsky City) as its urban core, surrounded by contiguous rural areas. A population, said to number 25,000 (including the majority of a population of 20,000 college students), lives within the city limits. The municipal limits of Wildavsky City, which is located at the extreme eastern end of the county, are very tightly drawn. An additional urbanized population of 50,000 people live in the immediate suburban fringe within 10 miles of the city center.

The population in the urban fringe live in four incorporated municipalities of 10,000 (Simonville), 6,000 (Amatai), 4,000 (Drortown), and 1,000 (Charles City), and approximately 25 subdivisions of varying sizes (10–200 households). The remaining 5,000 people of the county live in the outlying regions. An estimated 5,000 additional residents of the urban core of Wildavsky City reside in nearby Chestnut County. The Chestnut County seat is in Scottsvale, a town of less than 10,000, roughly 20 miles to the east.

At one of their weekly luncheons, Los Compadres invited Dr. Capri, a historian specializing in local and regional history. Vandalia, Dr. Capri told them, is in a long-term economic transition from heavy reliance on a single, primary industry and an extreme concentration of capital to a period of simultaneous deindustrialization, diversification of capital, and convergence toward national norms in income and education. It is also somewhat distinctive, according to Dr. Capri, that Vandalia was originally settled by a white, Protestant, Anglo-Saxon population, who became the upper class of a rural industrial economy. For several generations, this economic elite encouraged the immigration of a diverse combination of ethnic groups of African, southern European, and Asian descent. Members of Los Compadres agreed that although they were all members of ethnic groups once on the bottom of the Lindblom County pyramid, merely by the act of getting educated and remaining in the community, they had moved up into that upper class—a strange position for social workers, perhaps, but one not at all uncommon in the peculiar circulation of the elites characteristic of modern rural areas.

Increasingly, they found that their separate institutional loyalties were weighing heavily on their solidarity as a group and any sense of class consciousness they might have developed. The other members of the group periodically got on Alan's case about ivory towers and the practical irrelevance of theory and research. As the policy implications of deinstitutionalization almost imperceptibly shifted the focus of mental health services from what Andy called the worried well to persistent and chronic mentally ill cases, Lisa and Chris were increasingly at odds; Lisa had been very active in forming a local chapter of AMI, the Alliance for the Mentally Ill, and her agency aggressively supported a range of client rights, self-help, and empowerment groups for chronically mentally ill clients living in Lindblom County. Chris, on the other hand, increasingly voiced concerns raised by the business and professional community and corporate donors about the public visibility of the homeless and street people throughout the county.

At the same time, although her agency continued to be called Family Services, Nancy had become increasingly involved in the statewide campaign to address the growing poverty of children, and her program had shifted almost exclusively toward the problems of younger children and adolescents. Nancy and Andy almost came to blows at one meeting over her claim that "greedy geezers" were the real cause of children's poverty and his retort that statewide adult and senior services for the aged poor had been unfairly cut back by political pressures from a reckless children's lobby that had no real vision.

For a number of years now, Melissa had been particularly aggressive in pursuing commercial outlets for the work produced by some of her clients. This led to some grumbling among others in the group that she seemed more interested in making money in the art business than in helping her clients.

THE NAME ISSUE

Just when it appeared that the group might be torn apart by these internal conflicts, however, an external threat arose that brought them together at least temporarily. According to an article in the Wildavsky City newspaper, the group was the target of a resolution by the local Latino Political Action Committee condemning its use of the term *Los Compadres* since none of them was Latino.

The name controversy at first appeared to be just one more source of tension for the group. Chris, Andy, and Alan all made caustic comments about the language police coming to get them. Lisa and Melissa agreed that the issue was actually highly personal, and had come about because a classmate of theirs in the MSW program, Maria Sanchez, had always resented the group because she had never been asked to join.

Maria was now president of the Lindblom County LPAC. Like Alan, she had left the community following graduation but had returned two years ago. Maria was not born in Lindblom County, although she had gone to high school there, living with an uncle and aunt following the death of her parents in an accident. Since returning, Maria had little contact with her old classmates or others in the Anglo human services community. According to earlier accounts in the local paper, she had become very active in local politics, advocating for issues with the county commission, city council, school board, and in other venues. Like Maria, most of the Latino population were relatively recent residents of Lindblom County, moving there in large numbers since the 1940s to work in the primary industries of the county where employment was now rapidly declining. At the last census, Spanish-speaking residents made up 38 percent of the population of the county, and tended to be concentrated in two particular neighborhoods in Wildavsky City, as well as in Amatai and Charles City.

Maria's role with the Latino Political Action Committee was part of a general upsurge of interest in local politics within the Latino community, which now held two of the three county commission seats, two of the five school board positions, and one of the seven city council seats. Her principal opponent for local leadership of this increasingly important ethnic block was 62-year-old Alejandro "Mike" Ramirez, county clerk, who had moved to the county in 1963 to administer a summer youth-employment grant. Mike was a devout, traditionalist Catholic and very popular community leader who had been involved in controversy within the county virtually since his arrival. He recently initiated a local movement, with strong support from at least one local Knights of Columbus chapter, opposing women in professional and public life.

The most active and visible members of Mike's coalition were all male, although reportedly they also had a female auxiliary to make lunches for meetings, visit shut-ins, and carry out other tasks that the group defined as "women's work." Both the men's and women's groups were made up of active parishioners in Santiago de Compostella parish in Amatai, where Mike had lived since 1970. By contrast, Maria's group was made up of a mixture of men and women, only a portion of whom were religiously active and the majority of whom lived in Wildavsky City and had ties to Vandalia State.

Mike was probably the most popular elected official in the county and had a reputation as a local character—someone who spoke out for the little guy. He often said outrageous things, and one could never be certain whether he meant them or not, but people said there always seemed to be a good point behind them. When a national Protestant convention announced passage of a resolution that women should be subservient to their husbands, Mike had been quoted in the local paper as saying, "It looks like barefoot, pregnant, and in the kitchen ain't such a bad idea after all." Although he later claimed he had been misquoted, he also added that the Protestant group was right in passing that resolution.

Los Compadres believed that Mike actively courted much of the local publicity he received. Dan Jenkins, editor of the local newspaper, knowing good copy when he saw it, insisted that the paper's local political reporter, Howard Billis (who, in the experience of Los Compadres, was not distinguished by the accuracy of his reports), cover Mike's monthly speeches to his group, which officially had a long Spanish title no one ever used. Throughout Lindblom County, they were known simply as the Santa Maria Society.

Several months ago, Mike had singled out the members of Los Compadres for criticism in one of his speeches, calling them "pale, Protestant, pompous professionals" and demanding that they immediately cease using a Spanish name for their "obviously Anglo" group. He also said that he was in the process of filing a complaint with the regional federal EEOC office.

Andy lost his composure when Howard called him for a reaction to the speech. He was quoted in a sidebar to Howard's report of the speech as saying: "Is he nuts? It just means 'the friends,' for god's sake! And it isn't even an official name of record for anything. We've been getting together for lunch since we were students. It's just what we've called ourselves. It's a kind of group nickname."

Members of Los Compadres were at a loss to deal with Mike's comments. Chris suggested at their next luncheon that they start calling themselves "Les Amis" since there wasn't an active French ethnic organization in Lindblom County. "You're all missing the point," Nancy retorted. "This name started out when we were grad students and not very visible in this county. Remember? We just thought it was cool to take a romantic sounding label. Any one would do; this one happened to be Spanish. We certainly had, and still have, the right to call ourselves whatever we want to, regardless of what Mike Ramirez thinks."

"But you have to admit things are different now. We have the good of the community to consider. We're all community leaders now, whether we like it or not," another said. Someone else commented: "Maybe Mike's right; we should change our name. And, now that this has come up, maybe we should ask Maria to lunch with us too. I always thought we should have included her when she came back home to Lindblom County. Maybe it's not too late yet."

Everyone in the group was aware of the growing importance of an organized Latino community in Lindblom County. "But, if we asked her," Andy noted, "then we'll have to identify another male member too! Otherwise, women will become a permanent majority in what has been a gender-balanced group." The women in the group knew he was serious. Since the passage of Proposition 209 in California, Andy had been increasingly assertive in his criticism of Affirmative Action, but no one seemed sure to what extent Chris and Alan agreed with him because they maintained an obvious silence during such discussions.

"I'm less concerned about gender balance in our group than I am about Mike!" Melissa said. "You're right, we need another male also, but if it isn't someone associated with Mike's group, or at least acceptable to them, we're walking right into a trap. He'll say the Anglo service community is siding with Maria's faction; and he'll be right. God knows, we have more in common with them."

In part, Los Compadres *were* at a loss to deal with their internal group tensions because they were unable to fully come to terms with their position in the community, and Mike's challenge to them just made things worse. Like most social work students of community planning, they had been schooled to come to terms with power elites from the bottom up. But their group had become, or so it seemed, a local power elite by default. Such as it was, theirs was a kind of power.

Finally, it was decided to invite Maria to join the group and to postpone action on a possible eighth male member. She accepted, and within a couple of meetings, appeared to be fully integrated into the group. Maria told them at the very first meeting she attended how she had tried to get the name resolution tabled in the LPAC executive committee, but the more religious members felt that if they didn't vote for it, Mike would use the issue against them within their parish. The others were somewhat surprised to learn that since she returned to Lindblom County, Maria had been serving on the state human services advisory committee with Nancy and Melissa, and on Alan's visiting committee. Equally surprising was that Maria, Lisa, and Chris's sister had all dated Howard in high school, and that Maria and Andy had gone together to a couple of fraternity parties in college.

"GIVE FIVE"

Before they were distracted by the name issue, Los Compadres had been trying to gain a better understanding of the probable impact of welfare reform and devolution on social services in Lindblom County and to organize some type of response. They felt strongly that if there was going to be any kind of general community response, it would be up to them to make it happen.

As in so many areas these days, their opinions were sharply divided about how to respond. At one extreme was Alan, who (true to form, the others said) saw welfare reform as a great watershed in human services—a genuine opportunity to reassert local autonomy and build community, and to bring welfare recipients into the community in ways not previously possible. At the opposite extreme was Nancy, who expressed great concern about the wisdom of bringing the business community into the act of training welfare recipients for jobs. "You saw how they reacted to deinstitutionalization and homelessness!" she would say at almost every meeting. Melissa saw welfare reform as just another relatively trivial change in a bureaucratic monster that had taken on a life of its own and was totally resistant to change. This delicate balance was tipped when Maria joined the group. She enthusiastically endorsed the idea of organizing a community response from the start, and that became the group's position.

Gradually, after many weeks of exploring all angles of the issue, a group consensus began to emerge. Regardless of their views of welfare reform, it would be worthwhile to invest their time and energy in a campaign to increase local volunteering and raise the level of personal giving by community residents. "It's clear," said Andy, "that even if federal funds were available at the levels they had been in the past, many of our local agencies could always use more resources."

Early in the discussions, Lisa had said, "This is another good reason to include Maria. Increasing contributions from the Latino community is going to be critical: Everybody knows people in the Latino community don't give as much as the rest of the community. And Catholics don't give as much as Protestants or Jews."

"We don't have any evidence that's true," Alan noted. "But," Lisa replied, "we all know it is!" Now, with Maria in the group, it seemed more imperative than ever to gather data on giving and volunteering, if for no other reason than to counter group stereotypes with the facts. "Maybe we need to collect some data on it."

Shortly after Alan returned to Wildavsky City, the group had first become intrigued by the INDEPENDENT SECTOR Give Five campaign (www.indepsec. org/programs/givefive.html). Since the mid-1980s, this national umbrella organization had been advocating that citizens volunteer five hours a week and give 5 percent of their income in donations. A study by another professor in

Alan's department had recently confirmed both that the highest income quintile gave more than the general population (3.1 percent of personal income in Lindblom County, compared with 1.9 percent for the general population nationally) and that the poor gave even more (5.6 percent of personal income in Lindblom County).

Like many others, Los Compadres suspected that one of the implications of devolution was that there was bound to be a growing local *philanthropic insufficiency;* unlike others, they set out to measure it (Kimmel, 1997; Lohmann, 1992). Their methodology was quite simple: (1) establish the current national giving levels for human services philanthropy, (2) use the national norms to identify the portion of giving and volunteering that might be attributable to Lindblom County, and (3) compare those numbers with the actual local data. The total dollar volume and volunteer hours, which were also given a dollar value using a standard annual determination by the national group INDEPENDENT SECTOR, was called the *local predicted philanthropic capacity* (PPC) for Lindblom County. The combined sum of actual revenues of all identifiable community organizations they called the *real philanthropic capacity* (RPC). The difference between the two figures would either represent a *local philanthropic surplus* or a *local philanthropic deficit* (see Lohmann, 1980, pp. 218–219). (They hoped eventually to also derive a methodology for projecting actual need as well, but presently such a method eluded them.) From his position with the local United Way (which had recently been extended into Chestnut County following the recommendation of a committee headed by Alan), Chris was aware of the extent of the human services delivery system in Lindblom County. He prepared a draft report for Los Compadres to review as they determined what to do.

Results of the Study

The research undertaken by Los Compadres was going along very well. The data were collected and the group was in a position to announce within a week or two the results of its study of philanthropic capacity. They planned to do so at a kickoff breakfast for a campaign to recruit volunteers and major donors. Invitations had gone out to a broad cross-section of community leaders from government, religion, Vandalia State, local business, and other community interest groups, including the Santa Maria Society and its auxiliary.

Alan had arranged for a countywide random sample survey of nearly 1,000 households to be done by the fledgling Survey Research Center at the university, paid for in part by a small grant from the United Way that Chris negotiated. Andy had arranged for a large number of senior citizen volunteers to administer roughly 40 percent of the surveys, and many of the rest were handled by student volunteers. All in all, the survey generated a good deal of excitement in the community, and Howard Billis had already called to say he would be doing a front-page article on the survey results for the paper the Sunday following the kickoff meeting.

The preliminary results of the study were tabulated quickly. In most respects, Lindblom County fit the profile of the nation as a whole. However, analysis of the religious and ethnic subsets revealed some rather complex findings that would require a good deal of careful explanation: The aggregate of Latino givers in Lindblom County did, as Lisa suspected, appear to give less than the community as a whole (1.2 percent of income, against 1.9 percent for the county as a whole). And, Catholic givers did give less than any other religious group (including Protestant, Jewish, Muslim, Greek and Russian Orthodox, and a rather mysterious "Other" category that constituted roughly 17 percent of the total of religious preferences). However, when two intervening variables (professional status and education) were controlled for, *all* differences among religious groups disappeared.

MIKE'S COUP D'ÉTAT

Then came the most memorable week in local affairs that any member of Los Compadres could recall. The kickoff luncheon was scheduled for Friday noon. Monday's paper contained a brief news item that an EEOC investigation team would be in the county the following week to look into reports that local social workers were involved in fomenting possible hate crimes against Latino Catholics. A series of public hearings were scheduled at Santiago de Compostela parish and two other locations in the county. On Tuesday, the newspaper contained Howard's report of Mike's latest speech the night before. In it, he ridiculed efforts to measure community philanthropic capacity in the strongest language yet. "Those who believe that the compassion of Christian charity can be reduced to a set of numbers are," he said, "not merely misguided, but a dangerous element in the community." He went on: "For years, these professionals have been trying to impose their vision of social services on the good people of Lindblom County. Who died and elected them majordomos? This is nothing short of an inquisition against the Latino population of Lindblom County."

Members of Los Compadres spent most of Wednesday on the telephone attempting to find out what had set Mike off this way—What had angered him so much that he should say such things about them? Maria said she had no idea. No one else they talked to seemed sure either. "The whole thing is ridiculous," Chris said repeatedly. "How does he think a bunch of numbers are going to hurt them?"

On Thursday, the chairman of the County Commission, Antonio Diaz, who was also a member of Mike's group, announced plans to create a new County Social Services Planning Commission. "The purpose of this commission is to come up with a comprehensive plan for real social services in our county; services that will improve the quality of family life, and not lead to further family breakdown. This commission will be a practical one. They will not be wasting any more of our time and money on so-called 'social indicators' or 'outcome measures,' " chairman Diaz said. "This new Planning Commission will concentrate on the real needs of people in our community and not on the kind of nonsense that typically preoccupies those social work professionals."

The lead story on the front page of the Friday edition of the local paper contained a report of the proposed membership of the Lindblom County Social Services Planning Commission. No members of Los Compadres were included. In the second section, there was a small item indicating that the LPAC members at the meeting adopted a resolution that "strongly agreed" with recent remarks by Mike Ramirez that quantitative social indicators or outcome measures were part of a conspiracy against the Latino population of Lindblom County. A second resolution, also adopted at the meeting, demanded that Maria Sanchez resign as chair of the group. A letter to the editor in that same issue was from the chairman of the local AMI chapter: "I wouldn't have put it as bluntly as Mike Ramirez did, but he's right about those social workers. All you have to have is a diagnostic label and they think they can run your life."

Andy looked out from behind the curtains at the local high school auditorium at the sparse crowd of roughly 25 people. It was 15 minutes after the announced starting time and no one had come in for the past several minutes. He turned to the other members of Los Compadres and said quietly, "What are we going to do now?"

DISCUSSION QUESTIONS

Community Planning

1. What elements of community planning can be identified in this case? Are (or should) these elements be different in rural and urban communities. Why or why not?

2. How do Los Compadres mix and match social action, social planning, and locality development aspects of community practice in their work in Lindblom County?

3. What strategies might Los Compadres use to work toward creating a competent community? Is it possible to achieve enough consensus in community planning to actually create a competent community in Lindblom County? Explain your response.

4. Given the data presented in the case, what additional information would be needed to determine how much would be raised if Lindblom County were to achieve the national Give Five recommended giving target of five percent?

Power, Conflict, and Diversity

1. In what ways is the Latino Political Action Committee a stakeholder in Lindblom County human services? The Santa Maria Society?

2. Are the members of Los Compadres and other leaders of Lindblom County in fact engaged in oppression of the Latino minority? If so, what can and should they do about it? If not, why is so much conflict occurring? Does Paolo Freire's perspective on oppression apply here?

3. Why did the name Los Compadres spark so much controversy, and how might the group handle this conflict? Would it be feasible (or even possible) to invite Mike Ramirez to join the group, and what would the implications be? Should the group have changed its name?

4. How should Los Compadres respond to the antiprofessionalism expressed by Mike Ramirez? To the EEOC investigation team? To the move to create a new County Social Services Planning Commission?

5. Los Compadres became a community elite in a power vacuum. The Santa Maria Society became one through conflict. How could the two overcome their differences and work together?

Philanthropic Self-Sufficiency

1. What is philanthropic self-sufficiency and how might this concept be used in community planning?

2. How would the takeover of community human services leadership by another single ethnic group affect philanthropic capacity?

PART **IV**

THE ORGANIZATION AS
THE ARENA OF CHANGE

In this part, we focus on the primary locus of most social work practice—human service organizations. Organizations are critical practice arenas for most professional social workers in terms of the quality and quantity of services received by service users. Social service organizations legitimate and sanction the majority of professional practice; through either the implementation of policy governing multisource-funded programs or agency policy-governing, agency-funded programs, they have a great deal of influence on the final outcomes of efforts to help clients.

The next cases reflect two major themes encountered by all social service organization managers, leaders, and staff. The first case has to do with day-to-day administration of organizations, including leadership, coordination, control, motivation of employees, program structure and design, and resource acquisition and planning. The second case's theme is the management of external environmental relations, including interaction and exchanges with funding sources; political relationships; bureaucratic requirements; and dependencies on key suppliers, regulators, and cooperating agencies for client, monetary, and material resources.

The first case in this part, "The Consultants," is set in a public welfare agency and reflects problems often encountered within complex bureaucratic structures. In contrast, the next two cases—"The Women's Co-op" and "When Community Mental Health Meets Public Managed Care"—take place in nonprofit settings. Strains arise in "The Women's Co-op" case when environmental forces test the existing culture that has held the organization together, whereas in the community mental health case, strains are induced as the organization encounters public funds that are increasingly tied to conditions that mimic private-sector market forces. Following is "Computerizing Child

Welfare Services," which takes place in a public child welfare setting, but the march of technology it describes could occur in almost any agency setting—public, nonprofit, or for profit. Similarly, the last case in this part, entitled "Ecological Outcomes," could take place in any sector since any agency that does not know how to measure program effectiveness, using the language of "outcomes," quickly becomes obsolete.

Across cases, and in each agency, leadership is critically needed. "The Consultants" addresses a public bureaucracy in which an extensive change is occurring, and recently hired leaders earnestly look to outside consultants to assist their unit managers in meeting the challenges of a rapidly changing, performance-oriented environment. In contrast, "Ecological Outcomes" plays out a different scenario, illustrating how a void in nonprofit leadership (both on the part of board members and designated leaders) can make the demands of outcome performance-oriented measures appear overwhelming. "Computerizing Child Welfare Services" looks at the challenge of leadership in a situation in which change appears to be technologically driven—a not so uncommon situation in today's world. Finally, the situations faced by the community mental health agency and the women's co-op examine the reactions of leaders in nonprofit organizations as they attempt to understand and plan for the full implications of change.

As one reads these cases, one witnesses a variety of challenges that face social service agency managers and their staff. Further, change opportunities within agencies and within agency environments can appear in a multitude of ways for which the social service organization manager must be ever alert if improvements to staff conditions and client services are to be achieved. The organization as an arena for change is complicated by the fact that practitioners are often employees of the agency in which they want to see change occur and may encounter resistance at higher levels by those in authority who have a great deal of control over their lives.

9

THE CONSULTANTS

Reengineering Public Welfare

DAVID MENEFEE

THEORETICAL AND PRACTICE PERSPECTIVES

This case is based on a true story of a management consulting firm's (OD Inc.) work with a public social service agency in Maryland. Due to a new law passed by the state legislature (see Appendix 9-A), the King County Department of Social Welfare (KCDSW) finds itself in direct competition with private sector businesses, a situation that reflects the blurring of boundaries between public, private, and nonprofit sectors across the country. KCDSW has just two years to demonstrate the efficiency and effectiveness of its services, or some proportion of those services may be privatized. They have contracted with OD Inc. to help them plan and implement the organizational changes needed to accomplish this objective.

This case focuses on the organizational change and development process. *Organization development* (OD) is a team-based, organizationwide, systematic effort to improve an organization's performance using social and behavioral science theories and technologies (French & Bell, 1998) as well as those found in business management (Menefee, Ahluwalia, Pell, & Woldu, 2000). Successful organization development interventions consist of four major activities, "diagnosis, feedback, discussion, and action" (Burke, 1994, p. 8), respectively. Each of these processes is touched on here.

First, the organization must be assessed for its current conditions, processes, and structures (Netting, Kettner, & McMurtry, 2004). A comprehensive analysis reflects the current status and interaction of every subsystem within the agency. A variety of organization and management theories and models (Morgan, 1997) relating to management can be employed in the assessment including rational-structural, human relations, open systems, contingency, cultural, political, and Theory Z approaches (Netting et al., 2004).

Second, the diagnosis must be shared with key organizational figures for modification and validation (French & Bell, 1998). The OD consultant reviews the assessment in a focus group context and asks members to help refine the diagnostic model (Block, 2000). Feedback from those who live and work in the organization is critical for clarifying issues, identifying cause–effect relationships, and developing a shared understanding of organizational dynamics. The consultant would surely not want to risk designing and implementing an intervention if the organizational diagnosis is not on target.

Third, interventions must be planned in open discussion with the client. Successful intervention "starts where the client is" and addresses the organization's current and future needs. An effective intervention contains a framework for analyzing the agency's current task environment; assessing environment relations; and evaluating the agency's existing structure, processes, and conditions (Netting et al., 2004). The planning phase will identify those affected by the change, examine the agency's readiness for change; select a change approach; assess political, interpersonal, resource considerations; weigh the likelihood of success; and set realistic goals and objectives (Netting et al., 2004).

Fourth, the intervention (action) phase needs to be multidimensional and transformational, encompassing agency values, goals, structures, technologies, management style, and staff development needs as well as their interrelationship. Implementation must be incremental and yet still conform to the organization's timeline. Finally, implementation must have the support and active involvement of the entire staff; otherwise, the changes proposed will only be cosmetic.

As demonstrated in this case, the intervention will have to introduce new management technologies into the agency (Ginsberg & Keys, 1995), especially in the areas of continuous quality improvement (Kinlaw, 1992), business process reengineering (Harrington, Esseling, & Van Nimwegen, 1997), activity-based costing (Miller, 1996), and advanced automation technologies (Post & Anderson, 2000). The ultimate goal of the firm's intervention is to help the services division demonstrate the efficiency and effectiveness of its services in sufficient time to meet legislative demands or else they will go out of business.

It is important that the intervention helps the services division implement a successful outcome management system. The system has to inform managers of the resources consumed by various business processes and activities. It has to link activities with outputs and generate valid and reliable outcome measures. The system must also provide unit managers and employees with objective feedback so that they can improve performance on a continuous basis. Finally, the system must forecast the costs and benefits of new services based on the costs of activities and outcomes rather than traditional cost accounting procedures.

An organizing framework for these technologies is total quality/cost management (TQM) (Ginsberg & Keys, 1995), which includes an emphasis on continuous quality improvement (CQI) (Kinlaw, 1992), activity-based costing (ABC) (Miller, 1996), outcome measurement (Martin & Kettner, 1996), and business process improvement (BPI) (Harrington et al., 1997). TQM is a system of management that focuses the workforce on achieving service effectiveness through identifying and resolving performance problems that affect quality and cost outcomes. CQI is a team-based systematic problem-solving process that uses tools, such as fishbone diagrams, cause–effect analysis, data-collection techniques, control charts, and trend analysis, to pinpoint and resolve problems with a group's work processes. ABC is a nontraditional method of accounting that allocates costs directly to work activities based on their use of resources and then assigns costs to cost objects (customers, products, services) based on their use of activities (Miller, 1996). BPI is a methodology that is designed to bring about step–function improvements in administrative and support processes using approaches such as fast analysis solution techniques, process benchmarking, process redesign, and process reengineering (Harrington et al., 1997, p. 5). In addition, the consulting team will have to assist the managers of individual units as well as the division as a whole to develop valid and reliable outcome measures for both cost and quality (Mullen & Magnabosco, 1997). Such measures will inform the cost per unit of service, productivity, technical quality, service effectiveness, and client satisfaction.

Finally, whereas the technical cost-effective methods and techniques just cited are a necessity for processes of reengineering and organizational consulting, it is knowledge of and mastery of the change process that social work macro practitioners bring to cases such as this. Social work, a change-oriented profession, has much to contribute to the integration of the change process and technical methods in social service settings.

REFERENCES

ABC Technologies, Inc. (2002). Welcome to the ABC authority. [Online] Available: http://www.abctech.com.

Block, P. (2000). *Flawless consulting: A guide to getting your expertise used* (2nd ed.). San Francisco: Jossey-Bass/Pfeiffer.

Burke, W. W. (1994). *Organization development: A process of learning and changing.* Reading, MA: Addison-Wesley.

French, W. L., & Bell, C. H. (1998). *Organization development: Behavioral science interventions for organization improvement.* Upper Saddle River, NJ: Prentice-Hall.

Ginsberg, L., & Keys, P. R. (1995). *New management in human services.* Washington, DC: NASW Press.

Harrington, H. J., Esseling, E. K. C., & Van Nimwegen, H. (1997). *Business process improvement workbook: Documentation, analysis, design, and management of business process improvement.* New York: McGraw-Hill.

Kinlaw, D. C. (1992). *Continuous improvement and measurement for total quality.* Homewood, IL: Business One Irwin.

Martin, L. L., & Kettner, P. M. (1996). *Measuring the performance of human service programs.* Thousand Oaks, CA: Sage.

Menefee, D., Ahluwalia, U., Pell, D., & Woldu, B. (2000). ABM: An innovative business technology for human service organizations. *Administration in Social Work, 24*(2), 67–84.

Miller, J. A. (1996). *Implementing activity-based management in daily operations.* New York: Wiley.

Morgan, G. (1997). *Images of organization.* Newbury Park, CA: Sage.

Mullen, E. J., & Magnabosco, J. L. (1997). *Outcomes measurement in the human services: Crosscutting issues and methods.* Washington, DC: NASW Press.

Netting, F. E., Kettner, P. M., & McMurtry, S. L. (2004). *Social work macro practice.* New York: Longman.

Post, G. V., & Anderson, D. L. (2000). *Management information systems: Solving business problems with information technology* (2nd ed.). Boston: Irwin/McGraw-Hill.

THE CASE

THE CONSULTANTS

AGENCY BACKGROUND

KCDSW is a public social service agency serving a population of approximately 750,000. The agency provides a variety of services to families in crisis so that they may become independent and self-sufficient (see Appendix 9-B). Community Services include emergency assistance, food distribution, homeless services, and energy assistance. Family Investment Services include job counseling and placement, food stamps, medical assistance, temporary cash assistance, and temporary housing. The Services Division provides family and children services, adult services, and resource and support services (see Appendix 9-C). KCDSW's total caseload is approximately 8,500 per year. The agency currently employs 936 people; 294 work in the Services Division.

The director of KCDSW, Ann Smith, reports to the Maryland State Secretary for Human Services. Ann holds a master's degree in social work administration. She has recently assumed the director's position, having been recruited from a successful career in the private nonprofit sector. The deputy director for the Services Division, Paula Hayes, has a master's degree in public administration with approximately five years of management experience in the public sector. She was most recently promoted from the position of bureau chief for Family and Children's Services.

Both Ann and Paula are relatively new to their positions and are eager to make a significant contribution. During their first six months, they tried to get to know the division by interviewing the three bureau chiefs and the fifteen managers responsible for the service units. Not particularly encouraged by their initial findings and very concerned about the new legislation, they decide to call your management consulting firm OD Inc., for assistance. You meet with Ann and Paula at the agency the following week. The main purpose of the meeting is to find out what their perceptions are of the Services Division, what they think are the division's needs, and how they think those needs could be met.

FIRST CONTACT

During your conversation, Ann tells you that she is particularly concerned about the survival of the Services Division because "services are most vulnerable to private-sector interests. If we don't find a way to demonstrate in the next two years that our services are efficient and effective, we will be sitting ducks for privatization!" she exclaimed. Paula followed, "We need to develop a cost management model within the division so that unit managers can manage the cost of services at the unit level." "Yes," said Ann, "I want each manager to be able to do a cost–benefit analysis of her or his unit's services on a regular basis. That way the unit will be able to change the way services are provided and increase quality, improve productivity, and reduce costs!" she exclaimed. "We need a system of management here that is outcome-oriented," said Paula. You ask what that system might look like, but neither Ann nor Paula has a clear picture in mind.

At the close of the meeting, you agree to develop a plan for assessing the conditions, processes, and structures that might facilitate and inhibit the division's ability to establish an outcome management system. You commit to a two-week turnaround on the proposal so that Ann, Paula, and the bureau chiefs can review and respond to it. You agree that the assessment can begin next month and that it must be completed within one month.

During your drive back to the office, you think about Ann's and Paula's description of the unit managers, many of whom have been at the agency for 20 to 30 years. They have seen agency directors and deputies of service come and go. They have tried the latest management fads but have seen little success, and they are tired of broken promises. Worst of all, they have not seen a salary increase for six years and enjoy few extrinsic rewards for a job well done. You wonder about the level of resistance to change that has built up over the years and, knowing these managers will be key to the success of any intervention, you consider how you will gain their commitment.

ASSESSMENT PLANNING

You call a meeting of your professional staff and brief them on what you know about the client from your first contact. Your professional staff consists of management specialist Samuel Spector, organizational development consultant Mary Jefferson, business process engineer Bruce Abbot, activity-based cost accountant Jennifer Smith, continuous quality improvement specialist Joyce Freedman, and management information system specialist Edward Benson. Each team member also possesses a foundation knowledge and skill base in the specialization of his or her peers. To be successful in its work with KCDSW, your team needs to call on the expertise of each of its members. Your agenda is to define (1) the information you will need; (2) who in the agency is likely to provide the information; (3) the process, methods, and tools of data collection; (4) who in the firm should be involved; and (5) what action steps should be taken.

Three hours later your team is successful in completing the assessment plan (see Appendix 9-D). They describe it as a comprehensive assessment and believe it will yield the information necessary to begin planning an intervention that will help the division establish an outcome management system. They recommend that the assessment plan be presented to the Services Division management team. You contact Ann and arrange a meeting.

Your approach is to present the assessment plan to management, ask for feedback, and engage them in modifying the plan if necessary. You believe this approach will generate the greatest commitment to the plan. Your approach works as anticipated. With only a few minor changes, the management team approves the plan with enthusiasm. You return to your firm and announce to your team that the plan has been approved and that they can begin the assessment as scheduled. Each member of your team expresses excitement to be involved in the assessment.

THE RESULTS

Thirty days later you and your team finish the assessment as planned. You all meet in your conference room to review the findings. One by one, each member of the team presents his or her status report. The results are astonishing. You begin the briefing with the developmental history of the agency.

Developmental History—You

"KCDSW was formally established in 1952 and in its first ten years it grew into a large bureaucracy with formal structures, policies, rules and regulations, goals, specialization, etc. Although its basic function and form has been preserved, over the last twenty years the agency has gradually undergone changes that have eroded its capacity to function, including budget cuts, downsizing, job enlargement, reorganization, hiring freezes, and privatization of some services. The Services Division has been particularly hard hit since its services are seen as less vital than direct cash assistance to needy families. This has resulted in the disappearance and dissolution of many basic management functions as managers and staff struggle to provide quality services to a growing client population. Consequently, problems have arisen in the division's capacity to manage. In an attempt to compensate for these deficiencies, the division searches for and attempts to incorporate new management technologies. Unfortunately, most of the management talent has long since left the agency and new initiatives usually fail within a short period of time leaving employees discouraged and distrusting. Any questions?" You turn the meeting over to Sam to review his assessment of the management staff.

Management Competencies, Skills, and Style—Sam

"The unit managers do not function as managers but as lead workers. They resolve problems that arise between clients and the worker or agency. They are dedicated clinicians who have been promoted into manager positions with no formal education in management. They currently have no training or experience in planning, organizing, or controlling performance, but their MSW degree serves them well in the role of team leader. Results of the managerial style questionnaire confirm that the managers exhibit a democratic style of leadership. I found little or no experience in action planning, budgeting, fiscal management, management by objectives, or outcome-oriented management. My overall evaluation is that we have managers who excel in the interpersonal aspects of management but are sorely lacking in the technostructural areas. I'm sure that this comes as no surprise to most of you. Oh, yeah, one other thing. A high proportion of these managers are going to be resistant to any new management system we propose." Sam turns the meeting over to Mary who briefs the team on the division's working environment.

Culture and Working Conditions—Mary

Mary began by reading the core values of the division. "We believe all people have the right to be treated with dignity and respect. We believe in the strength of the family. We believe children and vulnerable adults are entitled to be protected and nurtured. We believe positive change is possible. We value partnerships and alliances with the community." She went on to describe the division's heroes. "They are hardworking, sometimes putting in 12-hour days. They go out of their way to satisfy the needs of the client, even if that means using their own resources! The heroes respect one another's opinions and seek out ideas from others. They are proactive and assertive, goal-directed, and achievement-oriented. They accomplish their objectives with few resources and little rewards.

"But, of course," continues Mary, "not everyone fits this description. Most of the staff see themselves as victims of a broken system. They believe that there is nothing they can do to change the status quo. They do not feel that management listens to their ideas and opinions. In fact, staffs generally bring problems to their supervisors instead of solutions. They feel undervalued due to the low wages they receive and the lack of recognition they get for their work. An employee told me that one of the rituals in the division is 'If you find a good horse, ride her till she drops, because everyone else around here is out to pasture!' " Mary said that although everyone claimed they had little time to do anything else but serve the client, she often observed people socializing in the halls and cafeteria for long periods of time. "The day-to-day life in the division is characterized by a lot of activity and interpersonal interaction that appears to be of little consequence. The grapevine is perhaps the most functional channel of communication since the formal channels do not work very well. All in all, I think we have a culture of co-dependents here, consisting of heroes and victims." With that, Mary turned the meeting over to Joyce.

Unit Job Descriptions and Worker Characteristics—Joyce

Joyce began her status report by saying, "I'll keep this one short. The personnel manager informed me that the last time the unit job descriptions were updated was fall 1987. They are mostly generic descriptions that do not even approximate what people are doing in their jobs. The only way you can determine what employees are actually doing is to ask them. Or if you can wait, the state Department of Human Services is requiring supervisors to update job descriptions over the next two years. With respect to worker characteristics," said Joyce, "there are 294 employees in the division. About 78 percent of the direct service staff are women, 64 percent are minorities, more than half have a master's degree in social work, and 72 percent have been employed by the division for five or more years. Well, that's about it on the job descriptions and demographics; Bruce, do you want to fill us in on structure?"

Unit Structure, Work Flow, Activities, Outcomes, and Goals—Bruce

"I'm afraid I don't have good news here, colleagues," said Bruce. "We do have organizational charts for each unit: the new deputy director asked each bureau chief to create them when she assumed her position. There are 15 units; the average span of control is 12. Beyond this, we have no work flow diagrams, no formal procedures, no activity analysis, no reliable and valid outcome measures, and no unit goals. It seems the way one learns how to do her or his job is by word of mouth, or folklore, if you will. Unfortunately, that's all I have to report. Jennifer, what's the status on the financial data?"

Financial Data—Jennifer

"The deputy, her bureau chiefs, and unit managers are not involved in the division's planning or budgeting process nor do they manage their own operating budgets. In fact, the entire planning, budgeting, monitoring, and reporting process is controlled at the state level, in the finance division of the Department of Human Services. Financial data at the program or service level are not available. Budget reports are provided only for the division as a whole. The deputy and the bureau chiefs never see a monthly report of their budgeted and actual expenses. When asked to quote the average cost of placing a child in a foster home, the deputy and bureau chiefs could only guess. When asked if they had any experience in planning and budgeting, they said, 'no, only with flex funds.' Things don't look much better in this area everyone. Edward, what's the status of information systems technology?"

Information Systems Technology—Edward

"If the division expects to automate cost and quality data, it is going to have to upgrade its hardware and software," said Edward. "It has a few PCs and a bunch of dumb terminals linked to a local area network server. It is currently running a UNIX platform that supports a client information system. The division is experiencing a variety of problems with the system; the network goes down two to three times a day and sometimes does not come up for several hours. Workers have to enter their client data on hard copy and then into the computer when the LAN comes back up. The system does not support some of the new financial management information software. In addition, the MIS manager resigned about two months ago, so there is no one there to maintain the system."

THE CHALLENGE

After the meeting, you lean back in your chair, contemplating all of the information your team gathered during the assessment. You clarify in your mind the objectives your firm has agreed to meet. Then, you schedule several meetings with your professional staff to design the intervention. Everyone is able to meet early next week, ready to work, but some team members appear to be a bit anxious about the project. You decide to prepare some additional "discussion questions" to review with your staff.

DISCUSSION QUESTIONS

Dealing with Organizational Change

1. How would you include Services Division staff in the change process so that they have some investment or ownership in what needs to occur?

2. What could be done to prepare major stakeholders in the Services Division to engage in moving toward an outcome-based management system? What resistances would you expect to encounter and why?

Assessing the Organization

1. If you were a consultant in this case, what frameworks or approaches might you use to conduct an organizational assessment?

2. The consultants in this case focus on developmental history; management competencies, skills, and style; culture and working conditions;

unit job descriptions and worker characteristics; unit structure, work flow activities, outcomes, and goals; financial data; and information systems technology. Are there other areas you would want to assess? If so, what would they be and how would you go about the assessment process?

Designing an Intervention

1. What strategy would you use to include key stakeholders in the design, development, implementation, and evaluation of the intervention? Is there a role for clients?

2. How would you design an intervention that would meet the needs of this division within a two-year time frame? What are the components of your intervention? Draw the relationships among the components and provide a rationale for why you have included each one.

3. What concerns would you have to address to ensure that the intervention was a success? How would you go about addressing these concerns? How would you sustain the changes?

4. How would you evaluate the effects of the intervention on the division? What would be your expected outcomes, and how would you measure them?

APPENDIX 9-A

Excerpt from *The Daily,* May 10

On May 8, 1997, the governor signed House Bill 164, the "Employee Competitive Reengineering Bill." This law establishes a *process for employees to compete* with private contractors for the delivery of targeted state services. Both public and private agencies can respond to the state's requests for proposals by submitting a plan to improve service delivery and reduce costs or reduce cost increases while maintaining the quality of the targeted service. In effect, the new law encourages private agencies to compete with public organizations to provide new and existing state services. State "expenditures could decrease to the extent that competitive reengineering creates a more efficient and cost-effective means of providing services to the public" (fiscal note revised, 1997) but at present these expenditures cannot be reliably estimated. The fiscal note ends with assurances that it is the policy of the state to use state employees to perform all state functions in state-operated facilities in preference to contracting with the private sector.

APPENDIX 9-B

King County
Department of Social Welfare
Organizational Chart

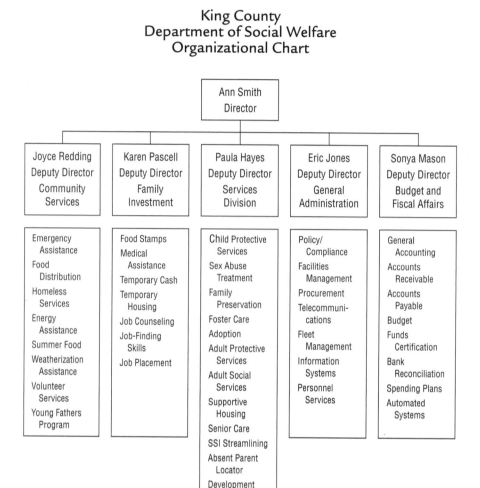

Ann Smith
Director

Joyce Redding Deputy Director Community Services	Karen Pascell Deputy Director Family Investment	Paula Hayes Deputy Director Services Division	Eric Jones Deputy Director General Administration	Sonya Mason Deputy Director Budget and Fiscal Affairs
Emergency Assistance	Food Stamps	Child Protective Services	Policy/ Compliance	General Accounting
Food Distribution	Medical Assistance	Sex Abuse Treatment	Facilities Management	Accounts Receivable
Homeless Services	Temporary Cash	Family Preservation	Procurement	Accounts Payable
Energy Assistance	Temporary Housing	Foster Care	Telecommuni- cations	Budget
Summer Food	Job Counseling	Adoption	Fleet Management	Funds Certification
Weatherization Assistance	Job-Finding Skills	Adult Protective Services	Information Systems	Bank Reconciliation
Volunteer Services	Job Placement	Adult Social Services	Personnel Services	Spending Plans
Young Fathers Program		Supportive Housing		Automated Systems
		Senior Care		
		SSI Streamlining		
		Absent Parent Locator		
		Development Unit		

APPENDIX 9-C

KCDSW Services Division
Bureaus, Services, and Description of Services

Family and Children Services Bureau	Adult Services Bureau	Resource and Support Services Bureau
Child Protective Services Investigations of allegations of physical/sexual abuse and neglect of children under age 18	**Protective Services** An investigative service directed toward preventing neglect, self-neglect, abuse, and exploitation of vulnerable adults	**Absent Parent Locator** Assists in locating parents for purposes of finding an alternative placement for children in foster care, terminating parental rights, and facilitating quicker adoptions
Sex Abuse Treatment Ongoing monitoring and treatment of families that have experienced child sexual abuse	**Social Services** The core voluntary service program for persons over age 18. It focuses on assisting disabled and elderly adults to remain independent and live in their community for as long as possible	**Development Unit** A grants coordinator and program developer are responsible for creative program development and public relations activities
Family Preservation Serves families experiencing a serious crisis involving child abuse or neglect requiring intensive family services		**Homefinding** The focus of this program is to recruit, study, and approve homes to provide foster care/adoptive homes for children and foster homes for adults
Foster Care Offers alternative placements for children (birth to age 18) who cannot remain in their homes	**Project Home** Supportive housing and case-management services for chronically mentally ill adults and adults with HIV	
Adoption Program Helps children who are in need of adoptive parents, and completes the legal process to become free for adoption and to be placed in adoptive homes	**Senior Care** Purchasing long-term care services for frail persons over 65 who are at risk of institutionalization	**In-Home Aide** Provides assistance with ADL for clients who either live alone or with their families
	SSI Streamlining Project Provides more efficient access to benefits for eligible disabled adults	**Respite Care** Provides short-term, occasional relief care on a scheduled or sporadic basis to families who need a break from the daily responsibilities of caring for a disabled child, adult, or elder

APPENDIX 9-D

Assessment Plan*

Information	Source	Process	Accountable	Action Steps
Division history	Sample of long-term employees	Group interview	You	1. Select sample of 30 long-term employees. 2. Conduct a structured open-ended group interview. 3. Record, integrate, analyze data. 4. Write status report on history of the division.
Management competencies, skills, and style	Bureau chiefs/unit managers	Face-to-face interviews and self-administered survey	SS	1. Schedule individual interviews. 2. Conduct structured, open-ended interviews. 3. Administer management style questionnaire. 4. Analyze interview/ questionnaire. 5. Write status report on competencies, skills, and style.
Culture and working conditions	Rank and file	Self-administered questionnaire	MJ	1. Select stratified random sample of 30 employees. 2. Administer and score questionnaire. 3. Write status report on climate, culture, and working conditions.
Unit job descriptions, worker characteristics	Personnel manager	Secure archival data	JF	1. Schedule appointment. 2. Obtain unit job descriptions. 3. Secure demographic data on employees in Services Division. 4. Summarize findings in status report.

Continued

Appendix 9-D   Assessment Plan *(Continued)*

Information	Source	Process	Accountable	Action Steps
Unit structure, work flow, activities, outcomes, and goals	Unit managers	Face-to-face interviews	BA	1. Schedule interviews. 2. Secure tables of organization, diagrams of workflow, lists of activities, outcome measures, and unit performance goals. 3. Write status report on structure.
Unit financial data	Chief of budget and fiscal administration	Unit budget reports and general ledger data	JS	1. Schedule appointment. 2. Secure chart of accounts, and budgeted, and actual expenses allocated to each unit by month. 3. Write status report on financial information gathered.
Information systems technology	Manager of information systems	Obtain hardware and software specifications	EB	1. Schedule appointment. 2. Map hardware and local area network configuration. 3. Obtain information on LAN software availability and usage. 4. Write status report on the information systems.

*To be completed within 30 days of approval at a cost not to exceed $10,000.

10

THE WOMEN'S CO-OP

The Clash of Two
Organizational Cultures

CHERYL A. HYDE

This case focuses on choices, often fraught with conflict, made in order to sustain an organization. The events illuminate the role that organizational culture has in the preservation of a group's identity and underscore how it is the communal glue necessary to survive a volatile, hostile, and competitive environment. Although the case examines a feminist organization, lessons derived from understanding its transformation under duress are applicable to other vulnerable political and service organizations.

THEORETICAL AND PRACTICE PERSPECTIVES

The organizational culture perspective promotes a holistic understanding of organizational dynamics as well as organizational–environmental interactions (Frost et al., 1985, 1991; Ott, 1989; Schein, 1992; Smircich, 1983; Trice & Beyer, 1993). Culture is "a pattern of shared basic assumptions that the group learned as it solved its problems of external adaptation and internal integration, that has worked well enough to be considered valid and, therefore, to be taught to new members as the correct way to perceive, think, and feel in relation to those problems" (Schein, 1992, p. 12). To comprehend an organization's culture requires an understanding of its history, specifically strategies for growth and development; processes of member socialization and cohesion; and day-to-day functionings that allow for stability *and* flexibility. An organization's culture creates a social order, sense of continuity, and collective identity. It is the lens through which members understand, interpret, and respond to environmental challenges (Ott, 1989; Schein, 1992; Trice & Beyer, 1993).

The elements of culture—norms, myths, behaviors, customs, symbols, and language—can be clustered into three levels: artifacts—"visible organization structures, and processes" (behaviors, art, technology); values—"strategies, goals, philosophies" (what "ought" to be); and basic assumptions—"unconscious, taken-for-granted beliefs, perceptions, thoughts and feelings" (notions of time, human nature, relationship to the environment) (Schein, 1992, p. 17). A cultural analysis captures the multilayered meanings of "obvious" elements, such as posters or seating arrangements, to the more subtle and ambiguous aspects of functioning such as who allies with whom, how money is discussed, or views of clients (Meyerson, 1991; Smircich, 1983; Trice & Beyer, 1993).

Organizations possess unique cultures, though there may be shared characteristics among similarly inclined groups. This distinct culture is generated by the intersection of the values, attitudes, and beliefs of society with respect to the organization's purpose; of relevant institutional sectors, such as human service, social movement, nonprofit sectors; and of the organization's founders and leaders (Ott, 1989). Considerable emphasis is placed on the role of founders and leaders, as signifiers of key values and assumptions that are to be preserved and transmitted and as change agents (Martin, Sitken, & Boehm, 1985; Schein, 1992; Siehl, 1985; Trice & Beyer, 1993).

Successful transformation is predicated on the change agent understanding the organization's culture. New ideas or solutions to problems, regardless of merit, will not be accepted into an organization if the culture (which by definition exists to ensure survival) is threatened. Organizational members may go so far as to engage in reactive or dysfunctional actions rather than risk the culture (Trice & Beyer, 1993). For cultural change to occur, the leader must possess an in-depth understanding of the status quo; be perceptive as to the new realities and why they necessitate change; be able to translate what she has learned about these new realities to other organizational members; be able to motivate these members to embrace change and participate in the change processes; manage anxiety that comes with learning and change; and stabilize the newly emergent cultural elements (Schein, 1992). Thus, the onus for transformation falls on the leader; but it will only succeed with the willing investment of the members.

Often, an organization engages in transformation to counter environmental threats or exploit environmental opportunities. Specifically, external crises can compel an organization to change in order to survive (Dyck, 1996;

Nutt & Backoff, 1997; Trice & Beyer, 1993). Organizational leaders or change agents must recognize the crisis, transmit the threat to organizational members, and convert the crisis into an opportunity for growth and development through the articulation of a vision and accompanying strategic plan (Dyck, 1996; Nutt & Backoff, 1997; Trice & Beyers, 1993). An organizational culture that promotes and facilitates cognitive and social learning by members greatly facilitates positive change outcomes (Lipshitz & Popper, 2000; Schein, 1992).

In this case, the organizational culture to be examined is that of a feminist health center. Feminist organizations are "hybrid" organizations in that as a "family" of organizations, they exhibit a variety of characteristics (e.g., missions, governance, strategies) while fitting under a common ideological umbrella. Further, these organizations operate in and are shaped by at least three different sectors: nonprofit, social movement, and human services (Hyde, 2001). Specifically, organizations, such as feminist health centers, are "social movement agencies" because they pursue their political agendas through the provision of programs and services to a disempowered or oppressed group (Hyde, 1992).

Within the feminist movement, there are two broadly defined ideological streams that shape the culture of feminist organizations. Simply stated, these streams are women's rights and women's liberation (also termed older vs. younger, bureaucratic vs. collectivist, reform vs. radical). These differences were particularly pronounced in the early stages of contemporary feminism, the late 1960s to mid-1970s (Echols, 1989; Ferree & Hess, 1985; Freeman, 1984; Hyde, 1992, 1995; Riger, 1984).

The women's rights branch embraced a more integrationist approach and favored strategies of public education, affirmative action, litigation, electoral politics, and public interest reforms. It generated hierarchical organizations with often clearly delineated roles and positions. Authority, including decision making, was largely determined by who held which positions (e.g., executive director, president of the board). Often, a national organization would be formed and a series of federated chapters, which followed the dictates of the central office, would then be started. The best-known women's rights organization is the National Organization for Women (NOW).

Women's liberation activists, largely influenced by their experiences in the radical Civil Rights and Student Left movements, rejected the integration strategy. They established organizations that reflected the revolutionary fervor of the times. Most of these groups were devoted to consciousness raising and political actions, though increasingly service organizations were founded. Services were understood as an expression of liberationist politics and were viewed as viable alternatives to, and critiques of, status quo offerings. There was little hierarchy in these organizations, which used some form of collectivist governance, including job rotations and consensus decision making. Authority rested in the whole group rather than with individuals. Liberation organizations were linked through decentralized, grassroots networks; prominent ones included Redstockings, the Chicago Women's Liberation Union, and the Furies.

Each stream exhibited certain strengths and weaknesses. For example, the women's rights branch made significant legislative inroads, yet is criticized for reproducing a male model of social control through its bureaucratic tendencies. Women's liberation developed some of the most innovative and politicized means of service delivery, much of which has been absorbed into "empowerment" practice. Yet the liberationist approach is viewed as inefficient, often reifying process over product.

As the feminist movement progressed, those organizations more closely identified with women's rights tendencies had a greater chance of survival. One major reason for this has to do with actions of the New Right movement, which attacked feminist causes and organizations through legislative, fiscal, and direct-action tactics (Hyde, 1995). Women's rights organizations, although vulnerable, had relatively more resources than liberationist organizations to counter New Right activities. Additionally, more of the New Right targets, specifically health centers (because of abortion), were in the liberationist branch (Hyde, 1992). Activists in liberation groups relied heavily on the organization's culture for emotional fortitude (Hyde, 1994; Morgen, 1995). In turn, they defended the organization's culture, even if it left them in a weakened state within the larger environment.

REFERENCES

Dyck, B. (1996). The role of crises and opportunities in organizational change: A look at a nonprofit religious college. *Nonprofit and Voluntary Sector Quarterly, 25*(3), 321–446.

Echols, A. (1989). *Daring to be bad: Radical feminism in America, 1967–1975.* Minneapolis: University of Minnesota Press.

Ferree, M. M., & Hess, B. (1985). *Controversy and coalition: The new feminist movement.* Boston: Twayne.

Freeman, J. (1984). The women's liberation movement: Its origins, structures, activities, and ideas. In J. Freeman (Ed.), *Women: A feminist perspective* (pp. 543–556). Palo Alto, CA: Mayfield.

Frost, P., et al. (Eds.). (1985). *Organizational culture.* Beverly Hills, CA: Sage.

Frost, P., et al. (Eds.). (1991). *Reframing organizational culture.* Newbury Park, CA: Sage.

Hyde, C. (1992). The ideational system of social movement agencies: An examination of feminist health centers. In Y. Hasenfeld (Ed.), *Human services as complex organizations* (pp. 121–144). Newbury Park, CA: Sage.

Hyde, C. (1994). Commitment to social change: Voices from the feminist movement. *Journal of Community Practice, 1*(2), 45–64.

Hyde, C. (1995). Feminist social movement organizations survive the new right. In M. Ferree & P. Martin (Eds.), *Feminist organizations: Harvest of the new women's movement* (pp. 306–322). Philadelphia: Temple University Press.

Hyde, C. (2001). The hybrid nonprofit: An examination of feminist social movement organizations. *Journal of Community Practice,* (84), 45–68.

Lipshitz, R., & Popper, M. (2000). Organizational learning in a hospital. *Journal of Applied Behavioral Science, 36*(3), 345–361.

Martin, J., Sitkin, S., & Boehm, M. (1985). Founders and the elusiveness of a cultural legacy. In P. Frost et al. (Eds.), *Organizational culture* (pp. 99–124). Beverly Hills, CA: Sage.

Meyerson, D. (1991). "Normal" ambiguity? A glimpse of an occupational culture. In P. Frost et al. (Eds.), *Reframing organizational culture* (pp. 131–144). Newbury Park, CA: Sage.

Morgen, S. (1995). "It was the best of times, it was the worst of times": Emotional discourse in the work cultures of feminist health clinics. In M. Ferree & P. Martin (Eds.), *Feminist organizations: Harvest of the new women's movement* (pp. 234–247). Philadelphia: Temple University Press.

Nutt, P., & Backoff, R. (1997). Facilitating transformational change. *Journal of Applied Behavioral Science, 33*(4), 490–508.

Ott, J. (1989). *The organizational culture perspective.* Belmont, CA: Dorsey.

Riger, S. (1984). Vehicles for empowerment: The case of feminist movement organizations. *Prevention in Human Services, 3*(2/3), 99–117.

Schein, E. (1992). *Organizational culture and leadership.* San Francisco: Jossey-Bass.

Siehl, C. (1985). After the founder: An opportunity to manage culture. In P. Frost et al. (Eds.), *Organizational culture* (pp. 125–140). Beverly Hills, CA: Sage.

Smircich, L. (1983). Concepts of culture and organizational analysis. *Administrative Science Quarterly, 28,* 339–358.

Trice, H., & Beyer, J. (1993). *The cultures of work organizations.* Englewood Cliffs, NJ: Prentice Hall.

THE CASE

THE WOMEN'S CO-OP

BACKGROUND

The Cooperative Health Project (CHP) is a feminist abortion and gynecological clinic located in a Midwest town of about 30,000 people. Its founding members embraced socialist-feminist values (liberationist branch), infused into the health services, political education programs, and collectivist governance. Members argued that feminist politics could be achieved through services that challenged "patriarchal medical models" and thus emphasized patient rights, education, and participation. The clinic was part of a broader feminist health movement; the approach was unique and controversial, pioneered in a few feminist and low-income health clinics in the country.

The organization was regularly targeted by right-to-life forces, which picketed the clinic and engaged in public harassment campaigns. One consequence of this opposition was that the clinic was unable to consistently secure medical malpractice insurance, mandatory for the provision of health care. The risk created by this hostile environment, combined with the type of services offered, rendered insurance too expensive. This, in turn, threatened CHP's ability to continue as an autonomous health care organization. In May 1990, after years of wrestling with the crisis, CHP members had to decide whether to continue as a health clinic, with substantially limited services, or accept an offer from Planned Parenthood Federation of America (PPFA) to become an affiliate.

Planned Parenthood is one of the most recognized providers of sexual and reproductive health care in the United States. Its mission includes the belief that "every individual has a fundamental right to decide when and whether to have a child, and that every child should be wanted and loved." Planned Parenthood offers a wide range of family planning, prenatal, HIV-AIDS, gynecological, abortion, infertility, and adoption services through "unique, locally governed health service" clinics. It has more than 100 affiliated clinics and national research and education centers.

The case opens moments before the decisive board meeting, with flashbacks to critical moments in the organization's history provided.[1] It is told through the recollections of Hannah as she awaits the start of the meeting. Hannah is a founding member and has served in numerous roles, including coordinator of the entire clinic during the 1980s. Her primary interest is accessible health care for low-income women. She often plays the role of conciliator and is valued for her capacity to see many angles. Although Hannah can be exasperated with some CHP processes, her commitment is unwavering. It has been her political and social home for 20 years. She describes the communal dedication in this way—"we worked at the collective; we played, we ate, we slept, we practically made love to the collective."

Board of Directors Meeting (May 1990)

An unusually large turnout, Hannah observes. She is more used to seeing decisions postponed for lack of a quorum than not being able to find a seat in the now packed conference room. In looking around the room, she recognizes many clients, volunteers, part-time workers, and the other full-time collective members; all are here to learn the fate of this organization. Hannah wonders if they are as tired of all the crises as she is. "Doubtful," she mutters to herself. "I've been around this way too long."

The board members have yet to arrive. Hannah knows from Gina, her partner and board member, that the group is having dinner together first to try once again to reach consensus regarding the acceptance or rejection of Planned Parenthood's offer. Yet people are getting restless; the meeting is going to start late and last well into the night.

Maria, another long-time collective member, joins Hannah—"What do you think they'll do about Planned Parenthood? I'd hate to work for that bunch of middle-class, professional, medical types." Hannah smiles; Maria is known to be a passionate defender of the clinic and a skeptic of anything remotely mainstream. "I don't know," Hannah responds. "The financial and political protection are tempting. It would be nice to have some security for a change." A volunteer, overhearing their exchange, exclaims, "Hannah, you of all people should know better than that. This is such a special place, and Planned Parenthood would just ruin that." Julie, a part-time worker, anxiously chimes in, "But my hours have been cut back for lack of money. We need this help." Maria, with barely veiled disgust, retorts—"Look, you haven't been around here as long as we have. It makes me sick that we might affiliate with an organization that has done terrible things to third-world women with birth control and sterilization. Planned Parenthood's a business, and that's not what we are." "Maybe that's what we should be," Julie responds. "If we had been more responsible earlier, we wouldn't be in this mess today. It's about time we grew up." Attempting to smooth over a conflict that would no doubt be repeated throughout the meeting, Hannah weighs in—"Well, you need to remember that we did have help getting into this mess. The right-to-life picketers did a lot of damage, and there's no reason to think they will leave us alone. There is a lot to consider, like the need for a regular doctor and consistent insurance coverage, as well as our principles. I'm sure the board is taking everything into account."

At that moment, the board members arrive. The nine women look grim and tense. "Who'd have thought that when we started, we'd end up in this predicament. It all seemed so promising way back then," Hannah thinks. As the board members get settled, she drifts back to the early, heady years of the collective.

A PROMISING START (EARLY 1970S)

The Cooperative Health Project opens its doors as a clinic of "women helping women." Those first few months are chaotic, but members[2] feel exhilarated. Finally, they can meld their politics with the provision of needed services. The women requesting care seem to appreciate their efforts. Within the first year, they have basic gynecological and abortion services, which include political education for patients on their reproductive rights and a small community education program.

Yet, founding members know that offering women's health care, in general, and abortion services, in particular, would meet with opposition. Indeed, they anticipate it: "We are quite aware of how controversial a service we are offering. . . . [But] we are just as much against forced abortion as we are people running around telling women they have to have children. We feel a woman's body is her own. . . . We are more than a simple abortion clinic. We hope to be a total women's clinic." Opposition comes quickly—a barrage of letters to the editor of the town newspaper refers to CHP as a "slaughterhouse." CHP staff believe that this is an orchestrated campaign and choose to ignore it, assuming that the quality and innovation of the clinic speaks for itself.

Board Meeting (May 1990)

Hannah sighs wistfully, "such excitement and dedication in those first few years. We really thought we were going to make a difference. And the opposition, while annoying, seemed minimal." She turns her attention to Renee, the board president, who is calling the meeting to order. Hannah, trying without luck to make eye contact with Gina to see if she can guess the decision, wonders, "Will tonight mean all those years of commitment and struggle are going to go down the drain?" Maria breaks through these musings and nods to the board members—"I wish they'd get on with this. It's like waiting for the ax to fall, and there's no good solution to this never-ending mess."

GROWING PAINS (MID TO LATE 1970S)

The collective grows from 5 to 25 members, becoming a bit more diverse in the process. Members remain committed to service provision and the fight for reproductive rights. Outwardly, the clinic seems as true to its politics as ever. Staff open a "problem gynecology clinic" to provide nonroutine care on the premises (rather than referring to other practices). The regular abortion, gynecological, and the newer well-woman's clinics are expanded.

They publish a position paper, "Feminist Health Workers as Political Activists," which articulates and defends how service providers do political work. The paper emphasizes the revolutionary nature of self-help, viewing clients as a constituency, political education as part of medical care, and the defense of abortion rights. The writers are highly critical of mainstream, reformist "women's" and "family planning" clinics.

Yet internally, conflicts emerge over political ideology, job responsibilities, governance, and staff credentials. Because of the clinic's growth, members decide to consolidate several administrative functions and designate areas of service specialization. Everyone is still trained in all fields, but for efficiency's sake, each member specializes in one or two areas. This restructuring is done only after a prolonged and rancorous debate about the nature of collectivism, which in its purest form calls for everyone to do everything. As part of this debate, and as a means of affirming nonhierarchical divisions, members reject a differential pay scale.

Members constantly revisit this restructuring, struggling with a balance between egalitarianism and efficiency. They experiment with specific job assignments, a further form of specialization, and also decide on a two-tiered staff structure: One is either a collective member, involved in all aspects of center governance, or a contract worker, involved only in clinic operations. Contract workers tend to have some professional training, which sparks another debate on pay equity. The collective again rejects differential compensation, noting that "there are many members of the organization who have special skills and training that we are not recognizing with pay differentials."

In addition to this more specialized staff structure, collective members also create a board of directors. The board is formed so that it can be used when the project applies for grant money, since most foundations require one. CHP members think of it as a "paper" board that is composed of former center members who are "people they can trust with the collective process."

At this time, the collective issues a policy and procedures manual, an attempt to address the increasing specialization within the organization. They set aside *Mao's Little Red Book*, which had been the personnel guide. Staff restates its commitment to "ideals of participatory health care, informed medical consumerism, patient's rights, and women-oriented health." Many members, however, express concerns that the manual, and other changes, signal the transformation to a more mainstream organization.

Another problem emerges during this time. Members are faced with the prospect of having no physicians (needed for abortion and some gynecological procedures). CHP relies on a pool of area doctors, one of whom requests that the clinic cover his malpractice payments (ob/gyn insurance is one of the costliest). The organization is caught between giving this doctor special treatment, something it does not want to do because everyone should be supported equally, and paying for all physicians' insurance, which is not financially possible. CHP does not have enough money to purchase its own insurance policy that could cover all staff. It provides a loan for this doctor, but fails to resolve the larger problem of acquiring available, self-insured physicians.

CHP experiences the first of many doctor shortages. At first, the clinic argues about whether to hire a staff physician. Many see such a move as institutionalizing hierarchy, male elitism, and professional credentials, all antithetical to the organization's philosophy. When the clinic is unable to consistently maintain a "guest" pool, it decides to hire a doctor who has "good technical skills" but is "abrasive and insensitive." This decision only happens after a hotly contested debate over skill versus philosophical compatibility, with skill apparently taking precedence. Members hope that the doctor is "trainable" in a feminist approach to health care.

The Board Meeting (May 1990)

"Well that sure didn't happen," Hannah recalls. "He didn't last but a few months, and the staff meetings were battlegrounds over his employment." She barely pays attention to the approval of the last meeting's minutes and the relaying of announcements. "No wonder we're all so burned out and tired of this decision," she thinks. "It's been with us for years. The problem is that most of the younger workers don't know that. They don't know how hard we tried to resolve it, and they just don't seem as committed to our original vision. And, they certainly don't know how difficult it became once the Republicans took power. It was all we could do to survive."

RIGHT-WING PRESSURE
(LATE 1970S TO MID-1980S)

In the late 1970s, anticlinic picketing begins. Picketers demonstrate on days when abortions are performed, harassing clients and staff. In 1979, the clinic is firebombed and picketing intensifies, part of a wave of anticlinic violence that is sweeping the country. The clinic responds by holding a pro-choice rally, which has a "wonderful turnout." The local paper runs a favorable editorial, noting that the clinic "has managed to stay pro-female without becoming violently anti-male."

With the landslide right-wing victories in the 1980 elections, the CHP (like feminist clinics) finds itself in an increasingly hostile climate. Clinic picketing, especially client and staff harassment, increases. Right-to-life organizations escalate their hostilities by launching a billboard campaign that condemns CHP workers as "baby killers" and threatening to publicly name CHP leaders and health care providers.

CHP members are now confused over how to respond. There is simply not enough staff to deal with this political crisis and to maintain quality services. Much time and energy are spent on clinic coverage because the physician situation remains a problem. In 1984, the clinic reluctantly agrees to meet with police in the hopes of gaining support and protection; this has limited success. Members also agree to emphasize political education with clients by encouraging them to write to legislators and local newspapers. In 1985, the clinic accepts voluntary help in the form of pro-choice pickets and patient escorts, most of whom are from the area's National Organization for Women (NOW) chapter. Aside from these momentary efforts, CHP is unable to formulate a plan for dealing with the continuous, and debilitating, presence of the right-to-life activists.

The Board Meeting (May 1990)

Renee thanks everyone who has offered opinions and support, "It's been an extraordinarily difficult process for all of us. There are many factors to consider. The Planned Parenthood offer is a generous one, but it has drawbacks too. Unfortunately, and despite some clear preferences, the board could not come to consensus as to what we should do." At this point, the barely contained group erupts into verbal chaos. Julie seems to lose all color in her face; Maria storms out of the room. Hannah thinks, "Well, our long-standing tradition of wavering continues."

ORGANIZATIONAL INDECISION (MID TO LATE 1980S)

The lack of malpractice insurance continues to trouble the CHP. Another self-insured physician, and former collective member, is hired. Collective members struggle with having a part-time professional in their midst. The doctor, who wishes to become a collective member again, expresses feelings of marginalization. This situation exemplifies the larger struggle within the CHP—finding the balance among feminist philosophy, an approach to collectivist governance that is more efficient, and the recognition of different kinds of expertise involved in maintaining the clinic. CHP members also wish to reinvigorate clinic service expansion plans that had stalled in the last few years, even though personnel and funds are not available.

After several months of painful negotiations, the physician asks to end her contract. Although still supportive of CHP, she cannot tolerate endless debates about her merits as a collective member. The clinic must again resort to guest doctors. In addition to losing this physician, the collective also loses several members who resign for a variety of reasons. To save money, the collective does not fill these vacancies and its membership falls to 15.

A consultant is hired to assist them with the tensions. After several weeks, he notes that, whereas there is considerable closeness among collective members, the decision-making process rarely moves beyond the idea stage. There is no clear evaluation of service quality. The collective is not able to engage in long-term planning, or to think strategically about its resources. The consultant commends the organization for its commitment to fulfilling a feminist approach to health care through programs and services, but expresses concern over the lack of clear accountability and future planning.

The affirmation of their dedication is like a life preserver. This commitment becomes the rallying cry for the collective—members want to save this at all costs. Yet they are not able (or willing) to incorporate the other components of the consultant's message. Short-term, crisis planning prevails.

The Board Meeting (May 1990)

"Sisters, please, we need to calm down and discuss things," implores Renee. "That's all we do is talk," someone yells. Shouts another: "What's the point of a board if no decisions get made." Beth, another organizational veteran, attempts to intervene: "We all need to participate in this; that's what we're about." The group settles a bit, and Renee attempts to start again. She says that what the board would like is some guidance from CHP supporters and members to see if there are any clear preferences for action. Maria, who has returned, mumbles, "This is like beating a dead horse; we've done this before." Hannah nods, and wonders if Planned Parenthood knew all along how vulnerable the clinic was and is.

THE CRISIS (LATE 1980S)

The CHP is still not able to acquire sufficient malpractice coverage for its doctors, and staff face the possibility of closing down the organization. As an independent clinic, situated in a politically hostile environment, affordable insurance cannot be found. Many doctors in town choose not to associate with or assist the clinic for fear of right-wing reprisals. Medical residents from a nearby hospital offer their services on a contractual basis, but the hospital refuses to extend malpractice coverage to work done at CHP. Thus, CHP relies on a shrinking pool of part-time physicians. Abortion and gynecological services are cut back, the well-woman's clinic and the problem gynecology program are eliminated. Education and public relations programs continue, but no longer have a collective member assigned to coordinate events.

The reduction of services produces a deeper fiscal crisis. Staff layoffs, based on seniority, occur, a plan that is referred to as "tragic but necessary." The collective is reduced to eight members. Some laid off workers are rehired on a part-time, hourly basis as contract workers. Within weeks, contract workers report feeling marginalized and alienated from the collective. Collective members feel overwhelmed by the crisis.

The board of directors, which has been largely inactive, is asked to help. Yet with little development having occurred, it is unclear what board members can and should do. Some make inquiries to various foundations, but little grant money exists. Others offer their services as mediators, trying to help the clinic survive on an interpersonal basis. As the CHP deals with the increasing likelihood of shutdown, the board grapples with the new knowledge that it may be fiscally responsible for organizational debts. Whereas board membership had started as a voluntary gesture of goodwill, it now signifies a serious financial risk for individuals.

A temporary solution comes along when an older doctor, nearing retirement, agrees to be the clinic's physician. He has no experience with CHP, but is pro-choice and, more important, has his own insurance coverage. However, he makes only a one-year commitment in order to buy some time for the organization.

Board and staff members report feeling burned out and frustrated. Although still committed to being a "feminist workplace," they are hard-pressed to find a more permanent solution to the malpractice crisis and to reinvigorate the collective's membership and offerings. At this time (June 1989), the Planned Parenthood Federation offers a possible resolution.

The Board Meeting (May 1990)

"It's hard to believe," thinks Hannah, "that all this nonsense with Planned Parenthood has been going on for just a year." She recalls the suspicion of the collective to the initial proposal. And then there were the meetings with Planned Parenthood, which became increasingly antagonistic. "Clearly," thinks Hannah, "we're good enough to be taken over. Why can't we be good enough to survive on our own?"

THE OFFER (1989–1990)

In 1989, the regional Planned Parenthood office makes overtures to the CHP to become a federation affiliate. Initially, CHP members ignore these efforts, but Planned Parenthood persists. Finally, CHP agrees to an information meeting with a regional Planned Parenthood director.

The meeting is held in a coffee shop in CHP's town. Hannah, Gina, and Renee represent the collective. Planned Parenthood's regional director, Josephine, is accompanied by Tracy, a clinic worker from an affiliate in another part of the state. After introductions, Josephine takes control of the meeting with businesslike efficiency. She lays out the benefits of affiliating with Planned Parenthood, emphasizing that this is a time of crisis for CHP, in particular, and feminist health clinics, in general. Her list includes insurance under the federation's policy, clinic protection money, and legal assistance. CHP could maintain, and probably expand, its abortion, gynecological, and educational services, but only in accordance with Planned Parenthood guidelines. Tracy then chimes in enthusiastically, indicating how much she's learned at Planned Parenthood and how exciting it is to do such important work. The CHP representatives mostly take in the information and ask few questions. They learn, however, that to affiliate would mean that CHP would no longer exist as an autonomous organization that espoused socialist/feminist principles and collectivist governance. As a unit of Planned Parenthood, they would have to adopt those goals and procedures. Josephine assures them that they would still be able to serve the populations they wanted to through even more comprehensive health programs.

In their report to CHP about the meeting, Renee, Gina, and Hannah attempt to lay out the pros and cons in a balanced fashion. Many of the members express relief that financial and insurance worries would be resolved. Others feel that they are "selling their souls." Affiliation means adhering to a more mainstream philosophy and entails more bureaucratic, medical-model approaches. Yet they also understand that alone they cannot come up with the resources to obtain malpractice insurance.

CHP tries to negotiate with Planned Parenthood around maintaining a version of its socialist ideology and collectivist governance. Planned Parenthood refuses. Affiliation means that an organization fully takes on the Planned Parenthood identity—including mission, services, governance, program evaluation, staffing, and political directives. All affiliates follow Planned Parenthood policies and procedures and are certified by the national office.

CHP members are increasingly uncomfortable about the Planned Parenthood offer, yet are not able to reach consensus in terms of accepting or rejecting it. Planned Parenthood then ups the stakes. It announces that CHP can either affiliate with the federation, or the federation will establish its own office in the community, thus directly competing with CHP. CHP members have no way of assessing the validity of this ultimatum, though they feel that they are caught and either way will lose. The collective turns the decision over to the board, with the understanding that all CHP members will be consulted and briefed before any decision is finalized.

The Board Meeting (May 1990)

Remembering those fateful negotiations with Planned Parenthood, Hannah thinks, "maybe desperate times call for desperate measures." She realizes that Renee has managed to regain some semblance of control over the meeting. The group has done a collective meditation in order to focus and now, for seemingly the millionth time, is listing the benefits and costs of affiliating with Planned Parenthood. Then, it is hoped, some direction will become clear. Hannah sadly realizes that no matter what the outcome is, the CHP will never be the same even if it decides to remain autonomous. She feels that she, and others, have been bled dry.

DISCUSSION QUESTIONS

Organizational Culture

1. Organizational culture is comprised of many different elements (e.g., norms, symbols, rituals, values). What are the key elements of CHP's culture?

2. When using an organizational culture perspective, it is important to understand and examine the underlying meaning of the cultural elements. For each element listed (in Question 1), indicate what its meaning is to individuals and to the organization as a whole. Identify the origins of these meanings. What is the essence of CHP's culture?

3. Organizational founders and leaders play a pivotal role in shaping the culture and in guiding its transformation. Who, individuals or groups, are the founders and leaders of CHP? What influence do these people have on the organization's culture?

4. Organizational culture is the lens through which a group understands and negotiates its environment. Who are the key environmental actors with whom the CHP must contend? How is the impact of these actors understood from the CHP's perspective?

5. Given what the organization wants to accomplish, what are the strengths and weaknesses of this culture?

6. Planned Parenthood also possesses a distinct culture. Although information is limited, answer Questions 1 to 5 with Planned Parenthood as the focal organization. For those questions that cannot be answered, indicate how you might discover that information.

The Decision

1. Identify the reasons or factors that favor affiliation with Planned Parenthood, keeping in mind the cultural analysis just completed on both organizations.

2. Identify the reasons or factors that argue against affiliation with Planned Parenthood.

3. What additional information would you like to have? Why? How would you obtain this information?

4. Should CHP affiliate with Planned Parenthood? Why or why not?

Implications

1. If you choose affiliation, how do you propose to address the concerns that CHP members have about losing their identity?

2. What steps are needed to ease this transition—on the part of Planned Parenthood and CHP—or does that matter (perhaps just saving the programs is sufficient)?

3. Does affiliating with Planned Parenthood essentially mean that CHP will need to give up its culture?

4. If you choose not to affiliate, how do you propose to sustain CHP? What changes need to occur in philosophy, governance, and service delivery to make survival more likely?

5. Where will you obtain doctors' coverage and insurance?

6. What plans do you have for resource development?

7. How will you address the frustration and disintegration that seems to have been building over the last few years?

8. In the end, what cultural transformations need to occur, and how do you propose that they be implemented? In other words, how would you turn crisis into opportunity?

NOTES

1. This case is set in the past so that the challenges and obstacles faced by the CHP accurately parallel broader developments in the feminist movement during the 1970s and 1980s. The decisions with which CHP members contended, and the threats that they experienced, were not isolated. Feminist clinics across the country faced countless battles in order to continue the provision of services.

2. The term *member* is a slippery one in this case. Member without a modifier refers to anyone working in the organization, either paid or volunteer. *Collective member* refers to those individuals who belong to the governing body.

11

WHEN COMMUNITY MENTAL HEALTH MEETS PUBLIC MANAGED CARE

DIANE VINOKUR-KAPLAN and PATRICIA MILLER

THEORETICAL AND PRACTICE PERSPECTIVES

The Organizational Life-Cycle Metaphor

The following case presents a contemporary example of a human service organization encountering a crisis of survival due to drastic changes in its external environment and funding prospects: A community mental health center faces the introduction of a competitive managed care system for low-income, mentally ill patients receiving Medicaid—a target group whom the agency has historically served. The actual agency on which this case is loosely based, Southwest Detroit Community Mental Health Services, Inc., Detroit, has evolved in its 25-year history from a small crisis clinic to a multiservice community mental health service center, serving a large, multicultural, low-income catchment area. Although this case draws from some of the experiences of this agency, some parts of the case are strictly fiction created by the authors. Therefore, this case is offered and should be used solely for purposes of education and discussion.

The reader is encouraged to look for the stages of organizational development through which the agency has already passed and the types of crises it has mastered at each transition point in its life cycle. Then, consider: (1) how one could possibly better understand its situation and avoid its decline and death;

and (2) whether the agency can remain true to its original mission of serving the local community, or must be reborn as a new, different organization.

Obviously, human service organizations are not really individual, living organisms, as are plants, people, or other animals. However, they too often seem to go through a life cycle, an ongoing process with various predictable stages of continuous development. There are at least four reasons why someone might want to approach a human service organization from this life-cycle point of view.

First, the metaphor of the life cycle presents a sequence that helps to conceptualize the dynamic development of organizations over time. It emphasizes that organizations are not static but rather evolving and often growing larger over time—just as yesterday's baby can become tomorrow's adolescent.

Second, it points to the vulnerabilities and challenges that each stage of development presents, and suggests some normative levels of functioning and attainment of typical milestones reached at each stage. Similarly, one may look at organizations' typical requirements and crises in their stages of formation, development, maturation, and structural elaboration over time (cf. Quinn & Cameron, 1983). Therefore, such a framework can help guide organizations through painful transitions that are necessary for further growth and self-maintenance.

Third, the life-cycle metaphor helps illuminate the changing array of stakeholders, their relative importance to the organization over time, and the criteria by which the organization's performance is evaluated (Jawahar & McLaughlin, 2001; Quinn & Cameron, 1983). (A stakeholder in an organization is generally defined as "any group or individual who can affect or is affected by the achievement of the organization's objectives" [Freeman, 1984—cited in Jawahar & McLaughlin, 2001]). Thus, just as parents, family, colleagues, employers, and friends satisfy different needs as a human being grows, so too the relative importance of different stakeholders changes as organizations mature. Indeed, their salience may be a function of their stakeholders' attributes of power, legitimacy, and urgency (Mitchell, Agle, & Wood, 1997—in Jawahar & McLaughlin, 2001). Similarly, the strategy used to deal with each stakeholder can change, as can the resources devoted to it. As different stakeholders become more or less critical to the organization's current needs, an organization may adopt strategies, such as proaction, accommodation, defense, and reaction, to deal with the stakeholders' influence (Clarkson, 1995—in Jawahar & McLaughlin, 2001).

Fourth, the impact of the environment on individual development cannot be ignored. As Hasenfeld and Schmid (1989) point out, much of this developmental process for human service organizations is induced by such environmental changes as new public mandates, legislation, and policy. Therein, "the organization undergoes transformations in its culture, strategy, structure, processes, and services which have implications . . . [for] the well-being of its clients" (p. 243). Moreover, the fast pace of change in today's environment—as captured by the slogan "the only constant is change"—does not permit organizations much time to adapt.

Finally, this perspective points to the potential frailty of all organizations, a reminder that in barring successful renewal, some may decline or die, even despite their efforts to change and adapt to new environments. Thus, the life-cycle metaphor cautions us against the assumption that any organization, once established and growing, will automatically go on forever.

In sum, there are certainly caveats and limitations to adopting this model—for example, there is probably no *inevitable* linear sequence of stages through which all organizations proceed, as there is in biological life cycles. Yet, this metaphor can help illuminate the process of human service organizations developing and adapting to changing legal, political, and social environments (cf. Hasenfeld & Schmid, 1989, p. 245).

Stages and Crises in the Life Cycle of Organizations

The usual perspective on organizational life cycles looks at the changes within organizations as they grow in size and complexity of structure, and not simply their chronological age. Typically, most theoretical frameworks of organizational life cycles describe processes affecting the survival and growth of the organization. They begin with the organization's creation, often in the form of a simple entrepreneurial structure, which is followed by limited growth that eventually spurs the development of a more elaborate, bureaucratic structure. "This transition is, in turn, followed by even more extensive growth, leading to even further diversification in strategies, to be followed, once again, by further division of structure that then paves the road for even greater growth (Chandler, 1962; Salter, 1970; Scott, 1971)" (Hasenfeld & Schmid, 1989, p. 244).

For example, in health care, one might think of pioneering physicians who develop clinics that eventually become hospitals, medical centers, and then comprehensive health systems. In human services, one can refer to small crisis clinics or hotlines that become mental health agencies and then continue to diversify and grow, or to soup kitchens that expand to become major distributors of food and diversify by also providing occupational training. As a resource for the reader, a diagram outlining the life cycle of a human service organization is provided in Appendix 11-A.

The metaphor of the organizational life cycle also highlights crises, or transition points, that need to be successfully met in order for the human service organization to continue to grow, not unlike the developmental crises of childhood, adolescence, adulthood, and maturity that developmental psychologists, such as Erik Erikson, have posed. For instance, one of the most common crises faced by small human service organizations occurs when they have developed from an idea into a reality, and they have survived organizational infancy to function informally as a grassroots collectivity. One might think of such examples as health collectives and runaway youth shelters. At that point, such organizations have some procedures in place; yet if they are to grow and diversify further, they must become more bureaucratic and more formalized to delegate tasks that have become larger than any one person or small group could handle. This situation may well pose a crisis for some members, especially to dedicated founders of the organization who have nurtured it through its infancy.

Strategic Planning

In order for organizations to better understand these changes in themselves and their environments and what is required for their successful growth or survival, they frequently employ strategic planning (cf. Bryson, 1995; Mulroy & Halpin, 1996). The purpose of strategic planning is to produce fundamental decisions and actions that define what an organization (or other entity) is, what it does, and why it does it (Bryson, 1995, p. 8). One of the advantages of using strategic planning is that it acknowledges the usually political decision-making culture of public and nonprofit agencies; unlike traditional rational planning, it does not presume consensus or authoritarian-induced agreement on goals, policies, programs, and actions necessary to achieve organizational aims (see Bryson, 1995, pp. 11–13). Rather, strategic planning focuses on *issues,* which by definition include some kind of disagreement, and it seeks to develop politically acceptable resolutions to these issues by involved or affected parties (see Bryson, 1995, p. 11).

The strategic planning process guides the organization through an examination of both its internal strengths and challenges, and the opportunities and threats in the organization's current (and future) external environment. Thereafter, the key stakeholders who can seriously influence the agency's fate and fulfillment of its mission are identified. In this manner, the organization can make a better, more genuinely accepted plan regarding if and how it could further survive, grow, or develop.

REFERENCES

Bryson, J. M. (1995). *Strategic planning for public and nonprofit organizations* (rev. ed.). San Francisco: Jossey-Bass.

Chandler, A. (1962). *Strategy and structure.* Cambridge, MA: The MIT Press.

Clarkson, M. B. E. (1995). A stakeholder framework for analyzing and evaluating corporate social performance. *Academy of Management Review, 20*(1), 92–117.

Daft, R. L. (1992). *Organization theory and design* (5th ed.). Minneapolis/St. Paul: West.

Freeman, R. E. (1984). *Strategic management: A stakeholder approach.* Boston: HarperCollins.

Greiner, L. E. (1972). Evolution and revolution as organizations grow. *Harvard Business Review, 50* (July–August), 37–46.

Hasenfeld, Y., & Schmid, H. (1989). The life cycle of human service organizations: An administrative perspective. *Administration in Social Work, 13*(3/4), 243–269.

Jawahar, I. M., & McLaughlin, G. L. (2001). Toward a descriptive stakeholder theory: An organizational life-cycle approach. *Academy of Management Review, 26*(3), 397–414.

Mitchell, R. K., Agle, B. R., & Wood, D. J. (1987). Toward a theory of shareholder identification and salience: Defining the principle of who and what really counts. *Academy of Management Review, 22,* 853–886.

Mulroy, E. A., & Halpin, M. (1996). Implementing Total Quality Management: A case study in strategic planning. In B. Gummer & P. McCallion (Eds.), *Total quality management in the social services: Theory and practice.* Albany: Rockefeller College Press, State University of New York–Albany.

Quinn, R. E., & Cameron, K. S. (1983). Organizational life cycles and shifting criteria of effectiveness: Some preliminary evidence. *Management Science, 29,* 33–51.

Salter, M. S. (1970). Stages of corporate development. *Journal of Business Policy, 1,* 23–38.

Scott, B. (1971). *Stages of corporate development: Part I, Working Paper.* Report 14-371–294 (BP 993). Cambridge, MA: Harvard Business School.

Vinokur-Kaplan, D., & Connor, J. A. (1997). The evolution of a community incubator of nonprofit organizations: A case study of NEW—Nonprofit Enterprise at Work. Paper presented at the 25th Annual Conference of the Association for Research on Nonprofit Organizations and Voluntary Action (ARNOVA), Indianapolis, IN.

THE CASE

WHEN COMMUNITY MENTAL HEALTH MEETS PUBLIC MANAGED CARE

"Good grief!" muttered Joe Smith, the affable, fortyish program director of Greenleaf Neighborhood Community Mental Health Center, as he entered his office. "What do they want of our lives today?!" He tossed the newspaper on his desk, leaving it open to the article on the State Department of Mental Health's new announcements on service contracts, and eyed the bulging, state-issued envelope sitting on his desk. John Aloha, the agency's visionary executive director, had left it there earlier that morning with a note: "Can we talk about this today at our meeting for planning the annual retreat, with Sonia, our new board member?" "Sure we can, John," mumbled Joe out loud, and then thought to himself: "Just when I imagined things were starting to calm down a little so we can celebrate this agency's twenty-fifth anniversary with our community, our main funders think of something new!"

Greenleaf Neighborhood Community Mental Health Center was indeed planning to celebrate its quarter-century milestone. It had emerged originally through the planning efforts of residents, civic groups, and service agencies in the post–War on Poverty era to meet the mental health needs of this oldest neighborhood in Big City, the large, surrounding metropolis. This community, where Joe was born and had spent his childhood, had once been a working-class neighborhood filled with many immigrants and migrants—some seeking good-paying jobs in the flourishing local car factories, others opening small service businesses (restaurants, dry cleaners, groceries) to provide for the growing families of the area.

But Joe's family, like many others, had left the industrialized Greenleaf area for a quieter neighboring town, seeking, as his parents had said, "more green leaf, and less factory smell." Over the years, the old neighborhood, like the city as a whole, continued to decline economically and socially. The aging car plants had closed, and with their departure, much of the area's economy degenerated. Then came the drug epidemic, and here and there, crime rose, houses were abandoned, and gangs grew. The community continued, partly buoyed by the strengths of its families, houses of worship, and community spirit. But the old, protective neighborhood of Joe's childhood was slipping away, and the most vulnerable populations—the homeless, the mentally ill, the friendless, and young, impoverished families seeking cheap rents—relied more and more on the few remaining agencies to help them face their poverty and other life crises.

The agency had first been established as a crisis center in the early 1970s, during the heyday of the development of local community mental health centers. Such agencies were established to help integrate the newly released residents of large state psychiatric hospitals into more normal lives in the community; this policy change was spurred by new appreciation of their aspirations and capacities and also by the medicinal balm provided by psychotropic drugs to calm their more extreme symptoms. The agency had also sought to generally promote the mental health of the community-at-large and prevent mental distress and illness through outreach at churches and other community sites, and through consultation and education services in local institutions such as schools.

Over the next two decades, Greenleaf Neighborhood Community Mental Health had established a reputation as an innovator in mental health services. It successfully collaborated with substance abuse and social services providers to holistically serve teens, the older people, and the homeless, and to counsel the families of the mentally ill. Multilingual outreach programs were set up to effectively reach residents who did not speak English. Rehabilitation of clients was seriously pursued through housing and recreation programs, including a Fairweather Lodge and club house, as well as job training and job placement for the chronically mentally ill. The agency grew from a small crisis center providing community mental health programs to a multimillion dollar mental health enterprise, promoting the well-being of many at-risk or underserved populations. It also started a subagency that focused on developing housing for the homeless and mentally ill and became one of the largest landlords in the neighborhood. Staff and programs grew, management information systems began to be set up, and the agency became known as Big City's "best kept secret of mental health service success."

Joe had started his own social work career as a mental health outreach worker at this agency, and over the years, he had been promoted to progressively higher administrative positions. His old clients still said "hi" to him when he met them on the street or saw them in the waiting room, and he remembered each one's name. He took a moment and thought back to those good old days at the doughnut shops and the parks, getting the lost and bewildered to come down to the agency. Many things had changed, to be sure, as he glanced around his report-littered office; the values he had brought with him at the beginning were still enshrined in this agency mission statement that had been adopted a few years before and still hung in a frame on a wall next to his desk.

Greenleaf Neighborhood Community Mental Health Center

Mission Statement

The mission of Greenleaf Neighborhood Community Mental Health Center is to enhance the mental health of adults, children, and families. GNCMH will accomplish this mission in a manner that reflects a commitment to the people of the community and surrounding area. Within the limits of our funding, we will provide comprehensive, community-based mental health services that promote the well-being of the individual and the community. These services shall be economically, culturally, and physically accessible; cost-effective; and promote the holistic development of the individual.

Beliefs

- Mental health is more than absence of mental illness; it is the presence of dignity and self-worth in the individual.
- Individuals are entitled to quality services without regard to their ability to pay.
- Services must be delivered in a manner that is respectful and sensitive to ethnic, cultural, and language diversity.
- Partnership with the community is integral to the delivery of mental health services and shall be reflected in the composition of the governing board.
- Competent, committed, caring staff are crucial to foster an atmosphere of excellence. To this end, GNCMH recognizes its role in the support and development of staff.
- Respect for, and preservation of, individual rights, such as appropriate care, confidentiality, informed consent, self-determination, and access to records, are guaranteed.
- Collaborative alliances with other agencies and organizations are essential to the delivery of community-based care.

The telephone rang, and Joe's secretary informed him that John and Sonia, the new board member, were ready to meet with him. "Be right there," Joe responded. He picked up the bulky envelope and a notepad and walked down the hall to John's office.

John greeted Joe with a grim smile when he saw him enter, carrying the heavy envelope. "Well, guy," he said to his co-worker of many years. "Looks like we have some new challenges to face." Joe winced with a smile in return. John continued, "I've brought in Sonia, our new board member, to help us think them through and present these issues coherently at next month's staff and board retreat. Sonia works as a management consultant, and she has volunteered to help us prepare for the meeting. She worked for our board president's company and comes highly recommended." Joe shook hands with Sonia as he joined them in sitting around a small conference table. "It's nice to meet you, Joe," Sonia said. "I should also tell you that I was interested in working on this because my own nephew was diagnosed as a paranoid schizophrenic several years ago, and he has spent a lot of time in the community mental health system. I know what an important role it can play in people's lives." Joe smiled and nodded knowingly, and then turned to John: "Okay, boss, let's begin!"

"Well," John began, "there's good news and there's bad news. The good news is that there is still a chance we can continue to serve this community and that there is still some money to help the mentally ill who are covered by Medicaid, the folks who have been our main constituency for nearly twenty-five years. Sonia, since you are new here, let me give you a little more background. As you may have seen in our annual report that I sent to you, the large proportion of the mental health clients we serve are age 25 and over, are not in the labor force, and often never have been. Roughly half of these men and women have finished high school and half have not. They and their families receive services that include psychosocial rehabilitation and psychiatric and psychological treatment, as well as family education, counseling, stress reduction, housing, and job preparation and training."

"I see," said Sonia, "and what about your staff?"

"Well," John replied, "we've continued to grow and to expand our programs and our staff, especially in the last decade. I am president (now they call me CEO), Joe is our vice president for programs, and we also have a vice president for administration; so we're the Executive Team. There are about seven additional folks who comprise the Management Team. They are the directors of various departments or programs, such as Outpatient Services, Psychiatric Services, and Development and Community Relations. We employ a dozen psychiatrists and psychologists, and about 30 folks as important support staff. And then we have a bunch of interns—maybe a dozen—from several different universities. We have about 14 different, specific program areas, each of which has between four to 20 staff (social workers, nurses, aides, and so forth). Some deliver services here at this site, others are at our vocational training sites, and still others are in the community, doing school-based services, outreach, homelessness prevention, and so forth. So altogether, there are at least 150 people regularly employed in some capacity or another. We also hire some of our clients, as well as have several serve on the board."

"Heavens," said Sonia, "this is really quite a complex place! I never knew that there were so many different things going on here!"

"Yup," said Joe, "but we should also say that we have been very lucky to have great, dedicated staff, many of whom have worked here for years. We have always prided ourselves on giving quality care to our clients."

"And, 'there's the rub,' to quote Shakespeare," John, the director, added. "With some of the funding changes that are being proposed by the government, we have to find a new way to make sure we can continue to provide all the care that our patients need. Let me start from the top. We are a nonprofit receiving the bulk of our funding from community mental health funds funneled down from the feds and the state to Big City's Community Mental Health Board. About one-third of the public funds supporting state mental health and substance abuse services come from Medicaid, which is jointly funded by the state and federal governments; it is administered by the state to provide payment for medical care for low-income or disabled individuals. Most of the mental health money comes from the state, and most of the substance abuse money comes from the federal block grant. In the past, as long as we could make a good case that we were providing adequate services for folks in our part of the city, those funds pretty much continued to come in, *as grants*, and we could use them rather flexibly to meet the needs of our clients. Now, the state Mental Health Department, in its wisdom and its efforts to cut costs, has decided to take a new approach, which is marked by two big concepts—managed care and competition."

John caught his breath and continued. "As far as managed care is concerned, Big City's Community Mental Health Board is going to be issuing managed care contracts for Medicaid recipients to receive behavioral health services (that's what they're calling mental health and substance abuse these days). This means that the Community Mental Health Board is also going to be acting as a huge gatekeeper for service provision. If we got a contract from them to provide such services for folks in our area, we would get a set amount of money per case for the year (that's what they mean by *capitated*). Using those funds, we provide services that we think the client needs. If we can be very businesslike, efficient, and watch our bottom line carefully (and by that I don't mean being miserly with our services), then we'll have enough money to cover emergencies, clients in need of more service than has been approved, and maybe a little extra, you know, for salary raises and repainting the waiting room. However, if we spend more than they give us, it's our loss."

"So," Joe said, "we will now be assuming more of the risks of financing our services than we have in the past. It's much more like a private practice model, where the county board will contract services from us, and then we'll have to bill them to get paid after we provide the service."

"That's right," responded John. "But, if they adopt a fee-for-service model, which they're also talking about in that heavy report in the envelope you brought in with you, we will have to first get approval from the county for the services we recommend. So let's say we've been seeing certain clients weekly and individually because we believe that is what they need to remain stable, stay in the community, and avoid hospitalization. Under managed care, the county has to preapprove the number of contacts they will pay for. They could come back and tell us that a client will be approved for only 20 visits a year, and that's it."

"But, wait a second," Sonia, the new board member, broke in. "Let me ask you something. Haven't you gotten money from some other sources in the past? I saw a bunch of foundations and other funders listed in your annual report."

"Oh, sure we do," replied Joe. "But, nearly all those foundation grants and other contributions are designated to support *specialized* programs, like postadoption services of mentally ill children and youth, or special bilingual outreach programs, or education and stress reduction for parents identified at risk for abusing or neglecting their children. All in all, about two-thirds of all our funds come to us to provide Medicaid services. So, overall, our agency's livelihood depends on that one source."

"So," Sonia continued, "let me understand. . . . You may have been treating a client for years, but now an outside source or payment constraints can determine the amount or type of service you can provide?"

"That's right," replied John. "But, there's more. Now it's also a free-for-all—any mental health organization, including private, for-profit ones, can come and bid against us to get the service contract—you know, like that Exclusive Health Associates Joe and I heard advertising on the radio last week when we drove to that advocacy meeting downtown."

"So," Joe interjected, "you're saying that our cost of providing a service really becomes a major issue, since they'll be comparing our costs to other agencies' costs before they decide to whom they let their patients go, and they will not automatically pay our actual costs. It sounds just like my cousin's health maintenance organization. It only let him have his heart bypass operation performed at some distant hospital where they had a contract because it was less expensive, rather than at the local university's hospital, where they didn't have a contract because the costs there are higher."

"Exactly," John, the director, responded. "So, like you have heard a million times in the past, we have to look at ways to reduce our overall costs—and this time, it's *really* serious!"

"Well, John," Joe continued, "you and I both know that there are only two ways to do that—either reduce the component costs of delivering a service (like using lower-cost staff, cutting overhead, turning off the lights), or increase our productivity (such as expanding the number of billable services we produce). So, for instance, case managers could improve their productivity by processing five additional cases a week. Indeed, we've been trying to both reduce costs and improve productivity for as long as I can remember, without compromising the quality of care—but I mean, c'mon, everyone has their limits! You can't constantly have everyone working in overdrive, or they'll burn out and leave. What else do Sonia and I need to know?"

Here the executive director paused, squinted his eyes, and rubbed his chin before he continued. "Joe," he said to his long-time colleague, "this place isn't going to be like it has been—plain and simple. We are going to have to act more like a business rather than a classic social welfare agency with grants coming in on a regular basis." Joe frowned, trying to take in these words' full implications.

"So, what are you saying?" Sonia asked John, also trying to interpret his meaning.

"Well," the director began, "think about the social work staff. They're dedicated and devoted to the clients, and don't really pay much attention to how much extra time they spend, or to what extra lengths they go for them. Now, they'll have to think twice, just like doctors do in an HMO before they order more fancy diagnostic tests; now we and our staff are the ones who have to live with the capitated amount that we can spend per patient per year, or the number of sessions that have been approved. If they or other clinicians order too many tests for too many people, after a while their salaries—and even their jobs—could be at stake. They have to start thinking about billable, reimbursable services, and we have to develop a more flexible workforce and new compensation plan that is in line with our new method of being paid.

"On top of that," John continued, "we're going to be redesigning our service-delivery system while there are still a lot of unknowns out there. The final system will depend on what state and county governments decide. And, at this point, we, as management, are going to have to ensure that our costs for each service are less than the fee-for-service rate that we're getting paid so that we'll have a little something for another rainy day, or a real emergency, not to mention pay increases for our very deserving staff. So we will need to generate a lot more reports and financial statements, learn about profit margins, and further automate our record system. We also have to start thinking about how to market our business better. Maybe we should open up a satellite office in the prospering suburbs. There, the folks could pay a bit more for our services, and we could use that to subsidize special needs we encounter here. We'd have to change our name, however—you know, get something less identified with this particular Greenleaf neighborhood.

"Oh, John," sighed the program director. "What are we gonna call ourselves, Have a Nice Day, Incorporated?!" Joe sighed and continued. "I mean, whatever happened to those days when we were flexible and met our clients' needs as they arose, and tried to do all those things we have in our mission statement? Doesn't anybody care about those poor, troubled folks wandering the streets, listening to voices from outer space, and getting beat up by local thugs or thrown in jail for being a nuisance? Don't people even realize that, in the long run, community mental health services are less expensive than building lots more jails?"

"But, my friend, that's the name of the game right now," replied John. "Either we somehow change with the times or we don't survive." He then added softly, "And Joe, we're the folks who know best how to provide Medicaid services—we've been doing it for a long time. We changed in the past, and grew from a little crisis center to a multimillion dollar operation, serving more than 3,000 local people. We now provide everything from prevention to rehabilitation services, and we help make this neighborhood a decent place to live for everyone. Just think of our upcoming Family Fun Day, at which all the neighborhood kids get to jump on the trampoline, ring the fire engine bell, and have fun with their families for an afternoon! We really promote the mental health of this community, and I don't want to be the one to fold up shop and abandon them. Somehow, we'll meet this challenge too."

"I know, John," murmured the vice president for programs. "But I just want to be sure that when we're done with all these changes, I can still look my old clients straight in the eye."

"You will, Joe, you will," said John gently. The director sighed, and then turned to the new board member. "Well, Sonia, do you have any ideas about how we can present all these changes to the staff and the board at the retreat?"

DISCUSSION QUESTIONS

1. If you were Sonia and were trying to think of ways to present this crisis to the staff and the board at the retreat, how would it be helpful in responding and moving toward development of an action plan to know which *stage* of the organizational life cycle this organization is encountering? Use the chart in Appendix A to substantiate your answer.

2. Which kind of crisis in its life cycle do you believe this community mental health organization is encountering? Justify your answer using the chart in Appendix 11-A.

3. Given the life-cycle stage you have identified, what types of actions would you recommend the agency leadership take? How will this agency maintain its close contact with the community, at the same time that it becomes more bureaucratic?

4. What specific types of programs would you suggest for staff to have in order to understand this current crisis and prepare for change?

5. When the Big City's Mental Health Board finally announces its plan, Greenleaf must choose between becoming the lead, coordinating agency with whom Big City would contract services, or else becoming one of the many service-providing members of a service network that some other agency would lead. How might the Greenleaf staff use strategic planning to help make this decision?

APPENDIX 11-A

Organizational Characteristics, Goals, and Crises during Four Stages of the Organizational Life Cycle

Organization's Size and Structure	Life-Cycle Stage of Organization and Structural Characteristics	Goal	Typical Crisis to Be Overcome Before Moving to New Stage
Small, Simple	*Start Up* **Organizational Infancy** • Entrepreneurial • Informal and nonbureaucratic	Survival—create single product or service; produce/launch and begin marketing	Need for leadership after initial creativity is expressed—but founders may not be interested in management activities demanded by growing size
	Emerging Growth **Organizational Youth** • Collectivity • Prebureaucratic, mostly informal, some procedures emerging	Growth	Need for delegation with control
	Maturity **Organizational Adulthood** • Formalization • Bureaucratic: Clear hierarchy and division of labor, rules, procedures, and control systems established	Internal stability, market/client expansion	Need to deal with too much red tape
Large, Complex	*Revival* **Organizational Maturity** • Elaboration of structure • Teamwork within bureaucracy, small-company thinking; a divisionalized structure emerges, based on type of services, clients, or geographic areas	Reputation; complete organization	Need for revitalization to avoid decline and death

Modified to refer to public-serving human service organizations.

Sources: Adapted from Hasenfeld and Schmid (1989, Table 1, pp. 248–249, 255); Jawahar and McLaughlin, 2001; and Vinokur-Kaplan and Connor (1997). The diagram presented in the latter source is adapted from Daft (1992, pp. 162–166, and Exhibit 5.5, p. 164). Original sources therein: Quinn and Cameron (1983) and Greiner (1972).

12

COMPUTERIZING CHILD WELFARE SERVICES

A Cyberworld Fairy Tale

STEVEN L. McMURTRY

THEORETICAL AND PRACTICE PERSPECTIVES

The first practical and commercially viable computers became available in the 1960s, and within a short time they were being used in everything from banking to spaceflight. Even at this early stage, writers began pondering how computers could also be used to help social workers. Some envisioned applications designed to support direct services, such as gathering background data, interactive role-playing, or administering standardized scales (Fuller, 1970; Schoech & Arangio, 1979). Others addressed specialized areas of practice such as child welfare, describing how tracking systems could improve service continuity and lessen the danger of children being "lost" in foster care (Young, 1974; Fein, 1975; Poertner & Rapp, 1980). A major federal law affecting foster care, the Child Welfare and Adoption Assistance Act of 1980, required that states develop computerized child-tracking systems (Pecora, Whittaker, & Maluccio, 1992).

Computers that were affordable for social service agencies began to appear in the 1970s at about the same time the accountability movement was pressuring managers for better documentation of services. Most early computer applications thus involved tasks such as running management information systems (MISs) and analyzing large data sets (Fuller, 1970; Hoshino & McDonald, 1975).

Three problems arose as computerization increased. First, as Schoech and Schkade pointed out, "Computer applications if left solely to managers will primarily serve the needs of managers" (1980, p. 572). MISs tended to be one-way streets—workers and other staff submitted information to be used by managers to meet the needs of those same managers. Some information did come back to workers, except as printed forms to be saved in their case files. Since the systems didn't assist with line-level functions, they were seen by workers simply as additional burdens. This led to the second problem, which was that the systems didn't work well for managers either. Workers saw no benefit about entering data for being conscientious, so the data tended to be fraught with errors or omissions (Courtney & Collins, 1994; McMurtry, 1986). A final problem with MISs during this period was that computer technology was still new, and neither computers nor the programs that ran them were ready to do many of the things promised for them. Most agencies were still dependent on large, centralized mainframe computers, and most software was specialized and laboriously written in highly technical computer languages. These dynamics led one writer to conclude that "perhaps the most notorious class of systems that do work is MISs" (Martin, 1982, p. 56).

Change came with three major developments: (1) the proliferation of powerful but affordable small computers that made mainframe models obsolete; (2) the creation of application-development software that increased the speed and ease with which new programs could be written; and (3) the development of hardware and software needed to allow computers to connect with each other through a local area network (LAN) controlled by a coordinating server or through the Internet. These are what Hammer and Champy (2001) call "disruptive technologies," meaning that they enable new ways of doing things that overturn traditional views about how organizations must operate. The following are three of their examples:

Old rule: Information can appear at only one place at one time.

Disruptive technology: Shared databases.

New rule: Information can appear simultaneously in as many places as needed. (p. 494)

Old rule: [Agencies] must choose between centralization and decentralization.

Disruptive technology: Telecommunications networks.

New rule: [Agencies] can simultaneously reap the benefits of centralization and decentralization. (p. 495)

Old rule: Managers make all decisions.

Disruptive technology: Decision support tools (database access, modeling software).

New rule: Decision making is part of everyone's job. (p. 496)

As we have all experienced, the influx of these "disruptive technologies" in our everyday lives has occurred with dizzying speed. In sharp contrast to only a decade ago, most social workers now have desktop or laptop computers in their workplaces, along with access to the Internet, e-mail, online databases, form-submission procedures, and other innovations. Not only has this dramatically altered the way workers and administrators carry out many of their tasks, it has occurred so rapidly that it has been difficult to judge the effects of these changes.

In the early days of computers, many observers expressed concerns about their impact on professional social work. For example, Braverman (1974) warned that computerization would further the mechanization of the workplace, a process through which workers increasingly became nothing more than appendages to machines. More specific to the human services, Fabricant (1985) called attention to the "de-skilling" of social work roles such as eligibility determination for public assistance ("welfare") payments. This process was once carried out by professional-level social workers but gradually became a largely clerical function in which staff simply enter relevant data into a computer. The same scenario could play out in other social work services, he argued, if the trend toward automation and compartmentalization of service functions continued. Still other writers suggested that the logic underlying computers and information systems fits poorly with the mind-set of helping professionals, either because of their nonmathematical orientation (Lamb, 1990) or because the nature of the work requires reasoning that does not conform to algorithmic logic used to write most software (Levitan & Willis, 1985).

Proponents of the use of computers contend that problems arise not with regard to *whether* computers are used but *how*. Roosenboom (1995) argues that a goal of computer use in human services is not automation—the mechanization of social workers' activities—but "informatisation"—the use of computers to make better and more useful data easily available to workers to help them do their jobs. Some research suggests that a critical factor is the way in which this information is presented. Bar-Tal (1990) examined the relationship between computer usage and employees' beliefs regarding control over their work. His findings indicated that the use of computers does not necessarily lead to a loss of sense of control over work as long as programs are written in ways that meet users' needs. He noted that "it is not computer usage in general that leads to [feelings of] loss of control, but the use of software that does not enable a sufficient level of flexibility" (p. 111).

Other findings support this conclusion. Taber and DiBello (1990) found that a group of workers, given sufficient training and time to adjust to a new computer system, lost their resistance to computerization and gained interest in using the technology. The authors note that perceived user-friendliness of the software was critical, as was an "agency look and feel to all screen displays, forms, and reporting formats" (p. 181). Monnickendam and Eaglstein (1993) found that the supposed negative attitudes of human service workers toward computers had little effect on acceptance of computerization efforts in a group of municipal social service agencies. Instead, key variables appeared to be organizational and process factors such as the involvement of workers in system design, the perceived receptiveness of implementors to worker feedback, and the ability of administrators to communicate a rationale and set of goals for the system. Frans (1993) found that worker perceptions of empowerment following a computerization effort were positively correlated with (1) the degree to which their agency's decision-making structure was decentralized, and (2) the level of technological sophistication of the new computer system.

Other studies offer further examples of successful computerization efforts in child welfare, together with additional guidelines for avoiding pitfalls. Smart, Russell, and Custodio (1998), documenting the incorporation of a child health database into the existing computer system used by protective service workers in Los Angeles, note the need for close collaboration between system technicians and line-level staff before, during, and after implementation so that problems can be addressed quickly and interactively. Kerslake (1998) emphasizes that a successful computer system is one that "not only meets management needs for information but also offers benefits to social workers by making inputting data easy and providing outputs that save on administrative tasks" (p. 237). Oyserman and Ben-benishty (1997) highlight the value of steps designed to allow workers to become comfortable with a new system. These include orientation, familiarization (in a hands-on, small-group setting using practice cases), interactive practice at the worker's site with a technician easily available, and ongoing user support.

The following case example is based on one state's experiences in creating a computer system for child welfare services. It is designed to show some of the possibilities and pitfalls of such efforts. The goal is not to warn against the use of computers, because, increasingly, they do play prominent roles in social workers' professional lives, but to illustrate what can be expected in such situations and, perhaps, how some problems can be prevented. To avoid embarrassment or notoriety for any real-life individuals, certain fictional characters have graciously consented to serve as stand-ins.

REFERENCES

Bar-Tal, Y. (1990). The effect of personal use of computers on employees' perception of control over work. *Social Behaviour, 5*(2), 103–115.

Braverman, H. (1974). *Labor and monopoly capital: The degradation of work in the twentieth century.* New York: Monthly Review Press.

Courtney, M. E., & Collins, R. C. (1994). New challenges and opportunities in child welfare outcomes and information technologies. *Child Welfare, 73,* 359–378.

Fabricant, M. (1985). The industrialization of social work practice. *Social Work, 30*(5), 389–395.

Fein, E. (1975). A data system for an agency. *Social Work, 20*(1), 21–24.

Frans, D. J. (1993). Computer diffusion and worker empowerment. *Computers in Human Services, 9,* 15–34.

Fuller, T. K. (1970). Computer utility in social work. *Social Casework, 51,* 608.

Hammer, M., & Champy, J. (2001). Reengineering the corporation: The enabling role of information technology. In J. M. Shafritz & J. S. Ott (Eds.), *Classics of organization theory* (5th ed.) (pp. 490–498). Fort Worth, TX: Harcourt.

Hoshino, G., & McDonald, T. P. (1975). Agencies in the computer age. *Social Work, 20*(1), 10–14.

Kerslake, A. (1998). Computerization of the *Looking after Children* records: Issues of implementation. *Children in Society, 12,* 236–237.

Lamb, J. A. (1990). Teaching computer literacy to human service students. *Computers in Human Services, 7*(1/2), 31–44.

Levitan, K. A., & Wills, E. A. (1985). Barriers to practitioners' use of information technology utilization: A discussion and results of a study. *Journal of Psychotherapy and the Family, 1*(1/2), 21–36.

Martin, J. (1982). *Application development without programmers.* Englewood Cliffs, NJ: Prentice Hall.

McMurtry, S. L. (1986). Substitute care information systems under Public Law 96-272. *Children and Youth Services Review, 8*(4), 349–361.

Monnickendam, M., & Eaglstein, A. S. (1993). Computer acceptance by social workers: Some unexpected research findings. *Computers in Human Services, 9,* 409–424.

Oyserman, D., & Benbenishty, R. (1997). Developing and implementing the integrated information system for foster care and adoption. *Computers in Human Services, 14,* 1–20.

Pecora, P. J., Whittaker, J. K., & Maluccio, A. N. (1992). *The child welfare challenge: Policy, practice, and research.* New York: Aldine De Gruyter.

Poertner, J., & Rapp, C. A. (1980). Information system design in foster care. *Social Work, 25*(2), 114–119.

Roosenboom, P. G. M. (1995). Solving the problems of computer use in social work. *Computers in Human Services, 11,* 391–401.

Schoech, D., & Arangio, T. (1979). Computers in the human services. *Social Work, 24*(2), 96–102.

Schoech, D., & Schkade, L. L. (1980). Computers helping caseworkers: Decision support systems. *Child Welfare, 59*(9), 566–575.

Smart, J., Russell, J., & Custodio, C. (1998). Developing a computerized health record in a protective services system. *Child Welfare, 77,* 347–362.

Taber, M. A., & DiBello, L. V. (1990). The personal computer and the small social agency. *Computers in Human Services, 6*(1/2/3), 181–197.

Young, D. W. (1974). Management information systems in child care: An agency experience. *Child Welfare, 53*(2), 102–111.

THE CASE

THE GNOMES
AND ROSE RED

BACKGROUND

Everyone knows the story of Snow White, whose fairytale adventures are immortalized in books, movies, and thrift-store kitsch. Less famous is Snow White's sister Rose Red. The Brothers Grimm introduced Rose Red in one of their stories, but her famous sibling grabbed top billing and poor Rose didn't make it into the sequel. But her later life paralleled that of Snow White in amazing ways—harrowing escapades, marriage to a prince, happy-ever-aftering, the whole storybook scene. Most surprisingly, she, too, crossed paths with a group of little people who were memorable characters in themselves. No, not the legendary seven dwarfs, though perhaps their distant cousins. These were the seven gnomes, and their names were Itchy, Twitchy, Strictly, Prickly, Groovy, Clueless, and Meds. Like their counterparts, they started humbly, working a mine in a distant corner of the forest. But, as with Rose Red, Hollywood stardom was not to be their fate. Instead, the lives of the gnomes took a much more unexpected turn, one that is instructive to the issue at hand. . . .

Lately, the seven gnomes had been thinking a lot about the good old days at the mine. Life seemed so simple then—wake up Twitchy and then calm him down, be sure Clueless ate his breakfast and not the breakfast table, listen to Prickly gripe about the volume level of Groovy's Rolling Stones CD, calm down Twitchy again, wait for Meds to take his macrobiotic vitamin supplements, watch Strictly rearrange the silverware drawer, calm down Twitchy again, then off to work they went. Okay, maybe it wasn't so simple, but at least once they got to the mine, the most advanced technology they had to confront was the handle of a pickaxe.

Unfortunately, they had been forced to leave the mining business long ago. The good veins of ore played out, overhead costs rose, and things got tight. Then there was that mound of tailing behind the mine they'd never paid much attention to until suddenly they had a desk full of citations accusing them of poisoning local streams with chemicals they couldn't pronounce. In short order, their public image went from colorful, lovable characters to rapacious environmental pirates. Yes, Rose Red had kept her promise to stay in touch, and a couple of times she used her influence to help out. But the Prince had gotten caught up in some scandal involving a palace intern, so the gnomes' problems weren't exactly highest on her list.

Going into child welfare had been Twitchy's idea. "Maybe it doesn't have anything to do with mining," he said nervously, "but if we don't find work soon there's no telling what sort of bad things could happen." He had seen the job announcement posted in the village square, then got some of the rest of the story through the grapevine. The children's division of the Kingdom Department of Human Services had lost a court suit filed by child advocates alleging that too many kids were being kept in group homes in cold, dank castles. One result was that a lot of new positions were funded for child welfare workers, and though the idea of going into an unknown line of work worried Twitchy considerably, he worried even more about the consequences of unemployment. Prickly was less certain and, characteristically, didn't mind saying so.

"What do we know about child welfare?" he complained. "If you're in such a hurry to get back to work, can't you at least pick a job we know something about?"

"We *do* know something about it," retorted Twitchy. "We took in Rose Red when she was just a teenager, and that's sorta like foster parenting, isn't it? We can say it was practical training for child welfare." Prickly remained unconvinced, but he went along when the rest of the gnomes decided to give it a try. If nothing else, at least the local welfare offices were slightly better lighted than the mine.

They all landed jobs in a unit that provided ongoing services to cases of kids in out-of-home care. Things went pretty well for a while. The gnomes, after all, were basically good-hearted fellows, and they came to feel that child welfare was a place where they could make a difference. One thing they hadn't counted on, though, was the paperwork. They thought the regulations and permits and codes at the mine had been bad, but they were unprepared for the volume of case recording, court reports, and triplicate copies of forms they had to complete. Moreover, each child, even if part of a large sibling group, was counted as an individual case, so forms multiplied not by the number of families but by the number of family members.

Perhaps inevitably, some of the gnomes began to leave the group. Prickly was first to go. His personality, of course, made him a natural for supervision and management, and he started to work his way up the ladder. Next to leave was Strictly. Having an obsessive-compulsive streak had made life in the dust, dirt, and chaos of the mine sheer hell. Dealing with his clients' often-chaotic lives hadn't been much easier, so at the first opportunity, he jumped ship for a position in the agency's bookkeeping department. Later he switched to the office that ran the division's computer services. But the remaining five gnomes stayed together and began to feel that they were getting better at their job. All of them took advantage of conferences and inservice trainings, and some began to take social work courses part time at the nearby college. Clueless even got to where he remembered that "home visit" didn't mean the client was supposed to come to *his* house.

They were having their usual pint of ale at the local pub one Friday after work when they first heard about the new computer system. Strictly said the division was planning to put in completely new hardware and software that would cover all the child welfare offices in the Kingdom. What he described sounded pretty good—at the start.

THE COMPUTER SYSTEM

"Here's what's happening," said Strictly enthusiastically. "We're going to be getting a whole lot of money from the Kingdom to build a full-service computer system for child welfare. It's gonna help you guys a lot."

Itchy, pausing briefly from scratching energetically at a spot on his left ankle, mumbled, "Yeah, well, I've been around long enough to know what it means when somebody says, 'Hi, we're from central administration and we're here to help you.' No offense, Prickly, but you know what I'm saying."

"Hmmph!" grunted Prickly indignantly. "Managers are always easy targets. Not that I'm all that high up, anyway. But I've heard the plans for this new computer thing and it sounds okay to me—if guys like you will give it a chance."

"Yeah!" said Strictly, almost knocking his fork and spoon out of their carefully aligned positions as he leaned forward in comic earnestness. "Really! You guys'll like this. For starters, you'll finally be getting your own computers to use. Every single worker'll get one! Supervisors, too."

Meds had been worriedly studying a slight discoloration on his left forearm that he was convinced was a cancerous lesion, but he stopped a moment when he heard this. "My own computer?!" he said hopefully.

"Yeah!" encouraged Strictly. "And not some broken-down old wrecks. These are brand new laptops, state-of-the-art. You're supposed to take 'em with you when you go out on home visits. You can get information from clients and complete all your forms right while you're talking. Then if you want to, you can go out and write up your case notes while you're sitting in the car and everything that happened is fresh in your mind. You can get all your paperwork done right there onsite!" He smiled triumphantly as he carefully arranged the salt and pepper shakers in a line perfectly orthogonal to the table edge.

"I don't mean to look a gift horse in the mouth," said Itchy, "but I don't see what good it'll do me to type all that stuff on a laptop. When I get back to the office, I still have to fill out the form for Central Records."

"But you can do that from the laptop!" said Strictly. "They'll all be able connect to the Web, and . . . "

"Wait a minute," interjected Clueless, a look of concern on his face. "I'm scared of spiders."

"No, no!" winced Strictly. "The World Wide Web. You know, the Internet. You can hook up your laptop anywhere there's a phone and upload your case notes and forms to Central Records, then it's all there for you the next time you need it."

"Oh yeah," he continued, "and I forgot to tell you the new system's name—CINCH. That's 'Client Information for New-Century Human Services.' "

"Pretty hokey," said Itchy, "but I do like the idea that they're finally gonna give us decent equipment."

"You haven't even heard the best part yet." Strictly was really getting excited. "They'll be wiring all the offices so all of our computers will be hooked into a local area network that runs on something called a token ring system that'll let you use all the software on the network to get rid of all the paper stuff and submit your forms and reports electronically."

"A token ring?" said Groovy. "You mean like wizards and elves and hobbits and stuff? Awesome, dude. I always wanted one of those rings."

"Will you guys cut it out?!" said Strictly. "A token ring system is one way to set up a computer network so you can each have computers at your desks that will do some of the work but then you can also share information and programs and stuff with a whole lot of other people and computers that are hooked together."

Strictly was just about to jump out of his chair now—he certainly didn't lack for enthusiasm about his work. "They're even gonna try to get some of those new cell modems. They're like those phones you see people talking on in their cars. . . ."

"You mean right before they run into a pole?" asked Itchy sarcastically.

"No!" persisted Strictly. "These are like cell phones for computers. You can dial-up and hook into your office network without even having a phone line to plug into. Say you finish a home visit and then go for a cup of coffee before the next one. You can take your laptop with you, dial into the system from your table, and get your case notes done before the waiter pours your second cup."

"I dunno," said Meds. "It's like I've been telling Prickly—what I need most from administration is just more time to spend face to face with clients. If something like this will take the paperwork and bureaucratic mumbo-jumbo off my back, then I'm all for it. But it sounds to me like this stuff isn't gonna be easy to learn, and it'll probably take a lot of time too." He paused to knock back an aspirin with a shot of seaweed tea. "And lemme tell you, it doesn't sound to me like the sort of thing you computer whizzes are gonna be able to get right the first time, or even the second. Is there anybody who's actually building this system that knows a home visit from a hole in the wall?"

"From what I know, they contracted with a big computer corporation to do it all," said Prickly. "They're supposed to have done all kinds of systems for all kinds of businesses and know how to avoid problems. . . ."

TIME PASSES . . .

Two years had gone by since the conversation in the pub, and now it was another Friday evening. Five of the seven gnomes were sitting dispiritedly nursing their mugs—even the usually cheerful Clueless was a bit glum. Neither Prickly nor Strictly joined them much anymore. Things always seemed a little tense, and arguments started too easily. It wasn't necessarily the new computer system that was to blame, but tonight it was a prominent topic.

"Man, I'm beat," sighed Itchy, rubbing hard at a spot on the back of his neck. "More cases and less time to work 'em. I thought somehow things would let up a little. I wasn't this tired when we finished a week at the mine."

"Chill, Dude, at least you got to go out to check on a couple of foster homes," drawled Groovy. "I spent the whole afternoon waiting for screens to scroll on CINCH so I could authorize payments to a provider, then I couldn't get the provider number I had to match up with the ones in the system. It was a bad trip, man." He leaned back, slipped his feet out of his sandals, and lifted them to the corner of the table. Uncharacteristically, he did not reach for his battered portable CD player and headphones.

"What I can't figure out is why we're having to handle provider payments in the first place!" said Meds angrily. "That's something I never bargained for when I heard we were getting a new system. I thought the idea of CINCH was to help us with the work we do as social workers—you know, like that stuff they promised us about doing our case recording online to reduce paperwork, and having easy access to archives to check for previous service records—that sort of thing. But that's not what the thing seems to be about at all. If you ask me, it's mostly about getting workers to do everything—billing, tracking payments, you name it." He thumped the table with his palm for emphasis, scattering a couple of vitamin E capsules in the process. Then he stopped to examine his somewhat reddened hand with concern.

"Yeah," added Clueless, "I'm confused. Sometimes they tell us we're social workers and other times they tell us we're case managers. I thought case management was part of social work, but the more of it I do, the less I get to see my clients. CINCH seems to be a lot about the case management part and not much about the social work part."

"And that's another thing," said Itchy. "The secretaries used to be able to do a lot of that stuff for us. They knew the old system and how to make it click. The people behind CINCH want workers to be able to do everything, but that means we've got to spend a lot more time than in the past with plain data-entry stuff. The new system won't even let the secretaries get into it. They'd like to help out but can't."

"Maybe it's just me," said Twitchy, "but I'm worried that I don't know the system as well as I should. You get stuck waiting for something to happen and you can sit there for two hours because the system's so overloaded. Or sometimes nothing happens because you did something wrong. The worst is when you've entered a lot of data and then the system freezes up and you've lost everything. You never know if it's yours or the computer's fault." He then stopped and glanced around apprehensively as though expecting to be reproached by an unknown authority who had decided it really was Twitchy's fault.

"Well, we should try to think positively," said Clueless, reprovingly. "They gave us those new computers, and they did bring us in for training."

"But that's just the point," interjected Itchy, his fingers chasing a loose nerve ending up one sleeve of his sweater. "They didn't do either at the right time. They had to go buy all the stuff when they got the money 'cause the Kingdom didn't want 'em just sitting on the cash. But that meant everything else was all scattered out. We got the laptops and stuff, when was it, almost two years ago? But it took a whole long time after that before they had all the offices wired, and longer still for the software to be ready. Matter of fact, that's still being done a little at a time. But two years is forever for hardware, so those fancy computers aren't state-of-the-art anymore, and I heard they can't do some of the stuff they want to do now because the computers won't handle it."

"Yeah," said Clueless, "I guess I did hear that sometimes those things at the back of your computer that connect to that—whadaya call it—that token ring system? Adapter cards, yeah. Well, sometimes those cards don't work right. They get the little token thing passed to them but they forget to send it along. So the big computer that runs the network has to make another token to send out, which slows down the system. A friend of mine who's sort of a techie said that newer systems can keep more than one token going around, so the whole thing runs a lot faster. . . ." Suddenly realizing that he was voicing a lot more opinion than was typical of him, he added, "Not that I mean to complain or anything."

"Sure sounds like a complaint to me."

The five gnomes all looked up to find Prickly beside their table, with Strictly standing a bit behind him. Prickly looked, well, prickly, but that was normal, so it was hard to tell if he was really upset about the topic of their conversation. Having been the last one to speak, Clueless felt a bit sheepish and scurried around awkwardly to find chairs and clear room for Prickly and Strictly at the table.

"Don't you guys have anything better to do than gripe about that infernal computer system?" asked Prickly.

"It's not 'infernal!' " protested Strictly.

"Yeah," said Groovy to Prickly. "How come it's infuneral or whatever? I thought you and the other big bosses wanted it."

"I'm no 'big boss,' " countered Prickly, "but, yeah, everyone in management thought the CINCH system was a good idea. Now, with all the complaining coming from the field staff, I sometimes wonder. What's this about the hardware getting old?"

"Aw, well," stammered Itchy, "it's not like it doesn't work or anything. But how come you guys didn't do all that programming stuff first and then get the computers?"

"Because half the field staff didn't even know how to find the 'on' button when we first started," answered Strictly indignantly. "We figured it'd be best to get computers in people's hands, even if the main CINCH software wasn't ready yet, because there was other stuff on the network like word processors and e-mail that they could use. The best software in the world isn't much good if people aren't comfortable with a computer."

"But what about those screens we used to go to in the office to check information in the client record system?" said Clueless. "Weren't those computers?"

"Those things?!" exclaimed Strictly. "Those were just terminals connected to the old mainframe. You could only use 'em to see if you'd filled out a form right—not to actually enter and change information. They didn't look or act like PCs do now. In fact, that's part of what CINCH was supposed to do—to give you a system with windows and pull-down menus and other things that six-year-old kids are doing on their home computers now."

"Think about it, Clueless," he continued. "Before CINCH, if you wanted to open up a record for a new case, how would you do it? You'd fill out a form, right? And then you'd walk it to your supervisor for checking and approval, and then give it to the secretary to enter, then go back some time later to one of the terminals to check it out, and then fill out *another* form to make a change if there were any errors. Right?"

Clueless nodded.

"And let's say you were placing a new foster child in a temporary shelter. How would you show that?"

"Uh, wasn't temporary shelter a code 863?" said Clueless.

"Right," answered Strictly, "but how long did it take you to learn that?"

Clueless blushed.

"That's what I mean!" argued Strictly. "The new system is supposed to make computers work for you, not the other way around. You don't have to remember any codes because the words "Temporary Shelter" are right on the placement options screen—all you do is click on that spot. And you don't have to fill out triplicate forms and schlep 'em across the office to wait for your supervisor to sign—the info's automatically routed to your supervisor to approve after you type it in."

Itchy suddenly ceased all scratching motions—a clear sign of agitation. "That's how it's *supposed* to work, if everybody knows the system," he exclaimed. "You know it, Strictly, 'cause you helped design it and work with it every day. Those of us in the field were supposed to learn it from a training session." He spoke the words "training session" in the same tone of voice he might have used in saying "proctoscopic exam."

"Yeah," joined in Meds, "and the training only covered the stuff that was working at the time, but all kinds of things just keep getting added to the system, so we've got to figure out all the new bells and whistles as we go along. There are so many windows and menus and screens in that thing that Daniel Boone couldn't find his way through it." He appeared ready to continue, then suddenly stopped to take his pulse rate, fearing he might have let it get too high.

"That's what's got me confused," added Clueless plaintively. "I tried to listen real hard at the training so I wouldn't mess up later. But a lot of the stuff we heard has changed since then, and it keeps on changing. I'm always wondering which button to push next, and . . . "

Twitchy had been trying to get into the conversation but couldn't seem to get a chance. Finally, he squared his shoulders and said, a bit too loudly, "And even when I know what button I want, a lot of times it's not there. This thing about building the system and working out the bugs as you go means that sometimes you're supposed to do something you can't do because that part hasn't been finished yet." He paused for a moment, shivered involuntarily, then added, "I hate to even think of the kinds of terrible things that could happen. . . . "

Strictly's chin had been sticking out farther and farther. He clearly was beginning to take some of the comments personally and was about ready to say something when Prickly quickly cut in.

"Okay, okay," Prickly said, holding up his hands. "Starting something like this is always going to be a pain, and I don't fault you guys for getting a few gripes off your chest. But most of the stuff you've complained about is what you'd expect any time any agency starts doing something different—whether it's designing a new computer system or changing the locks on the restrooms. You guys are lucky that Strictly's where he is, 'cause he's learned enough about computer systems to talk to the programmer types and tell 'em what'll work and what won't.

"In fact, that's part of the whole issue," he continued. "It wasn't *my* decision that you guys were gonna get a new computer system. Like we told you before, there was a pot of money from the Kingdom that wasn't going to be there forever, and we had to use it or lose it. What's more, there's folks from private industry who are in positions of power and who think that everything governmental should be done the same way it's done in the businessworld. Sometimes they're right and sometimes they're not, but if there's enough of 'em that think so, then that's the way it's gonna be no matter what we think.

"But the main thing is what all the computer jocks are saying about how the office of the future will be a paperless office—no file drawers, no manila folders, no two-hole punches, nothing like that. It'll all be in computers. We social workers always say we hate paperwork and want to spend our time with clients. Well, here's our chance. The only catch is that in order to get rid of all the paper, we have to learn computers—something else a lot of us say we don't like."

"Yeah, but do we control the computers or do they control us?" asked Meds, temporarily satisfied that a fatal infarction was not imminent. "I've been mulling over what Clueless and I were talking about a while ago—monitoring providers and doing billing and data-entry stuff and all that. You know those business types you talked about earlier? Well how do we know that computers aren't just a way for them to cut costs and get us to do a lot of other people's work?"

"That's not fair," protested Strictly, "it's not the computer's doing. Like it or not, social workers in child welfare these days are case managers, not therapists. We link our clients to resources—counseling, job training, transportation, child care, whatever—but we don't treat 'em directly."

"Yeah, and maybe that's what's wrong with this whole business," interjected Itchy. He frowned darkly while scratching with great vigor at the back of one knee joint. "We're not doing what we're supposed to be doing anymore, and your computer system is just helping get us farther and farther off track."

Strictly's chin went out defiantly farther, and he even ignored the fact that his tie was almost a full half-inch out of perfect vertical alignment. "Or maybe," he shot back, "CINCH knows your job better than you do and you just don't want to admit it."

Even Clueless's jaw dropped at that, but it was Meds who was the first to respond. "That's crazy!" he exclaimed, forgetting his blood pressure entirely. "It's like saying the coop determines the nature of the chicken! Can't somebody figure out a computer system that helps people like us do our work without taking over our job?"

"Nobody's taking over your job!" Prickly protested hotly. "This is a system that *will* help you guys. You just don't wanna give it time. Computers are here to stay, and they're gonna keep changing the way things are done. And it'll happen whether we want it to or not." He turned back to his mug and silence gradually settled over the group.

"Bummer," muttered Groovy, rummaging through his fringed leather tote bag. "Anybody seen my Jimi Hendrix disc?"

DISCUSSION QUESTIONS

1. Many other types of organizations and services have made effective use of computer information systems. Discuss why you think social work agencies sometimes struggled to make this technology work well.

2. Some people argue that, because managers and line-level staff have different needs and goals, no single information system will ever be able to serve the needs of both groups. Discuss whether you concur with this view and why.

3. Computers and computer software rely on a linear form of reasoning based on "if-then" connections. As noted in the chapter, some writers argue that for social workers to understand and address client problems they must think in creative, nonlinear ways, and this leads to an inherent limitation in computers' ability to be helpful to social workers. Do you agree or disagree, and why?

4. The gnomes voice concern that their jobs increasingly involve managing payments and services provided to clients by others and that this means they have less time to provide the services themselves. They are also concerned that the design of the CINCH system accelerates this change by making these new responsibilities part of its operating requirements. Do you think their concerns are reasonable? Why or why not?

5. Do you think the "de-skilling" process mentioned in the introduction poses a genuine threat to social workers? If so, do you think that computers are part of the problem? More generally, do you think computer technology tends to have a dehumanizing effect when it is implemented on a large scale in organizations?

6. Based on what you read about the gnomes' experiences, identify some "Dos" and "Don'ts" that you think should apply to any effort to implement an information system such as the one described.

13

ECOLOGICAL OUTCOMES

BENJAMINA MENASHE, RISA SANDLER,
and STEVEN RATHGEB SMITH

THEORETICAL AND PRACTICE PERSPECTIVES

Often, the nonprofit organizational form is used as a vehicle to pursue innovative ideas, funded by external grantors. Many nonprofit organizations are founded through the entrepreneurial impulse of one person or a group of persons, and these founders may secure public or private funds to start the organization from a major donor or government agency. As the competition for funding continues to increase, the dependence on one donor can create serious management issues, and diversifying the funding base and ensuring the initial commitment to innovation becomes a challenge (Gronbjerg, 1993; Letts, Ryan, & Steinberg, 1999; Young & Steinberg, 1995; Wolf, 1999).

Ecological Outcomes (EO) is just such an agency. EO is a Seattle nonprofit design and architectural community organization founded on Earth Day 1970 by a group of students and faculty from the University of Washington School of Architecture. Historically, EO had been dependent on extensive government support, primarily federal Department of Housing and Urban Development (HUD) funds disbursed by the city of Seattle. EO used these funds to provide technical assistance and design support to community organizations in Seattle. As in many other innovative agencies, the founder of the agency—a creative charismatic figure—served as its executive director for many years. The support of one donor—government—and the charismatic executive also meant that the agency did not undertake concerted fund-raising campaigns. The board was relatively uninvolved in fund-raising and tended to help support the work and vision of the executive director rather than set a tone for the organization. EO never developed a long-term strategic financial or organizational plan. The board's role thus becomes a basic element in this case. To better understand the issues surrounding the board's role, we suggest that the reader look at the ever-increasing literature on nonprofit boards of directors (Brudney & Murray, 1998; Herman, Renz, & Heimovics, 1997; Herman & Heimovics, 1991; Jackson & Holland, 1998; Jeavons, 1994; Ott, 2001; Ryan, 1999; Smith, 1995; Taylor, Chait, & Holland, 1996).

The challenges facing EO, including the position of the board and lack of financial planning, are suggested by two theories of nonprofit growth and development. First, scholars argue that nonprofits (and other organizations) go through predictable stages of development. In one model, nonprofits begin with an influential role for the board but once an executive director is chosen the power shifts away from the board to the staff, especially the executive director (Middleton, 1987; Oster, 1995; Perrow, 1963; Wood, 1995). A second model is based on the concept of resource dependency in which organizations structure programs and management to be responsive to the goals and objectives of their funders. The relative noninvolvement of the EO board in fund-raising could thus be explained by the reliance of EO on government funding, the congruence of EO's, HUD's and the city's goals as well as a lack of incentive that government funds provided for raising private donations (Oster, 1995; Powell & Freidkin, 1987).

The reliance on government funds, a powerful executive director, and a board without strong ongoing involvement in fund-raising created a vulnerability to changes in public policy and agency leadership. This came to the fore at EO years ago when the founding executive director left the agency, and at the same time government funding expectations changed. Government wanted to fund the end users of EO's services and programs with services conducive to more intense outcome evaluation. Looming cutbacks in direct public funds meant the agency might not be able to maintain its then current level of operations.

Thus, the EO executive director, Paul Foster, faced a classic dilemma of nonprofit human service organizations: How can the organization bring in new revenue without shifting its mission away from its commitment to the public interest and the Seattle community? Further, how could he successfully implement internal organizational changes in board–staff relations, product lines, and staff orientation that would position the agency to take advantage of new public and private funding opportunities? Is this even Foster's role, or should the impetus for changes come from elsewhere among EO's constituencies? Indeed, should the board of directors take the lead in reshaping the organization? As so often happens when an organization faces extreme environmental constraints on its survival, merger with another organization becomes an alternative (Adams & Perlmutter, 1991), but mergers can bring into play a new set of very complicated internal and external issues and problems (Schmid, 1995; Singer & Yankey, 1991; Wernet & Jones, 1992).

REFERENCES

Adams, C., & Perlmutter, F. D. (1991). Commercial venturing and the transformation of America's voluntary social welfare agencies. *Nonprofit and Voluntary Quarterly, 20*(1), 25–38.

Brudney, J. L., & Murray, V. (1998). Do intentional efforts to improve boards really work? The views of nonprofit CEOs. *Nonprofit Management & Leadership, 8*(4), 333–348.

Gronbjerg, K. (1993). *Understanding nonprofit funding: Managing revenues in social and community development organizations.* San Francisco: Jossey-Bass.

Herman, R. D., & Heimovics, R. D. (1991). *Executive leadership in non-profit organizations: New strategies for shaping executive-board dynamics.* San Francisco: Jossey-Bass.

Herman, R. D., Renz, D. O., & Heimovics, R. D. (1997). Board practices and board effectiveness in local nonprofit organizations. *Nonprofit Management & Leadership, 7*(4), 373–385.

Jackson, D. K., & Holland, T. P. (1998). Measuring the effectiveness of nonprofit boards. *Nonprofit and Voluntary Sector Quarterly, 27*(2), 159–182.

Jeavons, T. (1994). Stewardship revisited: Secular and sacred views of governance and management. *Nonprofit and Voluntary Sector Quarterly, 23*(2), 107–122.

Letts, C. W., Ryan, W. P., & Grossman, A. (1999). *High performance nonprofit organizations: Managing upstream for greater impact.* New York: Wiley.

Middleton, M. (1987). Nonprofit boards of directors: Beyond the governance function. In W. W. Powell (Ed.), *The nonprofit sector: A research handbook* (pp. 141–153). New Haven, CT: Yale University Press.

Oster, S. (1995). *Strategic management for nonprofit organizations: Theory and cases.* New York: Oxford University Press.

Ott, J. S (Ed.). (2001). *Understanding nonprofit organizations: Governance, leadership, and management.* Boulder: Westview.

Perrow, C. (1963). Goals and power structures: A historical case study. In E. Friedson (Ed.), *The hospital in modern society* (pp. 112–146). New York: Macmillan.

Powell, W. W., & Friedkin, R. (1987). Organizational change in nonprofit organizations. In W. W. Powell (Ed.), *The nonprofit sector: A research handbook* (pp. 180-194). New Haven, CT: Yale University Press.

Ryan, W. P. (1999). Is that all there is? Searching for more useful governance strategies beyond the board room. *The Nonprofit Quarterly, 6*(2, Summer), 8-15.

Schmid, H. (1995). Merging nonprofit organizations: Analysis of a case study. *Nonprofit Management & Leadership, 5*(4), 377-392.

Singer, M. I., & Yankey, J. A. (1991). Organizational metamorphosis: A study of eighteen nonprofit mergers, acquisitions and consolidations. *Nonprofit Management & Leadership, 1*(4), 357-369.

Smith, D. H. (1995). *Entrusted: The moral responsibility of trusteeship.* Bloomington: Indiana University Press.

Taylor, B., Chait, R. P., & Holland, T. P. (1996). The new work of the nonprofit board. *Harvard Business Review* (September-October), 4-14.

Wernet, S. P., & Jones, S. A. (1992). Merger and acquisition activity between nonprofit, social service organizations: A case study. *Nonprofit and Voluntary Sector Quarterly, 21*(4), 367-380.

Wolf, T. (1999). *Managing a nonprofit organization in the twenty-first century.* New York: Simon & Schuster.

Wood, M. (Ed.). (1995). *Nonprofit boards and leadership: Cases on governance, change, and board-staff dynamics.* San Francisco: Jossey-Bass.

Young, D. R., & Steinberg, R. (1995). *Economics for nonprofit managers.* New York: Foundation Center.

THE CASE

ECOLOGICAL OUTCOMES

HISTORY

Reflecting its roots in the environmental movement of the late 1960s and early 1970s, EO was formed as an ecological workshop and set up as a free clearinghouse of information to the community about current environmental issues. As stated in its bylaws, EO's mission was "to function as a community design and central resource center for the disadvantaged areas of our community, and to aid them in developing long-range community objectives, regarding planning, design, and the environment." Initial funding was from small cash and in-kind donations. Yet, the organization's focus soon changed. Shortly after EO was founded, it received a substantial grant from the federal Department of Housing and Urban Development (HUD). This grant was large enough to fund virtually all of EO's activities including overhead, capital, and staff salaries. HUD funding transformed EO from a grassroots information and referral/advocacy organization to a formal service-delivery agency providing architectural consulting services to the nonprofit community in Seattle.

Part of this shift was demand-driven as well. Initially, EO helped community agencies through the regulatory phase of development, but over time, the interests of these nonprofits changed and diversified; many agencies now wanted help with developing programs and actual buildings. The HUD grant allowed EO the flexibility to respond to these changing demands. Throughout the 1970s and 1980s, EO focused primarily on low-income housing and development. Its mission statement was amended to include the "development and improvement of low-income housing and facilities." EO staff designed and implemented all facets of community revitalization—from community gardens to townhomes in poor urban areas. EO worked with local nonprofit housing and community-development agencies that needed technical assistance and support on architectural design. For example, housing agencies that wanted to develop multifamily low-income housing units might consult EO, which would help craft appropriate proposals that the agency could use to attract funders. The proposal would include detailed cost analyses. This was especially valuable to many community agencies since they were usually not in a position to pay for critical technical design work. During this period more than three-quarters of EO funding originated from the HUD community-development block grant.

EO FINDS A NICHE

By supporting low-cost technical assistance, the funding from HUD to EO promoted the creation of a network of nonprofit housing and community-development organizations in Seattle. Through the assistance of EO, many small nonprofits were able to obtain funding and build or improve facilities to serve the needs of low-income and special needs populations. For many of these nonprofits, the assistance of EO was absolutely essential to the ability of the community nonprofit to successfully complete projects.

HUD grants enabled EO to build a reputation for itself as a leader in the community design and development field. It allowed EO to focus exclusively on nonprofit organizations—a market niche that enabled EO to prosper without unduly infringing on the market territory of for-profit design firms that felt they were not in a position to subsidize their work for community organizations.

In the 1970s and 1980s, EO, in keeping with its mission, formed partnerships with other community organizations, nonprofit and for-profit, to obtain land and financing for its projects. Partner organizations included major local firms and agencies: Washington Mutual Savings Bank, Seafirst Bank, US Bank, Central Area Public Development Authority, Providence Medical Center, King County, the Port of Seattle, development associations, hospitals, and local government. The partnerships were largely successful, building a positive reputation for EO in the larger community. Within the organization, these partnerships were viewed as a logical step for an organization originally focused exclusively on providing technical assistance.

In the early 1990s, EO's focus shifted again as it obtained non-HUD government contracts. In addition to its long-time support of low-income housing, EO developed relationships with other nonprofit agencies in the low-income, special needs housing community. EO's project base expanded to include childcare centers in a variety of settings including Harborview Medical Center. Once again, EO further expanded, from a community design/development organization to a more general design firm serving a wider portion of the nonprofit community in Seattle. Yet, even as it grew in scope, EO heard whispers that its core HUD funding might be reduced.

ORGANIZATIONAL STRUCTURE

Until 1997, EO was typical of many nonprofit community organizations dependent on government contracts: Its staff size was relatively small; it had few volunteers with the exception of the board of directors; and its board was modest in size, with close to a 1:1 ratio between the number of staff and board members (about 13 to 15 board members). The executive director supervised the architectural and support staff and reported to the board.

Historically, the board was comprised of local professionals, mainly architects, although individuals with backgrounds in human resources, banking, and law had also been board members at various times in EO's history. The board usually met monthly, with ad hoc committee meetings held on a loosely scheduled basis. Board member terms were staggered. Until recently, board recruitment tended to be an informal process wherein board members tapped their existing networks of professional colleagues and friends. Consistent with the informality of the board selection process, specific responsibilities and obligations were not presented to prospective members before or after acceptance to the EO board. Formal induction was by consensus, but dependence on the existing networks between the board and the founding executive director ensured that the selection process would be relatively noncontroversial.

The founding executive director was very influential in board selection and his vision helped provide the glue for the board and the organization that held it together. He was a highly respected leader, both for his tenacity and for his commitment to the organization. He essentially created EO with the founding board.

When he left about six years ago, difficulties began to develop on the board—a situation aggravated by the changing funding environment. With the founding executive director gone, the board was no longer shielded from daily operational issues. Consequently, the board had to devote considerably more time than previously to board service, just to maintain EO's standard operations.

Management during Transition

Problems began shortly after the second executive director was hired. Staff repeatedly approached the board about issues that arose due to conflicts between the new executive's style and the existing organizational culture. The executive director left, and the board had to manage EO without a leader until a new executive could be hired. During this period, it became apparent that the board was not fully aware of management practices or the organization's true financial status.

Conditions during this critical transition period necessitated intensive involvement from the board. They had met monthly and were, for the most part, unaware of EO's deteriorating financial posture. Board members now were forced to meet every week to review all aspects of the organization, from personnel issues to finances to day-to-day management concerns. By the time an executive director was hired, board members were collectively drained from their experiences of literally running the organization. Although there was some sense of satisfaction at EO's survival through the ordeal, many board members were burned out and wanted to discontinue their association with EO. Despite this clear sense of fatigue, most members remained on the board for two to three more years. However, most of the staff who stayed during this crisis period left shortly after the new executive director, Paul Foster, was hired in 1996.

Paul Foster Arrives

The arrival of Paul Foster did not solve EO's difficulties. Some board members complained that their individual areas of expertise were overutilized and that EO demanded too much of their time, especially in light of the relatively recent crisis situation from which it was still recovering. Some long-time architects on the board were frustrated that their architectural skills were *under*-utilized. Other board members voiced concerns that the actual state of affairs in EO was far more tenuous than had been initially presented to them when they had joined prior to Foster's arrival.

Overall, attendance at board meetings was poor, with only a small percentage of members having a 90 percent or greater attendance records. The board president was uninvolved in planning board meetings. Paul Foster usually set meeting agendas with the board president's approval and prepared all materials for the meetings: Neither support staff nor architectural staff attended board meetings. Staff had the option of going to board meetings, but it never seemed to be a priority.

In an effort to alter board recruitment and to provide board members with more information, Foster tried to formalize the process by inviting prospective members to meet the board president, the executive director, and selected board members and staff for lunch to discuss the organization prior to an official invitation to join. He also wrote a "notebook" that detailed board commitments such as committees and a financial obligation (i.e., a yearly donation). The board generally did not like Foster's push into fund-raising. His board initiative helped brief prospective members, but it did not solve basic problems in board selection including the tendency to rely on existing professional and personal networks. Several new committee members joined under Foster's leadership, but the majority of the board was still comprised of those who did not want to change the existing organizational system.

THE FUNDING DILEMMAS OF GOVERNMENT CONTRACTS

After the initial start-up phase, the HUD grant covered virtually all expenses, allowing the organization to operate free of monetary concerns. This situation encouraged complacency by the board of directors, staff, and the community. Even if board, staff, and community never raised or personally contributed a dime, they knew that EO would be financially viable. According to several board members, an unwritten rule existed that no board member "should" contribute money to EO because "it wasn't that kind of board."

In recent years, however, the criteria for government funding had changed and federal dollars were not as freely dispersed as in the past, especially to agencies with long histories of government support. Further, the new emphasis on measurement of direct-service outcomes strongly affects organizations like EO that provide intermediary services rather than tangible services directly to individuals.

According to Foster, "We cannot meet the new criteria because of this middleman role. EO provides consulting to other organizations that construct the buildings: How can you accurately judge the outcomes of our services?" Because it cannot compete for dollars based on typical performance measures, EO started receiving signals from the city of Seattle and HUD that their support from HUD's community-development block grant would likely end in the near future.

The quick succession of executive directors, combined with a board of directors that had not sufficiently planned for the future, left EO in a precarious situation. The gravity of its predicament became clear this year—with the city announcement that EO's entire block grant would be eliminated (or that possibly only a token amount would remain) at the end of the next grant year. After 25 years of sole-source funding, with no fund-raising or strategic financial plan in place, EO is about to become an organization with a budget of several hundred thousand dollars and incoming revenue of zero.

THE MERGER

Paul Foster understood from the outset that there was a strong possibility that HUD funding would be cut off. He considered his options: secure other types of public funding, undertake private fund-raising, and/or generate fee income. New public funding was a long-shot since EO is a specialized agency, and unlike direct human service agencies, it cannot bid on new direct service contracts. Private fund-raising was not likely to raise significant amounts of money, at least in the short term, given the historical aversion of the board and staff to fund-raising. Consequently, the only viable option for new revenue was tapping fee income from the private sector.

The opportunity to tap fee income was presented in a proposal for EO to merge with a local for-profit architectural firm owned and operated by Sara Clark, an architect who specialized in design work for child-care organizations and other small nonprofit community organizations. After many years of solo ownership, she was ready to change the focus of the firm. She was aware of EO's situation and concluded that a possible merger would allow her to continue to perform high-quality work without the personal stress of day-to-day management in the private sector. For its part, EO needed to consider new ways to do business.

Clark, Foster, and the EO board engaged in a series of negotiations, and the merger took place in early 1997. As part of the merger, a for-profit subsidiary of EO, The Outcome, was created. It was Foster's and the EO board's hope that, as a subsidiary, The Outcome could competitively bid on projects from which EO was prohibited. The Outcome's earnings would be taxable income, but the net profit after taxes could be used to cross-subsidize EO's existing operations. Under the merger agreement, Clark would serve as the salaried director of The Outcome, and Foster would serve as the executive director of the entire organization.

The pre-merger negotiations focused on complicated legal questions raised by merging a nonprofit and a for-profit organization, but the negotiators neglected to sufficiently address what would become significant and troublesome management issues that are inevitably involved in mixing two very different organizations. The management challenges of working with two formerly independent executive directors, an enlarged staff, and two distinct organizational cultures were never addressed. In addition, there was no discussion of whether the new direction that EO had chosen actually fit with its original mission and focus.

The merger created administrative havoc for the organization. Which staff were to work on which projects? How were for-profit and nonprofit projects to be divided among staff? Was everyone going to receive equitable salaries? What would happen if some staff had to be let go when the HUD revenue was finally eliminated? Would The Outcome be able to support the entire organization? If not, who would be fired and what would the organization look like in the future? It soon became clear that EO had two executive directors without a clear division of labor and guidance from the board. EO was in a state of flux.

DISCUSSION QUESTIONS

Boards of Directors and CEOs

1. The fiscal responsibility of boards of directors includes oversight of the current budget, including revenues and expenditures, the review and approval of the audit of past fiscal years, and the approval of the budget for the next fiscal year. These are factors required by most bylaws and by terms of incorporation. What additional fiscal responsibilities of nonprofit boards of directors should be identified? Which of these is the most important? What are the implications of these responsibilities for this particular case?

2. How can a nonprofit organization provide for renewal of the board of directors? Is it possible to develop and maximize the energies of current board members? How? Is it possible to plan for and structure board member replacement? If so, how could an organization go about doing this?

3. What is the relationship of the board of directors and the executive director in this case? What issues can you identify? How would you resolve them?

Funding

1. EO became so dependent on one source of funding that when HUD grants were being eliminated, the agency was in financial jeopardy. If you had been on the EO board, what might you have done or suggested that the executive director do to deal with this dependency? Would you have wanted to diversify the funding sources for EO, and if so, how could that have happened?

Mergers

1. Given the recent merger, the two executive directors, and your understanding of how this came about, how would you respond to the questions that emerge in the last paragraph of this case?

2. Identify and rank factors you think need to be addressed in discussions and negotiations concerning a merger involving a nonprofit organization.

PART V

CHANGING MACRO SYSTEMS

This final part includes three cases that are highly complex in that they occur across community and organizational arenas and include dilemmas in both. They contain organizational issues that also involve broader community issues, which take their characters into potential conflicts of interest. They also involve value-laden decisions about how to go about implementing change. It is important to note that both internal and external policy constraints are reflected in the dilemmas faced by agencies and their leaders in these last three cases.

The cases here reflect three overriding themes encountered by practitioners as they go about the business of changing macro systems. First, there is a focus on the complexity of determining how to change existing systems. Second is the importance of critical thinking as new approaches are considered. These first two themes are intertwined with intense value conflicts, which is actually the third theme. Value dilemmas swirl around those persons who must move beyond the intent of the planned change effort as they implement changes in environments infused with strong political, economic, and social forces—not to mention the very human feelings experienced by the participants in each case. This swirl of values is reflected in all aspects of policy making and implementation and in the tension between change agents and target groups. In each case, these are persons who face the opportunities and barriers inherent in moving change into viable and sensitive directions.

In "The Coffee Break," what appears to be a fairly straightforward supervisory problem of where and when staff take a break escalates out of proportion. Because community members become involved, the supervisor in this situation must balance public relations concerns with internal issues surrounding human resource management. Reactions of staff, and the consequences of the supervisor's actions, illustrate how differing definitions of a problem and how that problem should be addressed often vary so much that consensus on how to approach a change becomes an impossibility. In trying to solve one problem, the supervisor becomes painfully aware of the community and larger environmental driving and restraining forces, which influence what can and cannot be done.

"KingsHaven and YOU" is a collaboration case in which multiple service providers are involved in networking and coalition building. Public and nonprofit organizations come together to design what should be an exemplary program that would benefit community youth in danger of committing crimes. Things go smoothly at first, but as problems arise, previously collaborative relationships turn into tense exchanges as staff seek to protect the interests of their individual organizations. Similar to "The Coffee Break," this case involves a combination of internal management concerns with a major public relations issue that is quickly moving toward becoming a broader community problem.

Last, "Carol's Value Dilemmas" focuses on what happens after a client-directed policy is enacted and becomes the focus of program implementation. This case demonstrates how policies enacted at the state level are only the beginning of the story, that policy implementation is fraught with unanticipated consequences for practitioners as well as for service users. As Carol struggles with what to do, one wonders if perhaps she might benefit from clients' support. As the case draws to an end, community concern over practices occurring within the implemented program appear in the local newspaper.

We hope the reader will come away from these cases with a better understanding of the complexity of and critical thinking required for macro practice. Keeping in mind the importance of practitioner self-awareness, one can observe the stakeholders in each case as they reflect on their own values and behaviors. This poses the questions: How would you define the problem or problems in these cases? What would you, the reader, do in these respective situations?

14

THE COFFEE BREAK

Supervisor–Employee Relationships at Risk

DAVID P. FAURI

THEORETICAL AND PRACTICE PERSPECTIVES

The following case describes an experienced public welfare supervisor being confronted with a challenge to her leadership. The challenge comes not over a major question, such as resource shortages, the mission and direction of her unit, or service-delivery policies, but rather over an apparently simple matter of when and how staff will take coffee breaks. At first glance, this appears to be simple, but it becomes a major concern that may eventually affect funding, public relations, and the quality of services received by clients.

Certain themes emerge as the case progresses. Key among these are leadership and its use for goal achievement, the basis for and appropriate use of supervisory power and authority, and understanding employee motivation. Each theme is found in the classic organization and management literature that even today can be used to inform analysis and understanding of the events and to project possible alternative approaches to successfully addressing this or similar situations. Supervision and its various elements are also inherent in this case, and the latest edition of the classic social work text on supervision can be helpful to those wishing to pursue the topic. For a more recent social work perspective on these themes, see Kadushin & Harkness, *Supervision in Social Work* (2002).

Leadership

Leadership as it relates to goal achievement is paramount to understanding the case. As the classic definition points out, "Leadership may be considered as the process of influencing the activities of an organized group in its efforts toward goal setting and goal achievement" (Stogdill, 1950). The supervisor in the case feels responsible for providing direction in matters affecting goal accomplishment. We might ask why she is so concerned about this seemingly minor matter. In fact, she is caught wanting to support the group and maintain morale but also needs to use her authority for organizational ends.

More authoritarian leaders may be effective in creating high productivity in the short term but also may be injurious to group morale in the longer term (Kast & Rosenzweig, 1974, p. 349). This may be particularly true in organizations employing professionals who must exercise considerable discretion in their service work (Hasenfeld, 1992, pp. 18–19). Awareness by the social work macro practitioner of this potential duality can help in developing choices for leadership strategies and decision making. Tannenbaum and Schmidt (1958) proposed that managers could identify along a continuum between the extremes at each end (1) the degree of managerial authority and (2) the degree of subordinate freedom. Fiedler (1967) suggested that success of particular leadership styles was closely related to the situational setting in which leadership was experienced. Yet another excellent resource on the complexities of managing human resources in organizations is the work by Hersey and Blanchard (1977). The very human element of politics in organizational management is explored in detail by Gummer (1990). Finally, for a recent and practical approach to leadership, see Nanus and Dobbs (1999) on leaders who make a difference.

Management of Organizational Behavior: Utilizing Human Resources. Recent developments in organizational management, especially "teaming" or "team building," brings new recognition to the need for dispersion of leadership within the organization and recognition that leading others requires helping them learn to lead (see, for example, Katzenbach & Smith, 1993). This approach gives emphasis not only to the importance of teamwork but also to developing, or liberating, organizational members for leadership (Kouzes & Posner, 1993) and dispersing leadership ability downward and throughout organizations. Finally, the relationship between organization culture and leadership continues to draw attention, particularly in relation to leader responsibility for making a contribution to the building and use of organization culture (Peters & Waterman, 1982, pp. 103–106) and the manipulation of organization culture (Schein, 1985).

Power and Authority

Organization leaders may exercise different types of authority—the legal/ rational authority assigned to the position they hold, the authority of tradition ("it has always been done this way"), and the authority derived from an individual charismatic personality, which not all leaders possess. Legal/ rational authority is assigned by the organization to a position, and it remains with the position rather than the individual holding it because that person may move to other positions within or outside of the organization; in contrast, the authority derived from a charismatic personality is not controlled by the organization and goes with a person who leaves the organization. The basics of authority in organizations are best exemplified in the 1947 translation of Max Weber's work.

Some supervisors are very dependent on legal/rational authority. As you read this case, ask if there is evidence of this, and if so, why this is the situation. Although the supervisor attempts to use tradition by encouraging the workers to recognize the importance of traditional community attitudes and perceptions about public employees and their behaviors, she does not succeed in convincing them to change behaviors, and she does not appear to possess a charismatic personality.

Whether she knows it or not, the supervisor is working not only in a bureaucracy—a large, complex organization with multiple standardized roles, rules, and procedures—but in an organization that also is a "professional bureaucracy" (Mintzberg, 1979). Such organizations rely on professional expertise; this tends to diffuse power with each worker having professional expertise that they bring to practice in the organization.

Power is of course closely related to leadership and authority. Barnard (1938) first pointed out the importance of the acceptance of authority by those directed or supervised, and Bennis and colleagues (1958) emphasized the relationship between power and authority. Legal/rational authority may be "empty" if workers do not respect the person who holds the formal position in which authority is vested or if they do not respect the ability of the organization to enforce the use of authority. In this case, the supervisor confronts a dilemma—she holds a formal position of leadership complete with legal/ rational authority, but she does not have the power to pull it off when it comes to influencing the manner in which coffee breaks take place.

Those in administrative or supervisory roles in the social services have available different types of power. These are best addressed by French and Raven (1968) who identify: (1) reward power—having the ability to recognize accomplishment; (2) coercive power—based on fear of consequences; (3) legitimate power—norms and values placing "rights" of leadership in organizational positions; (4) referent power—based on respect for the person in a position; and (5) expert power—based on knowledge and ability perceived to exist within the person. You might want see how many types of power you can find exercised in this case.

Participative management that became popular with the work of Likert (1961), through research in industrial organizations, demonstrated the value to the organization of employee participation in decisions. McGregor (1960), who represented a high point in the acceptance of the human resources approach to management, argued that organizations that treated employees as being achievement-oriented ("theory Y") were more successful than those that made more negative assumptions about human nature ("theory X").

It should be noted that power can exist (and sometimes be more effective) separate from authority (Croizer, 1964). This, in turn, points out the importance of informal aspects of organizations (socially or relationship-based rather than hierarchically position-based) that exist separately from the formal organization structure—the structure and relationships on an organization chart. Perhaps the best explorations of informal organization, as well as its influence on power in organizations, can be found in James Thompson's *Organizations in Action* (1967) and Peter Blau's and Richard Scott's study of public bureaucracy in *Formal Organizations* (1962).

Motivation

Motivation of employees is a complex business, requiring knowledge of both human behavior and organizations. Assumptions about motivation were an important part of early management theory. Scientific management assumed that monetary income and opportunity to increase it were primary motivators (Taylor, 1911); yet, this was only the tip of the iceberg. Starting in the 1930s, the "human relations school" of management thought brought new understanding to the integration of people and organizations as demonstrated in the well-known Hawthorne Studies (Rothlisberger & Dickson, 1939).

Perhaps the best-known motivation theory, although it was not developed specifically for application to organizational leadership and goal accomplishment, is the work of Abraham Maslow (1954) that focused on lower- and higher-level human needs. Although this is known to most social workers, perhaps more influential, and particularly useful in the case at hand, is the motivator–hygiene theory of Herzberg, Mausner, and Snyderman (1959), which suggests that two parallel factors in organizations influence employee satisfaction. The first is "hygiene" (the job environment, including working conditions, supervision, policy, and relationships), which can easily lead to dissatisfaction but does not contribute much to employee satisfaction. The second factor is "motivators" (achievement, recognition, responsibility, advancement) that are major contributors to satisfaction. Addressing the hygiene factor to create a nonnegative work environment provides a base from which to provide motivation to spur goal achievement. In the present case, we can ask if the first, the hygiene factor, is provided for and why this is important to goal accomplishment.

An additional approach to motivation worth noting is the work of Vroom (1964). Expectancy theory emphasizes that the expected rewards for goal-directed individual efforts are most effective if they are both positive and compatible with both employee and organization goals. This could be useful in this case if one looks at rewards as more than simply monetary compensation and isolates the reward interests of the individual members of the work group and the goal achievement interests of the organization to ask if there is or could be congruence between the two.

REFERENCES

Leadership

Fiedler, F. (1967). *A theory of leadership effectiveness.* New York: McGraw-Hill.

Gummer, B. (1990). *The politics of social administration: Managing organizational politics in social agencies.* Englewood Cliffs, NJ: Prentice Hall.

Hasenfeld, Y. (1992). *Human services as complex organizations.* Newbury Park, CA: Sage.

Kadushin, A., & Harkness, D. (2002). *Supervision in social work* (4th ed.). New York: Columbia University Press.

Hersey, P., & Blanchard, K. (1977). *Management of organizational behavior: Utilizing human resources* (3rd ed.). Englewood Cliffs, NJ: Prentice Hall.

Kast, F., & Rosenzweig, J. (1974). *Organization and management: A systems approach* (2nd ed.). New York: McGraw-Hill.

Katzenbach, J. R., & Smith, D. K. (1993). *The wisdom of teams: Creating the high-performance organization.* Boston: Harvard Business School Press.

Kouzes, J. M., & Posner, B. Z. (1993). *Credibility: How leaders gain and lose it, why people demand it.* San Francisco: Jossey-Bass.

Nanus, B., & Dobbs, S. (1999). *Leaders who make a difference: Essential strategies for meeting the nonprofit challenge.* San Francisco: Jossey-Bass.

Peters, T., & Waterman, R. H. (1982). *In search of excellence: Lessons from America's best-run companies.* New York: Harper & Row.

Schein, E. (1985). *Organizational culture and leadership.* San Francisco: Jossey-Bass.

Stogdill, R. M. (1950). Leadership, membership, and organization. *Psychological Bulletin, 47,* 1–14.

Tannenbaum, R., & Schmidt, W. (1958). How to choose a leadership pattern. *Harvard Business Review, 36,* 95–101.

Power and Authority

Barnard, C. I. (1938). *The functions of the executive.* Cambridge: Harvard University Press.

Bennis, W., Berkowitz, N., Affinito, M., & Malone, M. (1958). Authority, power and the ability to influence. *Human Relations, 11*(2), 143–156.

Blau, P., & Scott, W. R. (1962). *Formal organizations: A comparative approach.* San Francisco: Chandler.

Blau, P. (1993). *The dynamics of bureaucracy* (rev. ed.). Chicago: University of Chicago Press.

Croizer, M. (1964). *The bureaucratic phenomenon.* Chicago: University of Chicago Press.

French, J., & Raven, B. (1968). The bases of social power. In D. Cartwright & A. Zander (Eds.), *Group dynamics* (pp. 607–623). New York: Harper & Row.

Likert, R. (1961). *New patterns of management.* New York: McGraw-Hill.

McGregor, D. (1960). *The human side of enterprise.* New York: McGraw-Hill.

Mintzberg, H. (1979). *The structuring of organizations.* Englewood Cliffs, NJ: Prentice Hall.

Thompson, J. D. (1967). *Organizations in action.* New York: McGraw-Hill.

Weber, M. (1947). *The theory of social and economic organizations.* New York: The Free Press.

Motivation

Herzberg, F., Mausner, B., & Snyderman, B. (1959). *The motivation to work.* New York: Wiley.

Maslow, A. (1954). *Motivation and personality* (2nd ed.). New York: Harper.

Rothlisberger, F., & Dickson, W. (1939). *Management and the worker.* Cambridge: Harvard University Press.

Taylor, F. (1911). *Scientific management.* New York: Harper.

Vroom, V. (1964). *Work and motivation.* New York: Wiley.

THE CASE

THE COFFEE BREAK

THE SITUATION

Two months prior to state primary elections, the supervisor of the Oyster County Social Service office received a complaint from a citizen of Sea View, the small town (population 5,000) in which the office was located, to the effect that jobs in the Welfare Department must be "pretty soft" judging from the amount of time workers could spend in the drugstore having coffee. The complainant was concerned by the fact that all six service workers were in the drugstore at one time. The supervisor decided that since it was election time, this was potentially a political issue and that she should share the complaint with the district director and ask her advice regarding handling the situation with the staff.

THE DISCUSSION

The supervisor related the citizen's call to the district director and explained that the workers were mostly the same age (mid-twenties to mid-thirties), belonged to the same athletic club and social organizations, and were a very congenial group. Three of the six held MSW degrees and the other three had begun part-time graduate study. The mid-morning ritual in the small county unit was for the most senior worker present each day to start the group moving toward the drugstore across the street with a phrase to the general effect that " . . . it's about time for a coffee break." The supervisor, an MSW with a clinical practice specialty, who was in her forties and had supervised the unit for three years, indicated that the staff was keeping up with their work but that she did recognize that the complaint had some basis as the workers went for coffee together and stayed nearer to 25 minutes than the 15 they were allowed each morning and each afternoon. The supervisor stated that she wished to address the problem effectively, but at the same time did not want to disturb harmony in the office. She also expressed that she was painfully aware of how lucky she was to have workers that liked one another and had rapport, given what the rumor mill had been around the state concerning job changes due to increased accountability.

The director recognized with the supervisor that the work of the unit in general was up to standard. There were no overdue case reviews or pending applications and regular spot-checking of records showed the quality of work to be comparable to other units in the district. She also recognized that it was sometimes difficult to get coffee, drink it, and be back in the office in 15 minutes. On the other hand, the agency was tax-supported and open to criticism by citizens who might at any time withdraw support, thereby possibly injuring the people the agency served. The director suggested that the supervisor present this point of view in a regular staff meeting and that, if this did not bring about the desired results, the supervisor could take up the matter again with each worker individually. The director said she thought nothing in the personnel manual covered a coffee break but that it was general practice throughout the agency and in local businesses. The supervisor and director together looked at the personnel manual to verify this. They discussed the possibility of coffee being made and consumed in the office but quickly came to the conclusion that the social aspect of going out for coffee and seeing and greeting others at the drugstore was probably as important to the workers as the coffee itself. The director then suggested that the supervisor might want to consider setting some clear boundaries for the workers concerning the matter.

THE STAFF MEETING

At the next staff meeting, the supervisor told the staff about the complaint, withholding the name of the complainant. Staff members wanted to know who made the complaint, pointing out that they worked hard and that their work was always current. The supervisor said that it was true that they were up with their work but that it was also true that they were the agency's representatives. At that point, the supervisor decided to ask the workers to divide into pairs and not all go at once to the drugstore as this called attention to them and led to misunderstandings because the person on the street was not able to know of work they were doing in the office or the field. The workers agreed to try this; one of them said that she always tried to be cooperative and preserve good working relationships in the office and they would still have a coffee break; another added that at least they would still be able to partake of the bagels the old-fashioned drugstore had recently added in order to compete with the new coffee place at the mall.

THE RESULT—AND THE TWIST

Immediately after the meeting, the workers spent some time conjecturing about who made the complaint and why. They continued to do their work well, but they did begin to complain that they were overworked. They were not working overtime, but as summer came on, they complained more and more of caseload pressures and tempers grew short. The supervisor was aware of "backroom talk," and tension and resistance increased.

After a period of complying with the supervisor's coffee break request, the workers, quite informally, developed a new twist on the habit of going for coffee together. They had been arriving at work promptly at 8:00 A.M., reading their office mail, going for coffee in pairs between 8:30 and 10:00 A.M., but now they met at the drugstore at 8:00 A.M. for coffee before reporting to work. Also, the supervisor noticed that they were managing to get back to the office from the field by 3:30 P.M. so that they could go for coffee together late in the afternoon near closing time. Shortly after this began, the supervisor received a new complaint that the staff was having breakfast on agency time.

During individual weekly conferences, the supervisor asked each worker how she felt about the coffee break. In conference, the workers quite uniformly said they had "missed each other," so had started this new coffee break pattern. Some defended this action by saying that they discussed work over coffee, but never discussed cases when they could be overheard, and that they and the agency derived benefit from this. They did discuss personal matters too, of course. Others stated that they did not think they were taking advantage of the coffee break as far as time was concerned because it was just about impossible to get coffee and return in 15 minutes and that it was much more efficient to do it at the beginning and end of the day.

THE SECOND DISCUSSION, STAFF MEETING, AND RESULT

Again the supervisor and the director conferred. By this time, the supervisor was very upset by the attitudes of staff. The director understood this feeling; they agreed that the problem must be met squarely and that the supervisor had the responsibility to do so. The director thought that no stress should be placed on the time of day that the coffee break was taken as long as the workers did their work promptly and well, but that the supervisor should insist that the workers report in before going for coffee and that the 15-minute limit should be enforced. She advised that the supervisor announce these rules at a staff meeting and not invite discussion of the matter at the time by saying that if anyone wished to discuss it, they might do so during their individual conference periods.

The supervisor put "coffee break" on the agenda of the next staff meeting. This gave staff members an opportunity for backdoor discussion and speculation before the meeting. One worker pegged the general direction in which the issue was heading by saying, "Well, it looks like this is escalating into a major conflict." At the meeting, staff were very quiet, and the supervisor carried out the plan suggested by the director. After that, staff rigidly complied with the instructions, reported for work, took 15 minutes for coffee in pairs, and often brought their unfinished coffee back to the office. In the afternoons, they returned from the field, did some work, and took 15 minutes late in the day. Although work remained up to par, the attitude of the staff toward the supervisor was one of frigid courtesy.

One worker, who resigned from the agency to accept other employment, later spoke informally about the tension in the unit with the district director after an elementary school PTA meeting. She mentioned that several workers had spoken of resigning; that there was no longer harmony between the supervisor and the staff; and that staff felt pretty unanimously that the supervisor had exaggerated the complaints, was overly sensitive to public opinion, did not appreciate their efforts on the job, and had rejected them. They thought her manner of presenting the matter to them had been at fault, and they resented her putting the coffee break issue on the staff meeting agenda a second time. It seemed unreasonable to them to insist that they report to work before taking morning coffee because she could look out the window, see their parked cars, and know where they were. What difference did it make when they took the time to which they were entitled, particularly when by taking it the first thing in the morning they could then get down to uninterrupted work? The former worker also said that she thought that at times the workers were wrong in their attitudes and treatment of the supervisor and that she had been wrong to join them in it when she really did not agree with them. She concluded that although she felt this way, she could not be expected to go against the group.

THE THIRD DISCUSSION

The supervisor, in yet another discussion of the coffee break situation with the director, said that she thought she had "failed miserably in leadership, motivation of staff, and use of authority" and that she could not continue to supervise the unit. She had heard "mutterings" and thought some workers were ready to resign. At any rate, she knew they were unhappy. It would not be easy to replace them. The director pointed out the areas in which the supervisor had contributed much to the staff and to the program over the preceding three years, particularly in supervision of case work and planning the mechanics of case handling, with the coffee break being the only real instance of rough going. The result of this discussion was that the supervisor remained on the job, for the moment, while both she and the director gave themselves time to reflect on the question the director had posed at the end of the meeting—"If leadership, motivation, and authority are areas you feel have caused difficulty, what might we do about those things? Perhaps this is a more important question right now than that of the coffee break itself."

ATTACHMENT

The Organizational Structure

The state Department of Social Services is divided into several administrative districts. State policies are mandatory for the districts and are set by the state board, which is appointed by the governor. The state board appoints a commissioner who directs the state office (finance, public assistance, child welfare, research and statistics, training) and is responsible to the state board on policy matters and for service delivery in the districts.

Each district has its own board, also appointed by the governor, and its own director employed by the district board under merit system regulations who is directly responsible to the board for the overall administration of state programs in the district. Manuals of procedure, policies, and personnel practices are supplied to the districts by the state office. The districts can use discretion in matters not covered in these manuals. Employees are covered by the state merit system, and the state is a right-to-work, "open shop" state without public employee unions.

Each district is further divided into several local offices, or "units," each covering an area that may be only a section of a highly populated county or that may be made up of several counties according to population and caseloads in the area. The units average eight workers each, with one clerical worker and a supervisor who is responsible directly to the district director. Individual caseloads average 50 family cases plus 15 adult protective service cases. Some workers have responsibility for independent adoption studies rather than adult cases. Child protective services is handled in the larger offices by specially trained workers in separate units or by single workers in smaller offices.

DISCUSSION QUESTIONS

Imagine that you are applying your professional knowledge and supporting yourself as an administration and planning consultant to social service agencies and that you are asked to consult with the director and supervisor about supervisory aspects of this case's situation. In considering these matters, it may be useful to recall the importance of integrating individual and organizational needs and to recognize that both a short-range, problem-solving perspective and a longer-range organizational development perspective may be appropriate. Likewise, it may be helpful to conceptualize theories that relate to leadership, authority, and power. What specific approaches might you suggest regarding:

1. the interactions among power, authority, and leadership, particularly when working with professionals? How might the supervisor define

power, authority, and leadership in this situation and integrate the three in coherent action?

2. the process of influencing human behaviors in the interest of achieving particular goals—in other words, is there an appropriate leadership approach that might be used to meet this contingency?

3. the formal organizational structure and the informal organization—could you draw an organization chart based on the information given in the following case exercise? Do informal aspects of this county office appear to fit with this formal organization structure?

4. understanding the complex needs that affect individual performance—that is, is there an explanation of human behavior and an accompanying applied motivation theory that may be useful?

CASE EXERCISE

This group exercise is designed for the participation of three groups, each of which work on the problems presented in the case from the perspective of the different case participants. Three scenarios are presented, each containing further developments immediately following "the third discussion." Each group assumes the role identified in the scenario they are considering and is asked to engage the problem and undertake certain next steps. Ideally, each group will complete written material to share in a short presentation to the larger group or class for discussion and comparison of the different roles.

Should it not be convenient to assemble three groups, selecting just two of the scenarios for use by two groups also works well. If group breakouts are not possible or desired, each scenario can be used as the basis for open discussion within a larger group or class, or can serve as the basis for take-home exercises.

The District Director

As the district director, you realize that you first learned of the situation from the supervisor, and you choose to work with her in dealing with it through discussion and consultation. Knowing this touchy issue may continue to need to be addressed in one form or another, you have decided to close your door for 30 minutes in order to think through the situation and set priorities that you wish to pursue related to this particular local unit, its supervisor, the staff, and the public. You are also mindful that your local district board chairperson is coming to see you about the matter. You think you had better make a list of the results of your priority setting, since one of your managerial methods is to be proactive rather than just reactive to issues and problems as they come along. To begin with, you decide it would be best to first determine your long-range goal as well as your shorter-range objectives relating to the unrest created over as simple a thing as a coffee break. First, you create these lists, and next you set about identifying and organizing strategies you will employ to reach each objective—and eventually the longer-range goal.

The Supervisor

As the unit supervisor, you remain on the job for the time being. You think you now see why you are paid more than line workers are paid. It has been tough going and this has been a trying experience. You had worked with the district director in dealing with the situation and know you have a good bit of support from that end, but you also know you are going to have to "mend some fences" with the staff.

Knowing things will be touchy for quite some time, you decide to close your door for 30 minutes in order to think the situation through and perhaps come up with some strategies and tactics that you wish to pursue related to the staff. You realize that it may be good to include some things that are positive and unrelated to the current tension-raising situation. You are also mindful that a friend has shared with you that he heard through the local grapevine that the local district board chairperson is going to see your district director concerning staff morale within the office. You realize that you have pretty much used a supervisory style that reflects the use of authority and leadership within a large bureaucracy, since the state Department of Social Services is a large bureaucracy. Yet, you now are thinking of your county office as unique and not really a typical bureaucracy. You thus decide to set a goal for yourself of adjusting your supervisory style to the culture of the county office and therefore, as a first step to help you understand this environment, you prepare a list of indicators of the informal organizational culture that exists within the office. You also consider the fact that the Department of Social Services is, in part, made up of a large number of professionals. Then, you identify as many supervisory techniques as you can that may have an adaptive fit with these indicators.

The District Board

As members of the local district board, you have learned of this situation because a local social service office employee, who is worried about morale in the office, made a call to a fellow board member with whom she is acquainted. The board member mentioned the call, in a very general way, at a board meeting, but there was no discussion, and the matter was held over for a future meeting.

Knowing that this could be a touchy issue both internally and externally, you discuss it casually over coffee one Saturday morning at a gathering of board members who get together once a month at a local restaurant for informal interaction. The chairperson expresses a sense that it is important to air the situation with the district director before things get out of hand and to that end has made an appointment to meet with her. You discuss the matter before moving on to the really important matters like planning the annual turkey shoot board outing!

You want to identify and list the internal organizational leadership and authority factors that may be important in this situation. Then you want to list important external, organizational environment factors that may be critical. Finally, you will want to look for and identify overlaps and conflicts between internal and external factors. The chairperson will use this in planning for the meeting with the district director.

15

KINGSHAVEN AND YOU

Managing Volunteers

NANCY MACDUFF and F. ELLEN NETTING

THEORETICAL AND PRACTICE PERSPECTIVES

In the following case, a public agency serves as the lead organization in the development of a public-nonprofit collaboration designed to target at-risk youth so that they do not engage in a life of crime. The intervention is to use volunteers as mentors to youth and to require that the youth receive professional counseling and other services, as needed, while participating in this project.

A number of themes emerge in this situation: (1) the development and maintenance of interagency relationships among collaboration members, (2) the inevitable conflict that results when problems arise, and (3) the oversight and management of volunteers. Each theme can be analyzed using the professional literature.

A first theme is that five agencies (one public and four nonprofit) form a collaboration. Bailey and Koney (2000) identify four levels of interaction between community providers: (l) affiliation; (2) federation, association, or coalition; (3) consortium, network, or joint venture; and (4) merger, acquisition, or consolidation. These levels move from affiliation in which organizations are highly autonomous to consolidation in which they actually merge. Depending on one's perspective, the efforts described in this case could be viewed as either a coalition or a consortium. The collaboration described here definitely goes beyond simple affiliation, but in no way consolidates the involved organizations. Reilly (2001) cautions that terms are often used interchangeably in the literature, stating: "Collaboration requires a more durable and profound relationship [than cooperation or coordination]. The process unites previously separated groups or organizations into a new structure to achieve a mutual purpose. Such relationships require comprehensive planning, a shared vision, and frequent and well-defined communication" (p. 53).

This case conforms to definitions of collaborations used by some writers (e.g., Mizrahi & Rosenthal, 1993), as well as to what Bailey and Koney (1995) call a community-based consortium in which local agencies and individuals come together to address a social cause. Given the use of individual volunteers and the geographical focus of this effort, one could argue that Youth Opportunities Unlimited (YOU) is both a coalition and a community-based consortium. For further readings on the theoretical development of these types of interagency relationships, we refer the reader to Reilly (2001), Waldfogel (1997), and Winer and Ray (1994).

Second, in this case, the theme of conflict management arises around volunteer oversight and the liability issues posed for collaboration members. Mizrahi and Rosenthal (1993) provide insight into the cooperation–conflict dynamic that occurs on multiple levels as power, legitimacy, leadership, and commitment issues interact. Reilly (2001) indicates that in a collaborative effort in which "authority is determined by the collaborative structure and risk is more substantial . . . each member of the collaboration contributes its own resources and reputation" (p. 55). Managing differences and tensions about structure and reputation come alive in this case.

Understanding the developmental stages of coalition building is particularly helpful in anticipating and managing conflict. Bailey and Koney (1995) develop a four-phase framework of assembling, ordering, performing, and ending. As the reader will see, the participants in this case encounter conflict as they move between these stages, and the commitment to their collaboration is severely tested. Roberts-DeGennaro's (1997) work is particularly informative in how to view this conflict within a political–economy perspective according to exchange theory. The reader may want to examine the coalition models identified by Roberts-DeGennaro and analyze this case in light of how earlier exchanges among agency members shift in the performing stage of development and how each organization's leader assesses his or her interests in light of changing events and potential risks.

A third theme that emerges is the use of volunteers by this group of agencies. Volunteer management could be viewed as the domain of one organization, but in cases of collaboration in which agencies engage in joint change efforts, volunteers may actually be managed (and shared) across organizations. Nevertheless, volunteer management is typically seen within the context of an oversight, or lead, organization. Volunteers often participate in human service activities alongside paid employees (Liao-Troth, 2001; Pearce, 1993). As with paid employees, recruiting, screening, motivating, recognizing, retaining, evaluating, and firing are all activities relevant to volunteer management (Macduff, 1996). For additional information on volunteer management activities, we refer the reader to Connors (2001a, 2001b), McCurley and Lynch (1998), and Scheirer (1993).

For the reader who is interested in learning more about volunteerism, we suggest the following journals as resources: *Nonprofit and Voluntary Sector Quarterly* (NVSQ), *Voluntas, The Journal of Volunteer Administration, Nonprofit Management and Leadership* (NML), and *The Journal of Community Practice.*

REFERENCES

Bailey, D., & Koney, K. M. (1995). Community-based consortia: One model for creation and development. *Journal of Community Practice, 2*(1), 21–42.

Bailey, D., & Koney, K. M. (2000). *Creating and maintaining strategic alliances: From affiliations to consolidations.* Thousand Oaks, CA: Sage.

Connors, T. D. (Ed.). (2001a). *The nonprofit handbook.* New York: Wiley.

Connors, T. D. (Ed.). (2001b). *The volunteer management handbook.* New York: Wiley.

Liao-Troth, M. A. (2001). Attitude differences between paid workers and volunteers. *Nonprofit Management & Leadership, 11*(4), 423–441.

Macduff, N. (1996). *Volunteer recruiting and retention: A marketing approach* (2nd ed.). Walla Walla, WA: MBA.

McCurley, S., & Lynch, R. (1998). *Essential volunteer management.* London: Directory of Social Change.

Mizrahi, T., & Rosenthal, B. B. (1993). Managing dynamic tensions in social change coalitions. In T. Mizrahi & J. D. Morrison (Eds.), *Community organization and social administration: Advances, trends, and emerging principles* (pp. 11–40). Binghamton, NY: Haworth Press.

Pearce, J. L. (1993). *Volunteers: The organizational behavior of unpaid workers.* New York: Routledge.

Reilly, T. (2001). Collaboration in action: An uncertain process. *Administration in Social Work, 25*(1), 53–74.

Roberts-DeGennaro, M. R. (1997). Conceptual framework of coalitions in an organizational context. *Journal of Community Practice, 4*(1), 91–107.

Scheirer, I. H. (1993). *Building staff/volunteer relationships.* Philadelphia: Energize.

Waldfogel, J. (1997). The new wave of service integration. *Social Service Review, 71*(3), 463–484.

Winer, M., & Ray, K. (1994). *Collaboration handbook: Creating, sustaining and enjoying the journey.* St. Paul, MN: Amherst H. Wilder Foundation.

THE CASE

KINGSHAVEN

BACKGROUND

KingsHaven is a small community in a largely rural county with a population of about 30,000. It is 65 miles from a larger city of 80,000. Like any community these days, KingsHaven has its problems, one of which is youth who are increasingly involved in crime. Community leaders hope that some way can be found to target youth at high risk of juvenile crime and to develop collaborative partnerships between government and nonprofits serving youth. Leaders hope that buzzwords like "collaborative partnership" will endear them to potential funding sources that might support a project that seems to be moving toward service integration. They also know that this problem is too much for one agency to tackle alone. One project, then, might accomplish these two goals—to work with at-risk youth and to engage community agencies in a partnership using both paid staff and volunteers.

Youth Crime in KingsHaven

"The Department of Juvenile Services has historically served about 300 children each year for misdemeanors and minor and serious felonies. Two years ago the number nudged up to 358 and last year it increased to 429. In the last two years, serious felony offenses for juveniles have gone from 28 percent of all children served to 39 percent. Males are disproportionately represented among the convicted felony offenders. Young females are especially challenging, as there are few services specifically designed for them. Lesser crimes, such as misdemeanors and malicious mischief, are up by 40 percent over the last two years. The high school dropout rate in KingsHaven has increased from 6 percent to 14 percent, thus raising the number of high-risk youth in the area. And there is increasing evidence that gangs are operating in KingsHaven." Mary Whitetower pauses for breath, having just rattled off these statistics. She makes eye contact with her audience.

"The decline in public dollars for programs to address these needs has resulted in low levels of current funding. We must find a way to be innovative in responding to the needs of at-risk youth so that the resources we do have can be maximized. If we can develop a successful project, then perhaps we can find an alternative funding source that would support a long-term program."

Mary Whitetower, director of the Department of Juvenile Services, is an experienced and respected leader in KingsHaven. She has an MSW and supervises several other social workers who are involved in the court referral process working closely with local counseling organizations. Mary is a likely person to facilitate building bridges between government and youth-serving nonprofit agencies. As Mary puts it, "There is no reason why we can't pool our resources to address the problem of reaching these at-risk youth! We just need to put our hearts and hands together." With her initiative and background, she envisions the potential for more sophisticated and intensive services for youth, and collaboration between sectors. She is optimistic that connections can be made between traditional public agencies, such as the Department of Juvenile Services serving at-risk youth, and nonprofit agencies that do not traditionally serve this population, including the Home and Family Association, Kids' Club, and the YWCA and YMCA. KingsHaven is not large and these potential players have a stake in reducing juvenile crime and in providing creative alternatives.

Mary continues her presentation to the group of assorted community leaders who have gathered at her request. "I believe strongly in the power of collaborative efforts to solve the problems of juvenile crime. It is my opinion that a coalition of government organizations serving youth and nonprofit agencies could make a significant dent in the increases in juvenile crime. In order to mobilize the necessary resources, our agencies will need to use volunteers to supplement what we can do with paid staff."

As Mary continues, she states that volunteers are especially important to her notions of how to work with troubled youth. She recalls having recently observed an alternative education program for felony offenders and for kids the public schools no longer want. This initiative was begun by two women who had been volunteering to help in the school and she thinks their impact has been "incredible." She ends her presentation by stating: "I think we can figure out a way to address the problems of youth in KingsHaven if we work collaboratively and if we mobilize volunteers who are truly interested in giving their time to turn children around before they enter a life of crime."

The community meeting concludes with commitments from several agencies to form a task force and to meet again in the near future. Mary's enthusiasm for change seems to be somewhat contagious. She knows there is a problem and she has been concerned for some months. She is anxious to move forward.

Mary's contacts in the state capitol report that in the next state budget cycle a substantial amount of money will be available to local communities to address the issues of juvenile crime. The money will go first to communities with disproportionately high levels of juvenile crime relative to their population and to those submitting proposals to collaborate with community agencies. Mary has only a few months to build a coalition before the "request for proposals" lands on her desk. She seizes this window of opportunity and moves forward.

THE KINGSHAVEN FIVE DEVELOPS "YOU"

Mary, from her base in the department, takes the lead in calling together a group of agencies to intervene with high-risk youth. She personally calls the leaders of several nonprofits to solicit their participation. She tells them that, under her leadership, the department will assume judicial responsibility and will refer to the appropriate agencies providing oversight of the entire project. Mary's organization, therefore, serves as the hub (or lead agency), and it is to the Department of Juvenile Services that any project staff and volunteers are ultimately responsible.

Mary is joined by Jim Johnson, director of the Home and Family Association; Clarice Jones, director of the YWCA; Pete Garcia, director of the YMCA; and Lois Wimberly, administrator of Kids' Club. They agree to call themselves the "KingsHaven Five" and to call their project "Youth Opportunities Unlimited" (YOU). YOU is essentially a joint venture of five organizations, with the Department of Juvenile Services being the lead agency. They define their purpose as "reducing juvenile criminal activity by assigning volunteer mentors to at-risk youth so that supportive adults can offer a positive influence."

Mary's KingsHaven Five colleagues all write letters to attach to a grant proposal in which they declare their willingness to participate in this project should it be funded. Mary's department receives a substantial grant to address the issues of juvenile crime and to develop YOU. The funded proposal is considered to be innovative and collaborative, much to the pleasure of the staff at the state Office for Juvenile Justice and Rehabilitation. Mary has been told she can expect visitors from around the state to see her project in action. Everyone sees the proposal as a model. Mary's stature, statewide, is in ascendancy!

Money flows to each organization for slightly different purposes. The Home and Family Association receives money for one and one-half staff persons; they hire two MSWs. There is also no stipulation that they work exclusively on YOU projects. The YMCA receives enough money to hire a

25-hour-per-week employee to work exclusively with children; the YWCA hires a teacher with experience in life skills and home economics. Kids' Club plans to hire a part-time secretary to work with Lois and hopes to have enough money to buy a computer. Mary has enough money left to hire a staff person to work with her in overseeing the project. Each agency also receives 15 percent of the value of its portion of the grant for administration and management costs.

Although money is not viewed as the motivating force behind the building of YOU, the KingsHaven Five are delighted to have these new resources because it means new money for additional staff. Mary rarely discusses money at meetings, but she doesn't need to. Everyone knows its importance. The KingsHaven Five agree to meet once a month to monitor the project for the first year. They hope to reduce the number of meetings once things are going smoothly, possibly meeting on a quarterly basis or as needed.

They agree that youth can enter the project through any of the five agencies. Mary contends that by the time youth are connected with the Department of Juvenile Services, they are already involved with the law. The other agencies, however, encounter at-risk youth much earlier (before they are involved with the law), so they can become part of YOU before major problems are identified. Essentially, a referral to YOU can come from any source. The point is to get youth involved with positive role models.

Although the Department of Juvenile Services and the Home and Family Association are reasonably professionalized, with multiple MSW-level social workers on staff, this is not the case for the other three agencies. Staff at both Ys and the Kids' Club are experienced in working with youth in small groups, camps, team sports, and informal classes, but they have developed their skills "on the job." Some staff are part-time, and all three organizations use at least a few volunteers. Lois at Kids' Club has the most experience managing volunteers.

Procedurally, the KingsHaven Five decides that once youth enter YOU, they will be required to participate in counseling sessions. The first step is for a social worker in Mary's department to assess each client to determine what types of activities may be most beneficial. Following assessment, all youth entering YOU will sign up for classes and recreational activities as approved by a counselor at the Home and Family Association and the counselor sees the youth on an ongoing basis. Because the Department of Juvenile Services' social workers agree to be responsible for assessment, they coordinate closely with the Association counselors who then are responsible for developing treatment plans with each youth. It is felt that this transition is easy since the social workers and counselors already know one another and have worked together in the past.

Central to the plan of action is the volunteer mentor role so that a supportive adult presence will be available to the youth. It is agreed that volunteers will be recruited by the Kids' Club since this is the type of work it already does. Lois, who is responsible for overseeing Kids' Club, started to provide educational and recreational activities for children after school in her own home 18 years ago. As interest in the program developed, she got space donated for meetings and activities and recruited parents, like herself, to provide guidance to the kids' activities. Over time, she became a full-time administrator, overseeing the work of 75 adults working with children after school, in the evenings or on weekends, and during the summer.

Although respected in the community for her innovative service to children, Lois has no formal training in the management of volunteers. There have never been problems with Kids' Club volunteers, so she assumes that the volunteer management pieces that are in place are sufficient. Lois describes Kids' Club as being a lot like Big Brothers/Sisters in other parts of the country because they recruit volunteers to mentor and befriend youth. Lois feels her participation in this project fits in with the Kids' Club's mission and agrees to work closely with the Association counselors to be sure that volunteer mentors are apprised of the plan for each child.

Mary knows Lois is the most experienced person working with volunteers in KingsHaven and sees her as the person to spearhead this part of the project—bringing in volunteers for a one-to-one match. Mary thinks all the parts of her vision for the program are important, but the volunteers are the ones who will really turn the children around. Mary accepts her lack of experience in this area and knows Lois is essential to the project. Without her, it won't work. Mary assumes that Lois knows the best ways to recruit, screen, train, and monitor the work of volunteers.

The Home and Family Association, under Jim Johnson's leadership, assumes responsibility for counseling targeted youth one-to-one and in small-group sessions. With a proven track record of counseling, the Association is the logical place from which youth will receive counseling services. Their staff is small, with only two full-time youth counselors, but they try to be available 24 hours a day.

The Ys are solicited to participate in the project through skill-development and recreational opportunities. Clarice Jones at the YWCA has worked her way up within the system from being a volunteer to being a part-time and then a full-time employee. Everyone knows Clarice, and she seems to know everyone in KingsHaven and the surrounding area. She agrees to provide skill development for youth in the areas of job searching, cooking, and personal hygiene. Since these skills are typically provided at the YWCA, Clarice feels it will be simple to open the Y's doors to new clientele as long as a few volunteers are added in the process.

The YMCA is under the direction of Pete Garcia. Known for his ability "to get things done," Pete is often looked to for his quick wit and insight. Because the YMCA sponsors ongoing recreational activities, both individual and group sports, Pete feels the Y can provide opportunities for at-risk youth without stretching its existing resources. However, he is happy to learn that Mary has some funds available just in case the YMCA needs to be reimbursed for the expenses of additional personnel hours.

Continuing to Develop YOU

The spring is devoted to frequent meetings among the five directors in order to orient themselves and existing staff, as well as setting up the volunteer mentor component of the project. Lois intends to use the same system to screen volunteers that was used at Kids' Club; anyone offering to volunteer will complete an application, be interviewed, sign a contract (see Appendix 15-A), and attend training. The procedure has worked for 18 years; therefore, she sees no reason to change it.

Mary tells Lois that the police will conduct a criminal records background check on volunteer applicants if she is interested. Lois has heard this is a good idea from other youth agency staff and decides to have one done on the volunteers who are working with YOU, even though she does not do this for her Kids' Club volunteers.

Lois is only one staff person and must use her time efficiently, so she combines initial orientation with the volunteer interview. Volunteers like this because they do not have to return, and Lois likes it because she doesn't have to set up yet another meeting. Initial orientation covers confidentiality, suggested activities with the youngsters, how to complete activity report forms, prohibitions against the use of drugs and alcohol when with the child, and how to report problems. Volunteers receive a series of handouts to reinforce the things they should and shouldn't be doing as a volunteer mentor.

Volunteers for YOU complete activity report forms on a monthly basis. These forms tell Lois how, when, and where the youth and volunteer have been spending their time. These statistical reports are primarily for Mary. Lois recruits a volunteer to tabulate the reports and rarely sees them.

As YOU begins, occasional territorial issues emerge when social workers and counselors think volunteers are not appropriately supportive of treatment plans or when they perceive volunteers as trying to assume more therapeutic roles. Staff work out problems separately and return to their respective agencies, having made the necessary adjustments. They remind volunteers of their appropriate mentor/friend roles.

Since protocols are somewhat loosely developed, YOU is sometimes in danger of losing its collaborative focus. At times, Mary just steps in and makes decisions without always having time to gain input from the other four directors. This happens when there are problems scheduling activities and developing appropriate treatment plans, when clients play off volunteers against social workers or counselors, and when there are intensified feelings of territoriality among the five agencies. Even amid these problems, however, the KingsHaven Five agree that their mission is important and that these are normal growing pains experienced when new ventures are started.

THE VOLUNTEER MENTOR PROBLEM

Six months into YOU's development, volunteer recruitment is going well. Lois has lined up 15 volunteers and seven of them are assigned to at-risk youth. Although Mary is responsible for their oversight, she has been so involved in working out problems that she quietly tells Lois to "feel free to work with the volunteers and just contact me if you run into problems." "Thank goodness," Mary adds, "that I don't have to worry about that aspect of the project."

Lois is very intentional in her methods; her years of volunteer recruitment have taught her a great deal. She casts her net wide in order to attract more people than needed because she knows that retention of volunteers is always a challenge. As background checks for criminal records are conducted, Lois personally calls references to verify volunteers' suitability.

Lois works with the social workers from Mary's department and the counselors from Jim's association to develop a series of volunteer inservices at which mentors learn about the assessment and treatment plan processes and get to know project staff. Volunteers are instructed that they are to be friends as opposed to caseworkers and there will be no religious proselytizing, drinking, sexual relationships, or drugs—any of these are grounds for immediate dismissal. Lois sets up monthly inservice sessions and requires volunteers to participate six times a year so that they can develop their skills and will be up to date on project changes. Volunteers express their appreciation at being taken so seriously and often talk about how much time and attention Lois devotes to this aspect of YOU.

Among the volunteers Lois recruits is a youth minister employed by a large Protestant church in the KingsHaven area. Roy Jamison is seen as one of her best recruits, given his extensive work with youth and his connection with the religious community from which Lois hopes to draw additional mentors. Roy is a seminary student in his late twenties, completing a student internship for the year. He is assigned to a 16-year-old male youth, Don Mann, who has no criminal charges in his background but is described by the social worker as "having a number of close calls and associations with youth felons." Roy and Don hit it off immediately. Lois is certain that this is one of those "almost perfect volunteer matches." If things continue in such a positive vein, Roy is the logical person to receive their first annual volunteer recognition award.

Don comes from a family that does not provide him much social support. Social workers view his situation as somewhat "neglectful" and "disengaged." From the beginning, Roy fills a major gap in Don's desire for social support and interaction. He is in the age range of an older brother that Don could have had, and their interests seem to parallel; both like to fish and go to movies. Often they talk about having done "fun" things—going to the arcades, taking long walks, going to sporting events, and seeing a movie at the State Theater in downtown KingsHaven. Even when Roy is heavily immersed in his seminary studies, he finds time to mentor Don and they get together at least once a week. Lois calls this one of her "most successful placements for the first year of YOU."

Simultaneous with his mentor relationship, Don is in regularly scheduled counseling sessions with one of the Home and Family Association's counselors. As planned, youth participate in periodic counseling sessions reimbursed by some of Mary's pooled resources at the department. Don reveals to the counselor that on several fall trips to the mountains to go fishing with his mentor, both Roy and Don have masturbated in front of one another. In fact, Don mentions this in passing as he describes a number of activities in which he and Roy have engaged. At no point does Roy touch Don, and Don does not feel coerced, only confused.

The social worker immediately notifies Mary. Although the social worker is an employee of the association, she knows that Mary at the department is responsible for YOU. Both Mary and the social worker are aware that this revelation of circumstances could ruin this young seminary student's career before it has time to begin. They talk about the fact that there is no law that addresses this circumstance and that it is technically not illegal. On the other hand, they are seriously concerned about this situation and what it could mean if word got out. They feel a need to protect Don from Roy even though he has not asked for their protection. In fact, he is very close to Roy and until now the staff has credited Don and Roy's relationship as keeping Don from spending much time with youth who are already in trouble with the law.

Mary calls an emergency meeting of the KingsHaven Five. Unlike previous meetings in which collaboration is viewed in a positive light, there is tremendous tension now. Jim, as director of the Home and Family Association, is curt with Lois. "Lois, I can't believe you managed to recruit a volunteer who is going to mentor by masturbating in front of a youth. How did this one slip by you? My God . . . if this gets out . . . don't you know the religious community is full of child molesters?"

Lois replies quickly, "Look, we've been friends for a long time. You of all people ought to know that you can't predict these kinds of things, and I resent your prejudicial remarks! We did background checks in the state and his references were stellar. I don't know why you are blaming me. This could happen to anyone."

"Because it puts the entire project in jeopardy. If one story like this gets out, YOU is dead, not to mention how our boards are going to look at us!" Jim retorts, "We're liable for what happens here!"

"Okay, look, it's not going to make things any better for us to yell at one another," Mary's voice breaks in. "We've got to solve this problem and blaming Lois isn't exactly a solution."

Pete Garcia responds, "Well, the YMCA hasn't had anything like this happen before, but my guess is that we've got another problem that no one's talking about. Don't we have a responsibility to report this behavior to Child Protective Services? I think it's sexual molestation. You all keep saying that it's not technically illegal, but folks I have to tell you that I think we're liable for not reporting this to CPS."

"I don't know that it falls under the law, Pete. I know that physical abuse includes sexual molestation in this state, but this wasn't physical abuse. If they had touched one another, that might be another matter. Or if there had been a sexual relationship, we'd have grounds for statutory rape. But, given these circumstances, I don't know that we have to report it to CPS."

Clarice looks anxiously at the group, "Besides I don't know that the YWCA needs to be pulled into this given that we don't even target males. If it's reported, then our name will be dragged into this mess when we've had a minimal role to play here. There are only a few women involved in the entire program and our mentors have been exemplary."

"Easy for you to say, Clarice! But we'll all hang together on this one, whether you or any of us like it or not. And you, Pete, I can't believe that you'd suggest we take this to CPS when all we have to do is forbid Roy from participating in the program. We can handle this ourselves." Jim's voice was adamant.

The group decides that a meeting among Roy, Don, the counselor, and Mary, as project coordinator, needs to be set up immediately. They discuss issues of confidentiality and administrative responsibility and the need to handle this situation with extreme care. The meeting is scheduled for the following day. Don explains that he revealed this information in the earlier counseling because he was conflicted about his own sexuality and the circumstances he described make him even more confused. Roy does not try to hide what happened, although he is visibly embarrassed. Mary indicates that

Roy cannot continue as a volunteer and that since Don is a minor, his parents must be told what has happened. Roy asks only that the agency be discreet, and not reveal any of this information to his employer.

When Don's parents are told, they are unconcerned. They feel as long as Don is getting counseling, and Roy is no longer a volunteer, the problem is resolved. Although the opportunity is offered, they do not want to attend counseling with Don or take an active role in any way.

Roy leaves the program quietly, but there are a number of volunteer mentors who ask what has happened to him. KingsHaven's being a small community and Roy's role in the local church make it difficult for him to just fade away. He makes up a story about being too busy with his studies to continue as a YOU volunteer.

CONCLUSION

Lois, on the other hand, is perplexed and smarting from Jim's attack of her volunteer screening abilities. She is also feeling put down by Mary who has stepped in to deal with the situation when it is Lois who has worked so hard to develop the volunteer component. She thinks Mary was audacious to have asked her to officially fire Roy, but not invite her to the session in which they confronted him about his inappropriate behavior. Lois wonders exactly who is coordinating volunteers for YOU, she or Mary. She further wonders why she has been stuck with the hiring and firing of volunteers when in actuality Mary is the project coordinator.

Lois decides there are some actions she must take, if nothing more than for her own protection. She begins by notifying the executive committee of her board of directors of the situation and swears them to secrecy. She knows that two of them belong to the church at which Roy serves as youth minister, yet she feels they must know the situation in case the information ever leaks out. She has to trust them not to tell anyone because of the legal liability issues that could emerge for the agency.

As leader of Kids' Club, she begins to obsess about her volunteer screening process; Lois never wants anything like this to happen again. She wonders if they should have told the church. When something like this happens, she reasons, should the volunteer's employer be notified—especially when they are employing him to work with youth! Would she want to take on such an incredible responsibility, and should she? She decides that she will definitely add an FBI check to the volunteer screening process, even though she realizes that this would not have surfaced her problem with Roy. She wonders how many other Roys are out there and how she can more closely monitor the activities of volunteer mentor and at-risk youth.

DISCUSSION QUESTIONS

Interagency Relationships

1. What were the strengths and limitations in the structure of this collaboration? Would you have structured this project differently? How? Why or why not?

2. Mary is confident that Lois should serve as the volunteer coordinator for this project, yet Mary consistently states that her department is the lead agency. When problems arise, Lois seems to be blamed. Could this have been avoided with a different project design and procedures? How might the relationship between volunteer coordination and project coordination have been better defined? Should Lois have assumed the volunteer coordination role at all? Why or why not?

Conflict Management

1. Early tensions arise between the social workers' and counselors' roles and the volunteer mentors' roles. Are these tensions inevitable? How would you address the tensions between paid staff and volunteers?

2. YOU is a collaborative project and the KingsHaven Five is a coordinating group that meets regularly. Would it be beneficial to have other coordinating groups or teams from the agencies composed of professionals involved in service delivery? Or would this pose difficulties that would suggest it is not a good idea?

Volunteer Management

1. What are the lessons learned about volunteer recruitment, orientation, retention, training, and oversight in this case? What would you do the same or differently?

2. Does the YOU project have a responsibility to tell the church about Roy's inappropriate behavior or to report what they know to CPS? What are the ethical implications if they do? If they don't?

3. Who do you think should be responsible for firing a volunteer from the YOU project? Why would this person be the likely choice?

4. What mechanisms could be put in place to screen out volunteers who might act inappropriately? How could the potential for inappropriate behavior be monitored in a project like this?

Program Monitoring

1. The KingsHaven Five agreed to meet once a month to monitor the project; however, they did not specify what would be monitored or how it would be monitored. What would you recommend that they monitor? How might they carry this out?

2. At the conclusion of the case, Lois wonders how she can more closely monitor the activities between volunteer mentor and at-risk youth. What could she more closely monitor, and how might she do this?

Note: In answering these questions, you could consider the following regarding effective management information systems:

a. What and where are the date sources?
b. Are there existing standards and procedures, or is it necessary to create new ones?
c. Are there existing input documents for data collection, or is it necessary to create new ones?
d. What would be the major categories for organizing the data?
e. How could the data be aggregated (merged and tabulated)?
f. How would reports be structured in regard to: (1) format, (2) frequency, and (3) distribution?
g. Who should be involved in planning the MIS?

APPENDIX 15-A

Volunteer Mentor Contract
Youth Opportunities Unlimited (YOU)

I agree to perform the following tasks to the best of my ability:

- Attend at least one full orientation session of the YOU project.
- Participate in at least six inservice sessions each year I serve as a volunteer mentor.
- Have at least one contact with my assigned mentee every week, either via telephone or in person.
- Develop creative opportunities in which my volunteer mentee and I can participate together (e.g., going to a movie, observing a sports event, working on a project, going out for a meal, meeting at the mall, attending an educational event).
- Listen to and assist my mentee in problem-solving issues of daily living, and refer the youth to YOU counselors as needed.

- Report all contacts on the encounter sheets provided and turn in sheets on a monthly basis.
- Report any problems, immediately, to the volunteer supervisor.
- Engage in no illegal activity, including the use of alcohol or other drugs, or any sexual relationship.
- Plan ahead in the event of my terminating from the volunteer program so that an adequate transition can be made.

                          Signature of Volunteer Mentor   Date

16

CAROL'S VALUE DILEMMAS

Implementing Public Services for Disabled Elders

SHARON M. KEIGHER

THEORETICAL AND PRACTICE PERSPECTIVES

Jansson (2003) makes the "moral case that policy advocacy seeking to advance ethical principles falls in the domain of all social workers, no matter what their role in the human services system" (p. 38), and "that social work is in moral jeopardy equal to that of other professions if its members do not try to change policies" (p. 39). The following case deals with the basic policy principles that undergird community care for disabled and frail elderly persons living in their own homes. It challenges the reader to weigh underlying assumptions of government policies, raising broad values-based questions about how government best supports elders, their family members, other "natural" caregivers, and paid paraprofessional care providers.

This case describes actual services in one American city, except that personal details and events are fictitious. Any similarity to real persons is purely and unintentionally coincidental. Within this case, three themes interact: (1) the importance of the context in the policy implementation process, (2) the value dilemmas faced by policy practitioners as they implement policies, and (3) the importance of continually analyzing policy choices and their consequences as various strategies are implemented. Each theme is explored in what follows.

Years ago, Lindblom (1959) argued that context is important in policy implementation, which can be viewed as an iterative process requiring a kind of artful dance or game playing among actors and institutions attempting to be rational. Actors and agencies engage in an ongoing process, which Lindblom called partisan mutual adjustment, constantly reacting to each other's agenda and repositioning themselves for better strategic advantage. Lindblom viewed action as facilitated less by clarity than by fuzzing over what one interest may be trying to accomplish just so that more interests can agree on it.

Other policy analysts emphasize the importance of context in understanding policy implementation (Fisher & Karger, 1997). Lowi (1969) used the term *interest group liberalism* to describe how conflicts are embedded in basic government mandates. Austin (1988) explored how these conflicted positions are a distinct feature of the political economy in which contemporary human service programs are conceived and develop.

Since policies are typically implemented in organizational arenas, Cohen, March, and Olsen's (1972) classic argument about organizations as *organized anarchies* is particularly relevant in this case. Their "garbage can model of organizational choice" views organizations as "organized anarchies" having three general properties—problematic preferences, unclear technology, and fluid participation. *Problematic preferences* means that political actors often fail to define their goals, resulting in a loose collection of ideas more than a coherent structure. Preferences are typically discovered through action rather than predetermining and driving action on the basis of those preferences. *Unclear technology* means that an organized anarchy's members do not understand their organization's processes very well or have only a fragmentary understanding of how their jobs fit into the whole. Operating by trial and error and learning from experience, practitioners respond to crises with pragmatic creativity. Finally, *fluid participation* means that participants come and go as their commitment wanes, depending on other conflicting demands. Problems can come at participants anytime, from anywhere, flowing from many separate streams through the system. Problems are sometimes resolved, but also drift away or may be ignored altogether. Outcomes depend on the "coupling of streams" in the choices (i.e., the garbage cans) that must be made—coupling the solutions to problems; interactions among participants; and the presence or absence of solutions, problems, or participants. As various problems and solutions become linked opportunistically, fortuitously, or serendipitously, the stage is set occasionally for abrupt policy changes.

Kingdon's (1984) revision of Cohen, March, and Olsen's garbage can model can explain how certain policy streams, when coupled at critical junctures, produce maximal agenda change. In government, Kingdon notes, there are three *families of processes*. Problem recognition is the process of drawing the attention of people in and around government. A second process is the formation and refining of policy proposals. This occurs within a community of specialists, each with his or her pet ideas or axes to grind, floating ideas to one another seeking support, and each fashioning his or her own solution stream. Finally, the political stream shapes the context in which consideration occurs. Changes in national mood, vagaries of public opinion, election results, changes of administration, shifts in partisan or ideological majorities, and interest-group pressure campaigns all converge in that mix. Each of these separate sets of processes, and the unique participants within each, can act as an impetus, or a constraint, on the emergence of policy decisions.

In agencies that contract with government, policy practitioners deal daily with value issues arising from such confluences of forces. The main character in the case that follows is no exception. Here Carol discovers that programs, such as elder care, experiencing growing, publicly legitimate demand are peculiarly vulnerable to conflicted mandates and therefore pose special implementation challenges. As she struggles to analyze what is happening, she would benefit from selecting policy analysis models that focus on the centrality of values (Flynn, 1992) or dimensions of choice (Gilbert & Specht, 1986). For example, she might study Moroney's (1991) analysis of the contradictions built into locally administered services, such as home care for elders (p. 235), or England and colleagues' (1986) adaptation of Gilbert & Specht's classic model examining dimensions of choice in locus of responsibility, values placed on family care, benefit target, policy objectives, and cost–benefit concerns.

The policy choice posed in this case is whether government should provide home- and community-based services only to elders who would otherwise be in nursing homes or risk serving applicants who might "come out of the woodwork" to use such services even though they had been getting by without them and would never go to a nursing home. Several congressional actions restricting Medicaid have aimed to keep states from making home care an entitlement program, "containing the woodwork effects." For example, a ceiling was imposed on Medicaid home and community care waiver programs when they began in the early 1980s requiring that per capita costs not exceed the state's anticipated average level had the waiver not been granted. Similarly, the Childrens' Health Insurance Program of 1997 requires states to exclude children in families whose parents are assumed to have employment-related health insurance, even though such parents often cannot afford to purchase such insurance.

By supporting home-based care only as a lower-cost substitute for institutional care, the Medicaid waiver policies have limited home support programs to serving only those so ill or disabled as to require nursing home care. The target for benefits must meet the "but-for" criterion, as in "this person would be in a nursing home 'but for' the services provided by the community care program" (Doty, 1985). The but-for approach effectively discounts the unpaid caregiving of friends and relatives from the total amount of benefits paid and raises questions about equity in benefits received, since an elderly person without friends and family available to provide care (for free) may receive a higher benefit than an equally disabled person who is receiving care from family members. Family care is not counted as a direct contribution to care and the programs providing it (even though it has a real cost to families), and family caregivers seldom receive recognition or compensation. If family care is not acknowledged in policy, even respite and caregiver training may become difficult to justify.

Implicit here is a conflict between the values of familism and feminism, thrusting caregiver responsibilities primarily on women, whose "job" is assumed to be at home, versus communitarianism or an assumption of social responsibility in supporting such care. If family care is framed as a private good (the responsibility of the nuclear family) instead of a societal or community responsibility, freedom from state intervention and preservation of private enterprise become more important in policy than assurance of access to care for all who need it. Home care becomes commodified and, in the interest of limiting government expenditures, reimbursement is restricted to medically related interventions.

Policy implementation in this case actually evolves in the months and years after formal policies are enacted, as the actions of various officials at different levels and positions in government—staff, program managers—and intended beneficiaries determine the ultimate program success or failure. Bardach (1977) argues that specific people can shape a policy's destiny by diagnosing why its implementation is flawed and developing implementation strategies that anticipate or blunt its worst effects. Prospects for success increase when several institutional actors take a personal interest in the policy's fate. Bardach argues that policies need a "fixer," a powerful person willing to invest time and political capital following an implemented policy, identifying obstacles, and seeking remedies. He argues that individuals with the requisite depth of knowledge to be effective are rare, partly because the U.S. political system inhibits their emergence. Thus, policies need to anticipate and avoid implementation problems and the need for more fixing. "Unfortunately, designing implementable policies is scarcely less difficult than finding a fixer to repair damage as it is detected" (Bardach, 1977, p. 6). Bardach sees this fixer in elected representatives who are willing to work tirelessly attending to details, and who have the political capital with which to persuade others.

Pressman and Wildavsky (1973), on the other hand, seek such "fixers" among bureaucrats willing to take up such tasks. Their analysis relates to what Bardach calls the "assembly process," and mastering the use of implementation politics to literally construct a machine that will consistently produce some specified program output. In the face of highly defensive postures among other actors who may exert a great deal of energy maneuvering to avoid responsibility, scrutiny, and blame, governments can only rely on their own officials and practitioners. Such practitioners must be skilled at the politics of implementation, persuasion, and bargaining. Pressman and Wildavsky detail the range of cracks in the system through which good intentions very often fall because of the human limits in anticipating and fixing so many potential cracks.

In the following case, Carol is the bureaucrat fixer struggling to implement policy while confronted with numerous value choices and ethical dilemmas. The case also raises administrative feasibility challenges, such as how to measure need, direct financial support to family caregivers, provide adequate wages to home care workers, and mediate political factors in programs largely funded by other levels of government. Readers are urged to consider the structures and resources necessary to allow agencies to fully address clients' problems in innovative, nontraditional ways.

REFERENCES

Austin, D. M. (1988). *The political economy of human service programs.* Greenwich, CT: JAI Press.

Bardach, E. (1977). *The implementation game.* Cambridge, MA: The MIT Press.

Benjamin, A. E. (2001, November/December). Consumer-directed services at home: A new model for persons with disabilities. *Health Affairs, 20*(6), 80–95.

Cash and Counseling Demonstration. (2002). University of Maryland Center on Aging, College Park, MD—www.inform.umd.edu/HLHP/AGING/CCDemo.

Cohen, M., March, J., & Olsen, J. (1972). A garbage can model of organizational choice. *Administrative Science Quarterly, 17,* 1–25.

Doty, P. (1985). *Family care of the elderly: The role of public policy.* (Available from the Office of Legislation and Policy, Health Care Finance Administration, Washington, DC.)

Doty, P., Kasper, J., & Litvak, S. (1996). Consumer-directed models of personal care: Lessons from Medicaid. *Milbank Quarterly, 74*(3), 377–409.

England, S., Keigher, S., Miller, B., & Linsk, N. (1986). Community care and gender justice. *International Journal of Health Services, 17*(2), 217–232.

Fisher, R., & Karger, H. J. (1997). *Social work and community in a private world: Getting out in public.* New York: Longman.

Flynn, J. P. (1992). *Social agency policy: Analysis and presentation for community practice* (2nd ed.). Chicago: Nelson-Hall.

Gilbert, N., & Specht, H. (1986). *Dimensions of social welfare policy* (2nd ed.). Englewood Cliffs, NJ: Prentice Hall.

Jansson, B. (2003). *Becoming an effective policy advocate: From policy practice to social justice* (4th ed.). Pacific Grove, CA: Brooks/Cole.

Kingdon, J. (1984). *Agendas, alternatives, and public policies.* Boston: Little, Brown.

Lindblom, C. (1959). The science of muddling through. *Public Administration Review, 14,* 79–88.

Lowi, T. (1969). *The end of liberalism: Ideology, policy and the erosion of public authority.* New York: Norton.

Mahoney, K. J. (2001) Consumer direction in managed long-term care: An exploratory survey of practices and perceptions. *The Gerontologist, 41*(6), 32–38.

Moroney, R. M. (1991). *Social policy and social work: Critical essays on the welfare state.* New York: Aldine de Gruyter.

Pressman, J., & Wildavsky, A. (1973). *Implementation.* Berkeley: University of California Press.

Simon-Rusinowitz, L., Mahoney, K. J., & Benjamin, A. E. (1999, Fall). Payments to families who provide care: An option that should be available. *Generations,* 69–75.

THE CASE

CAROL'S VALUE DILEMMAS

BACKGROUND

The Personal Care Program (PCP), one of the more established comprehensive home- and community-based care programs for the aged and disabled, is a *consumer-directed care* program as well as a *direct-payment* program (see Box 16.1). The state's PCP case managers, who are all county or nonprofit agency employees, facilitate clients' choosing, hiring, and managing their "own" personal care workers (PCWs). Although the county pays these workers (using largely state and federal funds) and has a fiduciary responsibility for them, the boundaries, risks, and liabilities inherent in such fiduciary relationships are typically less specific than in agency provided care.

BOX 16.1   Glossary of Terms

Consumer-directed care, self-managed care, and **cash and counseling** are all
models of paying users of disability services directly to choose, hire, pay,
and supervise their own personal care workers (Mahoney, 2001). Consumer-
directed care is an evolving term coined by the Working Group on Long
Term Care of former President Clinton's ill-fated Health Care Reform Task
Force in 1993–1994. Consumer-directed care and cash and counseling are
models recently promoted by a collaborative initiative of the Department
of Health and Human Services Assistant Secretary for Planning and Evaluation, the Robert Wood Johnson Foundation, and the National Council on
Aging funding demonstration and evaluation projects (Cash and Counseling Demonstration). Self-managed care is a term in current usage in several Canadian projects serving the physically disabled.

Direct payment is the provision of payments, by government or other third-
party payers, directly to independent personal care workers or attendants
who are chosen and supervised by the individuals they work with rather
than by a home care agency. Direct-payment provisions are widely but unevenly used in the states, and differ from government contracting for
the whole home care program of services to a private agency or vendor
that hires its own salaried employees. For an evaluation of the strengths
of direct-payment programs as seen by consumers, see Doty, P., Kasper, J.,
and Litvak, S. (1996); Simon-Rusinowitz, Mahoney, and Benjamin (1999); and
Benjamin (2001).

In this county, the payroll for PCP's personal care (supportive home care)
workers is handled by a fiscal agent, an outside accounting firm that writes
the actual checks, deducting FICA and federal and state taxes; the county
pays the employer's share of FICA and unemployment compensation, thus
protecting its clients (most of whom are indigent) from financial liability.
PCP workers are not covered by worker's compensation; the county is
self-insured, paying any liability claims out of its own reserves, and officials
worry sometimes that its deep pockets might attract liability claims. Laid-
off workers may qualify for unemployment compensation if they have
worked sufficient hours, but the county neither contributes to nor provides
health insurance or retirement benefits for PCP workers.

The county featured in this case is the largest in the state with a population of more than 900,000 within a standard metropolitan statistical area
of about 1.6 million; the state's population is 5.5 million. Eighteen percent of
the county's residents are 60 or older, and 28.6 percent are age 19 or under;

30 percent of all residents are people of color, including 20 percent African American and 5 percent Hispanic or Latino. That composition is evolving, however. Only 12 percent of older persons (aged 60 and over) are minority as are 46 percent of children, and 48 percent of children under age 6.

State officials are proud that PCP, a consumer-driven program, has been replicated by other states and even other countries. PCP uses all available funding flexibly to provide vital services needed to maintain frail and disabled older persons in their own homes; a similar program for disabled adults under age 60 is in the Adult Services Department. A case manager assesses the applicant, determines eligibility on the basis of net available income and functional impairment, and with the client develops a plan of care detailing everything it will take to maintain this person outside of an institution. In about 40 percent of cases, the case plan requires provision of a PCW to help regularly with activities of daily living (ADLs), including eating, toileting, dressing, bathing, and transferring, and instrumental activities of daily living (IADLs), such as shopping, laundry, cooking, household cleaning and maintenance. The PCP program makes extensive use of payments to family caregivers who, when available, are usually the providers of choice. This is a local policy decided by each of the state's many counties, and favored especially by counties with depressed local economies and high unemployment and/or high unemployment among certain minority communities.

Most of the county Department of Aging's (DOA) 85 case managers have bachelor's degrees; some have master's degrees (including social work) or many years of experience. Supervisory nurses provide monitoring and direct supervision in cases of fragile medical condition. Case managers have caseloads of about 55 elderly clients, and personal care is just one of several services they plan and oversee for their clients. They also arrange and authorize home health care, adult day care, home-delivered meals, respite, transportation, and other services. Elderly clients with interested family members tend to get very little attention from the department's case managers, whereas those without nearby relatives often receive a disproportionate share of the case managers' time. On the other hand, some clients' relatives seem to be effective advocates in getting a lot of service for them.

PCP was administered by the county Department of Human Services for more than 15 years, until 1991, when the DOA became an autonomous county agency and took it over. A new department director was appointed in 1999.

CAROL'S VALUE DILEMMAS

Carol glances reflexively at the calendar. It would be a year already on Monday, April 1. She smiles, remembering how her colleagues teased her last year about the date, as they had helped her unpack in the freshly redecorated office. This year certainly went fast, she thinks, exhaling slowly.

At least it no longer smells of paint, Carol thought, letting her eyes peruse the compact office, passing the framed diploma above the small conference table. It occurred to her how much her judgments really mattered in this office, how many old peoples' lives virtually depended on the programs here. More than she'd ever imagined back in 1993, when, after working over a decade in direct services with the aging, she had decided, finally, to return to school for her MSW—the year, she recalls, when her hair first started turning gray. Still, who ever imagined her running a $24 million a year program!

Carol's visual tour stops abruptly at the computer printouts Judy has just balanced on the pile on her desk. Carol's "In" basket has been leeching its way across the desk's surface, spreading like algae out of control.

It seemed like only yesterday that the new Management Information System (MIS) was implemented, but it had been two years really, and they were still fine-tuning it. Carol knew the improvements it had made. She had been assistant director of the PCP Program for only 13 months when Tom Johnson, the department's new director, had asked her to become acting director of the PCP. She was downright embarrassed, but he said she had a head for numbers, could articulate the program's purposes well, and case managers respected her many years of experience in the Aging Network. She could still hear him imploring her, "I need you!" And now she's been acting director for a year, long enough to start making some recommendations of her own for this program.

Among other things, the reorganization had expedited the privatization of many of the department's messy paperwork functions, allowing case managers to focus more on their clients. Like all area Agencies on Aging receiving funds from the federal Administration on Aging, the department was charged with providing universal services to older people with special attention to persons in poverty. The MIS highlighted some of these disparities in poverty rates among the county's diverse populations, and some of their implications. Regular statistical profiles on PCP enrollees showed they were about 41 percent black, 13 percent Hispanic, and 46 percent white, in a county where 88 percent of the elderly were white.

All this had facilitated managers seeing how much more needed to be done. By June 1999, before Carol had become acting director, the waiting list for PCP services had grown to more than 2,000, including clients who had been waiting since January 1998. Fortunately, the state had released special funding on July 1 for the department to conduct a one-time needs assessment, or audit, of everyone on the waiting list.

Through this crash effort, in three months they had learned that half of the persons whose names eventually worked their way to the top of this list were no longer eligible: They had already died, been placed in nursing homes, or no longer required care. The report was equivocal as to whether the latter group had recovered; were receiving sufficient care from family members; or no longer met, or perhaps had never met, the income-eligibility guidelines.

The other half, however, was still definitely waiting for service, and although data on how they were coping while waiting were sketchy, Carol heard plenty of nail-biter reports from her case managers. The department had suffered damaging publicity last winter for not doing more to expand services faster. An unknown share was spending down their savings in the meantime, paying for their own care as best they could. The PCP waiting list continued to receive new applicants every day. To be eligible and placed on the waiting list, a single person had to have an annual income below $10,000 and need functional assistance with ADLs. The speed with which applicant cases could be activated depended directly on how much the legislature appropriated annually for new slots, and the waiting list now stretched back more than two years. The state usually released new funds every three to four months, which usually absorbed about six months' worth of elders from the waiting list; however, this depended largely on turnover. Cases had to be closed to take on new ones. By October 1, 2000, with 2,725 prospective clients on the waiting list, PCP had an active caseload of 3,638 clients. For these, it was paying an estimated 1,300 PCWs at any given time.

Carol brings her attention back to the computer printouts, reverently picking up the dog-eared March 1 waiting list. Names were listed in the order of their dates of application and assessment, accompanied by a cost estimate for each. Case managers had become quite detailed in estimating the cost of releasing applicants from the waiting list. Carol's careful tricolored handwritten notes in extra columns attested to this list's almost sacred status in the department; handwritten tick marks along the right margin recorded each phone inquiry that had been received since March 1 about each case.

She always looked forward to receiving the updated waiting list on the first of the month, although typically it cleaned out only half of the bugs from the previous month. The real trouble was that when the state released new slots, it actually made available the average cost of serving a typical case, about $800 per month. In FY 2000, the state released 1,900 new slots statewide, of which the county got one-third with the DOA getting half of this—actually one-sixth, or 310, of the state slots; the Department of Adult Services got the other half. In FY 2001, the state would release only 500 total slots, but for FY 2002, it was already committed to releasing 1,400 new slots.

The problem for the county was that a case on the waiting list could cost anywhere from $200 to $2,500, or even more per month, depending on the needs assessment done when the case was activated. It cost at least $1,600 if the newly eligible client was already in a group home. The allocation for FY 2000 had been for only 83 new slots, at an average of $800 per month, but that cost $796,800 for a full 12 months.

Eyeing the clock, Carol begins straightening her desk. She is due in the director's office in 15 minutes, just enough time to look over the strategic plan her leadership team has been hammering out for the last month. The director holds executive team meetings every Monday at 9 A.M., and she hopes to broach her team's key strategic issues with these colleagues at this meeting. It would be interesting to see what Mike, the director of finance and budget, thought. More troubling than Mike is the latest projection from the fiscal agent—the downtown auditing firm that now handles payroll for the PCP personal care workers. They indicate that monthly payroll would probably edge up from $759,000 in the last quarter of 2000 to $865,000 in the first quarter (January 1 to March 30) of fiscal year 2001. Their analysis included separate pages for January (actual), February (actual), and March (encumbered). Carol hates these reports because they tell her nothing about what accounts for the changes, or variance, from what was originally budgeted a year ago. Were the increases due to more hours per case, more dollars per hour (meaning the client had an unanticipated increase in needs, or maybe a different worker), or admission of new cases and caseload growth? All these are very different factors, so it feels like a shot in the dark every quarter. She'll hold those questions for tomorrow's meeting downtown with the fiscal agent.

Carol pours what turns out to be the last cup of coffee from the communal coffeepot in the hall and snaps off the unit, glancing furtively toward the three administrative assistants sitting just beyond the room divider. She hasn't time to fix another pot so is relieved they haven't seen her. She rounds the corner quickly into the executive conference room. Sliding into the last of eight chairs at the table, she places her mug on a coaster on the highly polished table just as Tom emerges hurriedly with an armful of papers from his office at the other end of the room. He looks tired.

Resting her hands around the warm coffee cup, Carol takes a long sip, ready to savor her first welcome caffeine infusion of the day. It has an acrid metallic taste.

"Well, don't everybody get too comfortable," Tom says, opening the meeting. "This will be short. I've got to meet with the county board supervisor at 9:30 about the overages in the nutrition program. . . ."

Carol's heels click on the marble as she exits the elevator and, through subdued lighting, approaches the dark oaken door etched in heavy gold, "Snodwick & Ellis." It was hard not to be intimidated by the opulence with which the private sector was free to spend in order to get contract work from the county. She sighs.

The payroll for PCP workers is handled contractually with this firm's two newest accountants and a data-entry specialist. Carol doubts if all the work takes more than two person-days per month, but for this service, the county now pays them one percent of the annual payroll, or about $30,000 per year.

Entering the conference room, she is greeted by a familiar smiling young man in a sharp white shirt.

"Hey, Carol. You're just in time." He points to a shiny new appliance in the wet-bar area of the conference room. It gleams like the control panel on a high-end sound system. "Have a cappuccino. We are trying out our new machine."

"Sure, okay," Carol says, feeling her jaw drop as she removes her coat and guardedly pulls out a heavy leather chair on one side of the mahogany table. Accepting the delicate bone china cup and saucer he sets in front of her, she sits down.

"How do you like it?" he grins. "State of the art."

She sips the coffee. She hates to admit it, but it tastes great. So, is he actually wearing a silk suit? Incredible.

"Thanks," she says, clearing her throat. "This shouldn't take long. I hope you can help me understand better what data we have on these care arrangements, in terms of the money I mean. What is absolutely necessary and what is not? Is it possible to get more information from your payroll records than I get in these monthly reports from you?"

"Garbage in, garbage out," answers Joe, a little too flippantly. "I mean, if you want information about your workers, you have to collect more information on them. That costs money. . . ."

"If it ain't broke, why fix it?" chimes in the newer accountant.

Carol stiffens slightly. "I can't even tell if it's broken," she thinks.

"Why do you want it, anyway?" asks Joe, more deliberately this time. "I thought you were responsible for the clients, not the workers."

"Well," Carol pauses, reframing the question. "Okay then, what can you tell me about how much we've been paying the workers?"

Joe pulls out the February report; Carol recognizes it from the pile back on her desk.

"No, not that," she protests. "I need to see the individual cases behind the report."

The female assistant, who has not yet said a word, snaps on her laptop. A small portly woman with loose yellow hair and a furrowed brow, she wears a floral dress and a gold cross on a chain around her neck. Within 10 seconds, she is scrolling through payroll records listing each client, the hours of care authorized per half-month period, the name of their PCWs and other providers, the total hours worked by each PCW in March, gross payroll, itemized deductions, and the net amount paid to each worker. The system has screens (limits built into the program) so that no client's worker, or workers, can be paid for more than the authorized hours.

"What else do you want to know?"

"What's the average hourly wage per client, and per worker? How, and how much, do we pay family members? What percentage of workers earn at least $7 per hour, or more than $10 per hour, and who is that? . . . and why? And what percentage get less than $5, and why?" Carol pauses, breathless for a moment.

"Fundamentally, I guess, I need to know why our costs seem to be going up beyond our budget. Are we spending more per client than we were budgeted for? And if so, why? And for which ones? What is going on?" Carol's mind is racing faster than she can talk.

"Whoa," says Joe. "If you want more information on the workers, beyond their Social Security numbers and proof of citizenship . . . you'll have to go get it. We can code it, but it'll require revisions to your forms. Collecting it is what's expensive."

"Do you have any record of co-payments paid by consumers?" she asks tentatively.

"You know we don't," says Joe. "They submit that information to you and your case managers."

"Yeah, but that needs to be tied into your information . . . if clients don't pay, or can't, we need to know. That has implications, and the system's not telling us anything about that now. I have no way to connect it. Maybe we should have the client pay the co-payment directly to the workers themselves, then we could just adjust the wage, downward, accordingly. That would get the case managers out of the messy business of keeping track of co-payments, and also reinforce the idea that the consumer has a responsibility here." Carol is thinking out loud, something she knows better than to do in public.

"Right," says Joe. "And if they don't do it, let the worker worry about not getting paid. That seems reasonable."

"They'll get it," chirps the other accountant, sounding like a chorus boy. Slowly Carol asks another question, partly to herself, "Which of the providers are related to the clients?"

"How would I know?" Joe responds bluntly. "We certainly don't have that data."

"Are you really paying relatives?" blurts out the woman at the laptop, cutting in, suddenly sitting a foot taller. "Good heavens, why? I take care of my Uncle Joe. He's 89 years old and I'm over there three nights a week fixing his meals and cleaning up. But I certainly don't get paid for it. I *love* the guy. I wouldn't think of asking for money . . . not like some bums in this town." Her voice is dripping with sarcasm.

Silence.

"Well, why are you paying relatives, anyway?" asks Joe.

"When you have no idea which ones they are?" the chorus boy smirks. "I'm sure you could save a helluva lot of money by cutting that loose. Period. Nada. That just ain't right anyway, if you ask me."

Carol is stunned. Struggling to keep the disgust she is feeling from showing across her face, she considers telling him she is sorry she asked. "Well, do we have any other suggestions?" she asks politely. "I think I'd like to reassess these options."

"Well," Joe breaks the painful silence, tentatively. "You might also consider eliminating payments to workers whose clients need care for less than an hour a day." He looks at her, seeking her reaction. "I mean, how great can their needs be, after all? They'll find a way to manage, if that's all they need. Let their families help out."

"And which ones would those be?" Carol shoots back icily.

"Oh, I can identify them," says the woman at the laptop.

After the meeting, safely back in her car in the dim light of the adjacent parking structure, Carol fumbles for aspirin in her purse. Adrenaline is still throbbing through her head. "I know this program better than any other county employee," she reminds herself. "So why is everyone else always full of fatuous advice about how to manage it? Why can't I come up with better suggestions?" She is furious at that sanctimonious woman. Imagine suggesting "just" cutting off payments to relatives, asking, "Why are you paying relatives anyway?" as if not paying relatives was an option department bureaucrats had just been too thick to think of themselves.

It occurs to Carol that the public probably has no idea how strained and fragile some of these care arrangements are or that this little bit of PCP income, plus the client's SSI, is the sole income in many households. Not to mention how hard it is to find paraprofessionals willing to go into some neighborhoods where the poorest and neediest clients tend to live.

Carol knows that disallowing payment to relatives is a perennial suggestion, a simple and tempting one to conservatives who favor enforcing family obligations for purely ideological reasons. The last couple years have been even more difficult than usual with the state's implementation of TANF and the perilous reduction in welfare cases. She feels more urgency than ever to maintain payments to families whose members have lost AFDC, in which the sole income is now from PCP, plus something from Social Security.

This very morning Carol read in the paper that the state is now fourth highest among the states in the proportion of custodial parents in full-time employment. Fully 80 percent of mothers are already in the workforce. The county can't easily replace these family caregivers taking on second full-time jobs to support their own families. Yet, the community would be paying, as women needed to make more income. Carol wonders what evidence could be gathered to show that impact on her program.

On the other hand, the elimination of AFDC is also an incentive to women without other skills to seek employment through PCP. For all I know, maybe this is creating an incentive to those already employed on PCP to increase their hours or wages. The reforms have probably increased the supply of available workers, but these workers are likely to be untrained and to need higher wages, not to mention full-time work.

Recently Kathy, her intern, had described meeting a family that everyone considered a success story. Mary Sweet, age 48, had lived with and cared some 15 years for her very ill mother and disabled brother while working part time as a grocery clerk. Mary had never married or gone on to school, and her most recent wage was $6.50 per hour. The family lived modestly, mainly on the mother's Social Security and brother's SSI. Finally, a year ago, the mother began receiving PCP funding for 27 hours per week, so Mary hired a PCW for $9 an hour. This worked well except that Mary was increasingly exhausted from helping her mother get to the toilet throughout the night, then getting up and going to work herself. Recently, though, the PCP hours were increased to 40 per week, just as Mary's employer went bankrupt and laid her off. Mary had decided not to seek other work, and became the full-time caregiver instead. Now, with the care supplemented with nursing and therapy visits, she subcontracts for respite with the former PCW when she needs her. "That's how the program is supposed to work," Carol thinks to herself. "That was the family's own choice, and Medicaid makes out well too, saving lots of money by not institutionalizing that elderly woman."

Glancing at her notes, her hand still in her purse, Carol gropes for the small tape recorder she keeps for moments like this. She is still seething at Joe's suggestion that she "just" eliminate payments to workers whose clients need care for less than an hour a day. How could he say that, that their needs were not that great? Of all of them, he's been involved with PCP long enough to know better. "Okay, okay," she says to herself. "Get a grip! Don't get mad at them. This is a strong program, one of the best. Think! What is the goal of this program, anyway? I need to make a list of the issues." Unwrapping a fresh microcassette, she snaps it into the tape recorder, and starts talking. . . .

The next morning, Carol retrieves a neatly ordered list from her "In" box (see Figure 16.1). "I must thank Judy for this," she thinks. "Thank God for an efficient secretary." Laying the freshly printed list on her desk, she takes a deep breath.

Carol knew it had been a county policy decision all along to establish a waiting list. It maintained equity in determining eligibility: Everyone was evaluated with the same functional impairment and financial resource criteria. Basically, the waiting list protected the credibility of this whole system. It also protected the wages of workers who would inevitably be paid less if the department was ever pushed to stretch the funding to cover more cases. "And it irritates the state agency no end," she said out loud. Despite its claims to the contrary, the state agency was always questioning wages in the city, pushing the county to cover more clients.

4/6/01
TO: Carol
FM: Judy
RE: Things to Check Out

1. What caused the quarterly increase? Must examine Sally's numbers from the budget office data to see if there are seasonal trends in PCP spending across recent years. Then compare that trend with the reports we are getting from the fiscal agent.

2. Examine the available demographic data on who is being served. What proportion of them are being cared for by paid relatives? Can we distinguish daughters/sons from other relatives? Which clients have a live-in, or live with, a caregiver? How many and which clients have more than one worker?

3. What is the distribution of hours authorized per week by the functional impairment level of the clients? What does determine "high need"? What is the biggest need? What do the "low-need" clients typically get?

4. Examine what we know about the 1,621 PCWs. How many are relatives of their clients? How many have more than one PCP client? Do any PCWs earn PCP payments for more than 40 hours per week? Could/should this be disallowed? (One could imagine circumstances where it might be essential.)

5. Control for the assisted living cases; exclude them from this analysis. They are automatically costly and we are stuck with them. We have to budget for them first, then see what's left after that.

6. Examine the waiting list. What "demand" is out there, and is it really growing every year? How are these individuals coping until PCP steps in? Which ones and what proportion actually spend down their resources and become Medicaid-eligible before, or by the time, they become program eligible?

FIGURE 16.1

The latest missive had directed them to "maximize use of Medicaid funds by expediting service activation for any applicants within $2,000 of having spent down their assets." In other words, because 60 cents in federal matching funds could be drawn down for each dollar spent on them, Medicaid clients went to the front of the line. "Was this fair?" Carol wondered. "Maybe I've lost sight completely of what's fair. After all, there was a time when the county simply sent you to the poorhouse, or an asylum, but only when you and your relatives were clearly penniless. Residualism, deterrence, means-testing . . . had always been the American way until well into the 1970s.

And what happens if the state funds this new countywide "assessment unit" where we can assess everyone? In fact, we'll insist on assessing everyone, and we'll promote this process, advertising everyone's right to have an assessment—only then to tell at least two-thirds of them to pay for services with their own money. Can we actually do that? It's ironic how little we know about what's happening to elders already on our waiting list, and those who drop off, Carol thought with chagrin.

On Friday morning, Carol is just taking off her coat when Judy knocks on her door. "Did you hear the rumor? Some local union has been contacting PCP clients, trying to get the names of their PCWs. I guess they're trying to organize them. Something about signing them up. Several case managers over in the Southside office were here for a meeting yesterday; they heard about it from their clients."

Carol is stunned. Quickly putting in calls to a couple of supervisors, she confirms the rumors. Organizers from the Service Employees International Union (SEIU) have been talking with several PCP PCWs. "That's all we need," thought Carol, "having the workers organize, demanding more rights on the job, maybe forcing us to raise wages I can't afford now! And reaching them through the clients! That violates the clients' right to privacy, doesn't it?" As progressive as she thinks she is, Carol finds it hard to be sympathetic.

That afternoon, locking her door and looking forward to doing some data analysis, Carol cleans off a work space and neatly spreads out the printouts for January, February, and March, along with a fresh research report from Kathy. All she needs now is a caffeine shot to get started.

Thinking deeply about unit costs, she goes out to the coffeepot with her cup. The pot is empty, again, nasty stains cooked to its bottom. Okay, it is her turn. She'll make the fresh pot this time. Reaching under the counter, she finds about two tablespoons of coffee left in the can and one last filter behind the paper towels. "Oh, poop, I hate when this happens." Dutifully retiring with the pot to the ladies' room, she scrubs it out, and fills it a quarter way up. Back at the divider, she throws in the coffee and water, and flips the switch.

Finally, back in her office, she looks over the data. She had asked Kathy to do some random sampling of cases to learn what she could from comparing client records and case plans to payroll records of the PCWs. Kathy has sampled from the fiscal agent's records to get a good cross-section and then looked up the actual case files. Apologetic that the assignment has taken so long because each case required pulling data from three different sources, she only completed a few. Her report shows each case number, age and race of each worker, total hours authorized, and hourly wage data, including the wage paid per hour and the number of hours authorized per two-week period

4/1/01

TO: Carol

FM: Kathy

RE: Information on Personal Care Workers from Study

Personal Care Worker by Number	Gender	Race	Age	Hourly Wage, First Interview	Hourly Wage, Second Interview	Hours per Week, First and Second Interview	Health Insurance Coverage
1	Female	C	64	$8.00	No longer PCW	2 prn – 0	Medicare
2	Female	C	75	$10.00	$10.00	12 – 6	Medicare
3	Female	C	42	$8.00	$8.00	30 – 4	Private
4	Female	AA	60	$10.00	$12.00	4 – 30	Husband
5	Male	C	56	$7.00	No longer PCW	15 (0)	VA
6	Female	AA	61	$9.00	$9.00	60	None
7	Female	AA	67	$7.00	No longer PCW	20 (0)	T-19
8	Female	C	63	$10.00	$11.00	20 – 20	Private
9	Female	C	49	$10.00	$10.00	30 – 22	Husband
10	Female	AA	59	$7.00	$8.00	15 – 25	T-19
11	Female	C	53	$8.00	$8.50	32 – 40	Private
12	Female	AA	72	$8.00	$8.00	24 – 6.5	Private
13	Female	AA	57	$8.00	$9.00	35 – 35	Husband
14	Female	AA	46	$8.00	$8.00	40 – 32	Other Employment
15	Female	C	38	$8.00	$10.00	15 – 15	Husband
16	Female	AA	45	$9.00	$9.00	16 – 26	Other Employment
17	Female	AA	57	$10.00	No longer PCW	28 – 0	Husband

FIGURE 16.2

per case. Arranging all this on a spreadsheet (Figure 16.2), Kathy has calculated ranges, means, and standard deviations. This is new information to Carol and quite informative.

Deep in thought, she is jarred by the phone ringing.

18	Female	AA	39	$8.00	$8.00	14 – 14	Other Employment
19	Female	C	57	$9.00	$9.00	6 – 9	None
20	Female	C	57	$9.00	$9.50	55 – 55	Husband
21	Female	C	51	$11.00	$11.00	15	Medical Assistance
22	Female	AA	39	$7.00	$7.00	20	T-19
23	Female	AA	21	$6.50	$6.50	22	Medical Assistance
24	Female	AA	63	$7.50	$7.50	28	None
25	Female	AA	31	$7.50	$7.50	16	Medical Assistance
26	Female	AA	47	$5.00	$5.00	30 – 40	Medical Assistance
27	Female	AA	70	$6.50	Worker Illness	25	Insurance
28	Female	AA	36	$5.00	$5.00	20	Medicaid
29	Female	C	40	$7.50	No Client	25 – 30	Husband
30	Female	AA	55	Lives in	No Client	24	Private
31	Female	C	61	$9.00	$9.00	10	Husband
32	Female	C	24	$12.00	No Client	14	
33	Male	AA	28	$6.00	No Client	20	None
34	Female	C	48	$10.00	$10.00	25	Husband
35	Female	AA	48	$8.00	$9.50	32	None
36	Female	AA	22	$10.00	$10.00	10	Parents
37	Female	AA	43	$5.50	$6.50	40	None
38	Female	C	44	Lives in	No Client	27 – 7	Other Employment
39	Female	AA	52	$6.50	$6.50	?	Other Employment
40	Female	AA	75	$7.00	$7.00	21 – 24	Other Employment

FIGURE 16.2 *Continued*

"Sorry to bother you," says Judy urgently. "It's the director's office. He's got a Mrs. Smith from the SEIU in there, and he'd like you to come over right away. They are talking about establishing a bargaining unit to represent the PCWs in the PCP program."

"Yikes!" Carol quickly grabs a notepad and races down the hall.

It isn't until she returns to the analysis on her desk that she remembers the coffee. Cup in hand, she returns to the coffeepot, only to find it all gone, again.

Two weeks later Carol spreads out all the documents, including the "actual spending" report for the third quarter, across her small conference table. "Do I have a problem? If so, exactly what is it?" she wonders.

Tom wants to see her tomorrow at 10:00 A.M. and she needs a proactive strategy to keep him from overreacting. If she can name this problem herself, and offer her own solution for it, she can assure him not to worry. There were a lot of spending controls the department could impose, but the key question was whether they were really necessary, and if so, how far to go. Carol marveled at the pressures she could see converging on this flexible, individualized, but vital home care program. Other administrators seemed to view it as an open spigot of revenue to be raided. Should the DOA try to stretch its limited state funding the next time it is released to cover the steadily increasing number of elders eligible for PCP? And if so, how could it actually do this without imposing arbitrary service limits on clients whose own preferences should be respected?

If spending controls were necessary, one alternative—for a time at least—would be to increase the co-payments required of clients receiving home care services. This would allow extending services to more elderly in need while still ensuring some oversight of their workers. Of course, this might also deny service to families and individuals who felt they could not afford, or simply would not make, co-payments. This might really hurt some people. On the other hand, maybe by requiring clients to make co-payments directly to the workers, she could take that responsibility off the case managers.

Another option was to simply let the waiting list keep growing. Many believe this is the most fair and equitable option, letting everyone waiting for service exhaust their finances equally by paying for care themselves, or relying on family members for help. Some would spend down their liquid assets faster than others, at which time they would be eligible for Medicaid, and the 60 percent federal matching funds. This approach had the advantage of having worked so far, and it put pressure on government, which had the fundamental responsibility, after all, to expand the program.

Finally, it wasn't out of the question to do some class advocacy. They could still devise a strategy to persuade the legislature to appropriate some of the state's growing budget surplus to the PCP program. That surplus was expected to reach $350 million by July 2001, partly a result of welfare reform and the disappearance of thousands of Medicaid recipients who had lost AFDC. It was unlikely any of this would be allocated to social services programs, however, given the Republican majority in both legislative houses, and the governor's commitment to prison construction and tax relief, not to mention his recent decision to run for reelection.

It was depressing to believe so little could be done to shift societal priorities when the resources were clearly available. Carol recalls the home visits she'd made with Kathy just last week, meeting Mary Sweet and her family. They were still hanging in there. "If it ain't broke, don't fix it," she reminds herself ruefully.

Carol decides to write a briefing paper to Tom, partly to clarify her own thoughts. She'll copy it to the whole DOA Senior Management Team. This would do it. She started drafting her analysis, appending documentation as she went along.

Three hours later, at nearly 8:00 P.M., Carol hits the print key on her computer, stands, stretches, and begins assembling the various sections for her report (see Figure 16.3). Judy could clean this up by 10:00 A.M. Gathering dirty coffee cups scattered around the room, she turns to the new single-cup drip coffeemaker on her credenza. With fresh blotchy brown stains, it already needs a good cleaning with vinegar. Dumping the filter and icky grounds in the trash,

---

4/19/01
TO: Tom
FM: Carol
RE: Briefing Paper Outline

CC: DOA Senior Management Team

This is my outline for the Briefing Paper for the director. It needs to encompass at least the following:

1. Extrapolate from Sally's data from Finance and Budget, projecting the probable utilization growth for the next year, showing how much could be covered, and how much could not.

2. Use Kathy's report on the circumstances of the PCP workers if I can to do #1.

3. Lay out a list of alternatives.

   - Include some possible controls or priorities for the waiting list that could be used to expedite service to those needing it.
   - Consider whether we should reprioritize criteria for the waiting list.
   - Should we adjust wages with part of it, or authorize more hours for some cases?
   - Lay out a plan for monitoring the effects of this plan.

FIGURE 16.3

she gathers the cups, the half-empty pot, and filter rack, and heads down the hall to the ladies room. It is dusk, and the building is quiet. She envisions the coming summer, spending time outside in the evenings. It will feel good to get out of here, go home, and relax.

There was a nice feeling of satisfaction to this, nevertheless. After such a long intense period of indecision, she has finally clarified some policy options. She knows now that workers' wages average $7.50 per hour, and that one-third of them earn less than this while two-thirds earn more per hour. But it is the range of wages that is somewhat troubling. Even in this small sample, workers earn from $5 to $12 per hour. The higher wages reflect responsiveness to client preferences; clients typically choose a worker they have already employed. However, is paying the wages previously paid entirely the department's responsibility? Older clients have every right to hire a worker they know and want even if he or she normally charges $10, $12, or more per hour, but does the department have to underwrite every dollar of that?

She would explore the implications of setting some limits for the workers. She could also project the implications of having a maximum wage, something on the order of $7 or $8 per hour for certain workers, or perhaps for, say, family caregivers. Period. No more. If hourly wages could be controlled better, management could better project utilization, and identify what seemed to be expanding demand once older service users were active PCP clients.

At the sink, Carol juggles the three cups and coffee equipment in the soapy water, thinking how ridiculous this is, to be doing dishes in the restroom on a Thursday night. It had been annoying last week to hear the office manager announce she was no longer responsible for the coffeepot. "What does it say about a department that can't voluntarily maintain its own coffee pool? Better to overlook the small stuff," she reminds herself. It felt good to have finally moved her policy problem a few steps toward closure.

Standing close to the mirror and glancing up, Carol's eye catches on her hair; it is getting noticeably gray, even white, on the sides. She tosses her head, flipping the hair loosely off her shoulders, rearranging it slightly. Perhaps she should start coloring it. Momentarily she is startled by a fleeting glimpse, her own furrowed brow in the mirror. She'd really prefer to have her hair colored regularly by someone else, not to be messing with it herself.

"This program honors client preferences," she reminds herself, putting away the cups in her office. "We're all entitled to those, aren't we," she wonders, snapping off the lights and heading for the department's front doors. Outside the building she puts two quarters in the newspaper box and takes out the last copy of the *News-Review*. Quickly scanning the front page, her eyes are drawn to a headline below the center fold. Suddenly she stops and stares in disbelief: "Questionable Spending in County Program for Disabled Elders" (see Figure 16.4).

Questionable Spending in County Program for Disabled Elders

by Jeff Sanderling of the *News-Review* staff

Dr. Edward Phud, the new chief of the state Department of Health has started immediate investigations into expenditures of one of the state's county Personal Care Programs (PCP). PCP is the consumer-directed care program run by that county's Department on Aging to hire personal care workers (PCW) to assist home-bound disabled citizens. The program is financed largely with federal and state Medicaid revenues.

According to an unnamed public official, in the past year state dollars have been used for the following:

1. Dog and cat food for pets of PCP participants.
2. Recreational outings for participants to baseball games, churches, and pet stores.
3. A veterinarian bill to debark one PCP participant's dog, which was interfering with her neighbors' sleeping at night.
4. Work clothing for PCWs and provision of cell phones for some of them.
5. Purchase of a cage for a litter of kittens whose mother was killed in front of a participant's home.
6. Lottery tickets for an unknown number of PCP participants.
7. Special boating and camping gear for disabled participants so they could engage in these activities.
8. Purchase of microwave ovens for several clients living in assisted living, which already provides all meals for them.
9. An overnight conference for PCWs last summer at Ballyhoo Resort at which free liquor was provided.

The items above, along with other examples, were cited by Dr. Phud as "incredibly questionable and in dire need of correcting." Officials in the Department of Health's Medicaid program contacted for comment explained that federal rules require that Medicaid funding be spent "directly for the amelioration of medical conditions or medically related needs." One unnamed official said, "If we get caught using Medicaid funding for such frivolous things, our whole PCP program could be decertified by the feds. That would cost us millions."

Asked for comment, one personal care worker explained that the provision of work clothing is no different from any other job that requires you to wear a uniform, except that PCP workers are ex-pected to "fit in" as a normal part of their clients' home and community. "You do get dirty," she said. "You often help with bathing and toileting, so sanitation is real important." But, she added, "I don't approve of the lottery tickets." She is concerned that one of her older clients might be addicted to gambling. "Purchasing lottery tickets with him is something I just can't do because I don't believe in gambling. He's not happy that I won't do it, but gambling is something I just can't abide."

There is concern as well about how much money is used for what Dr. Phud called "pet care." He added, "Their job is to care for disabled people, not their pets!" Asked for comment, Merv Jones, president of the Area Center for Independent Living, responded, "Pets are really important to people with disabilities who often have very few opportunities. Must they be denied the simple affections of animals too?" Another member at the center pointed to her own dog tied to her wheelchair, noting that "sometimes a dog can be a more reliable attendant than a PCW." Mr. Jones added, "Consumer direction means being able to live your own life, period. Simply do normal stuff. And lots of 'normal' people do all these things."

Asked about this, another PCW stated, "I just refuse to work for people who have a pet because it's too messy. I told one lady, it's me or that cat, honey. Besides, *she* had allergies and the mangy thing was bothering her neighbors. When she refused to give it up, I hear they finally put her in an institution." Asked about other expenditures of the Department on Aging, some PCWs said that having cell phones has made them a lot more efficient, although one complained, "I see a lot of gals yakking on the phone now."

A source in the Department of Aging, who prefers not to be identified, stated, "The department has trained our service users and their PCWs to help clients manage their own care and make their own decisions. This program is very different from your regular home health agency, but perhaps Dr. Phud doesn't understand that yet. It's easy to inflame the public before all the facts are in. Besides," she added, "the state can always spend its own funding on home care if federal Medicaid won't provide matching funds."

The county PCP program's acting director, Carol Smith, could not be reached for comment at press time.

FIGURE 16.4

DISCUSSION QUESTIONS

Analysis of the Political-Economic Context

1. How does the policy context influence Carol's daily activities as a program manager? How much control does she have over these influences?

2. What analytical frameworks, models, or other tools might you find helpful if you had Carol's job? Why would you select these particular tools?

3. Discuss the role of government in providing personal services to elderly and disabled persons by addressing the following questions: (a) Should services be means-tested, rationed, and reserved for the worst or most destitute situations, or should they be provided universally to persons with a wide range of long-term personal care needs without regard to income? (b) Is government's basic interest saving revenue by limiting eligibility or bringing a certain level of care to a high percentage of elders in need of such care at home?

4. What are the arguments for and against paying relatives in a service user-directed care program? Do you think family caregivers are treated fairly now? Would it cost Carol more or less to change the county's current policy of simply ignoring family information in letting clients select their own caregivers?

Values Dilemmas in Policy Implementation

1. How would you frame the basic value dilemmas that Carol faces in this situation and how would you address them?

2. How does government (or any care management agency) determine the hours of care required, hourly rates of pay, the difficulty (value) of the effort, and the skill required to do it? How are these choices value-driven?

3. What are the implications of some of the measures Carol is considering in an effort to (a) institute wage controls or maximums on PCW wages per hour? (b) institute maximums on hours that a worker can be employed in a day or a week?

Implementation Strategies

1. What are some strategies that might be implemented to reduce the waiting list? What are their potential implications?

2. It is likely that Carol needs to conduct several studies of data available in the MIS. Identify at least three issues you would study, detailing as explicitly as you can exactly what data you would use, its source, and how you would tie it together.

INDEX